Christian Outdoor Leadership
Theology, Theory, and Practice

How to Use Time in the Wilderness and
Backcountry Adventure Camping for Leadership
Development, Evangelism, Discipleship, and
Spiritual Formation—with Experiential Learning
and Bible Study Resources

Ashley Denton

Foreword by Robert Coleman
(Author of *Master Plan of Evangelism*)

WORD ON THE STREET
ABOUT *CHRISTIAN OUTDOOR LEADERSHIP*

"In *Christian Outdoor Leadership*, Ashley Denton achieves a *coup d'etat* by surprising even seasoned readers of the New Testament about how much of Jesus' teaching and discipleship takes place outdoors. We all have seen the amazing results of organizations like Outward Bound, but Denton takes it a step further by demonstrating the theological basis for outdoor ministry and mentoring. If you are looking for an alternative to the inwardly focused, self-referential spiral of today's hedonistic spirituality, then go no farther. *Christian Outdoor Leadership* calls an 'inward' and 'indoor' generation back out into the great outdoors—and reminds us that this is God's world and it is still his favorite workshop!"

–TIMOTHY C. TENNENT, Ph.D., Author, *Christianity at the Religious Roundtable,* President and Professor of World Christianity, Asbury Theological Seminary

"Ashley's years of experience in youth ministry and wilderness adventures set the stage for this journey through the Scriptures in search of a theology of wilderness ministry. For many of us who are involved in leading wilderness expeditions, this book fills a long-standing gap in the literature of our field by providing a scriptural basis for the significance of the wilderness environment as a ministry platform. In this, Ashley Denton has given us a great gift."

–AMY SMALLWOOD, Assistant Professor of Outdoor Leadership, Simpson University, President, Christian Adventure Association

"*Christian Outdoor Leadership: Theology, Theory, and Practice* is the first comprehensive Christian text on outdoor leadership. It should be required reading in every college and university that seeks to prepare outdoor leaders. This is a superb book that will benefit both seasoned practitioners and those seeking to be equipped to serve as outdoor ministers in congregational, parachurch, or mission contexts. Denton's book steps in to fill the vacuum of Christian literature on outdoor leadership. It will likely be a cornerstone for years to come. Denton's sound theology mobilizes and motivates as he writes in a well-organized, crisp, and conversational style. He speaks from experience and a deep and passionate faith in the truth of Scripture, the love of Jesus, and the power of the Holy Spirit. This is a seminal book."

–JIM DOENGES, Assistant Program Manager, Solid Rock Outdoor Ministries

"Ashley Denton exposes something that we have clearly lost sight of today. Human beings have known since the beginning that God made his creation as an invaluable gift to help us encounter him personally and learn the secrets of his Kingdom from his handiwork. In *Christian Outdoor Leadership,* Ashley takes us into the reason why we need outdoor adventure and wilderness ministry. He provides a thorough theology of recreational ministry, and then brings us into a well-developed and comprehensive practical application of what it all means. *Christian Outdoor Leadership* is more than a book—it is an outstanding resource for every follower of Christ in that it calls us back to a simple and timeless lifestyle of ministry that patterns the life of Jesus. This is a foundational book that I highly recommend!"

–CHAP CLARK, Ph.D., Author, *Hurt: Inside the World of Today's Teenagers*, Professor of Youth, Family, and Culture, Fuller Theological Seminary

WORD ON THE STREET

"Ashley Denton carefully builds a prominent cairn for practitioners in the field of Christian outdoor leadership and wilderness ministry by expertly pointing new and experienced adventure ministers to the ancient model of how Jesus used the wilderness for outreach and discipleship. This book is refreshing and impressive."

–MATT ISMERT, Director, Young Life's Wilderness Ranch

"Ashley Denton knows Jesus, theology, the wilderness, and young people. In *Christian Outdoor Leadership* he artfully and powerfully ties the ropes of his knowledge into a knot that can bear the weight of outdoor ministry in any culture. More importantly, however, Ashley's love for God, his adoring wonder of creation, and his passion for young people make this sturdy book a reliable and authentic field guide for anyone who aspires to spiritual leadership. Read it and be equipped to thrive, no matter the wilderness in which you find yourself."

–HOWARD BAKER, Author, *The One True Thing,* Instructor of Spiritual Formation, Denver Theological Seminary

"The lessons in, *Christian Outdoor Leadership*, are timely and universal. Ashley uncovers and examines in detail absolute truths that apply equally as well in the boardroom as they do in the great outdoors. If you are in a business leadership position you need this book to survive everyday in the wilderness of American business where everything (including morals) gets tested each day. Teams bond in the wilderness just like they do when they face daunting challenges in the office. I highly recommend this book. Reading it will equip you to survive in the many wildernesses we encounter."

–HAL MASSEY, Former Vice President, Hewlett Packard Integrity Hardware Business

Copyright © 2011 by Ashley Denton

Published in the United States by Smooth Stone Publishing, Fort Collins. www.smoothstonepublishing.com

ISBN-10   0615413250
ISBN-13   978-0-615-41325-9 (paperback)

LIBRARY OF CONGRESS CATALOGUING-IN-PUBLICATION DATA
Denton, Ashley
Christian Outdoor Leadership: Theology, Theory, and Practice or How to Use Time in the Wilderness and Backcountry Adventure Camping for Leadership Development, Evangelism, Discipleship, and Spiritual Formation with Experiential Learning and Bible Study Resources/Ashley Denton/Foreword by Robert Coleman

LIBRARY OF CONGRESS CONTROL NUMBER: 2010915853

Ashley, Denton, 1970
p.   cm.
Includes bibliographical references and index

1. Religion. 2. Christian Ministry. 3. Discipleship. I. Denton, Ashley. II. Title.
Bible references are New International Version (NIV) or New American Standard Bible (NASB) version unless otherwise noted.

Cover Design: Luke Flowers
Editor: Jeff Chesemore
Proofreader/Copy Editor/Interior Design: Jessica Williams

To Becky

My best friend, my bride, and my guide partner as we journey together in Christ. Thank you for filling our home with laughter, joy, and prayer from the overflow of your relationship with Jesus. In the last eighteen years of our marriage you have blessed me with more life, peace, and adventure than I could have ever imagined. I have been blessed to see many beautiful wilderness areas in my life, but the greatest beauty I have ever seen in the wilderness is still you strolling down the path with a backpack on.

Publisher's Note

Dr. Ashley Denton's book on Christian outdoor leadership is the first of its kind.

Christian Outdoor Leadership: Theology, Theory, and Practice offers a relevant and innovative approach to leadership development, evangelism, discipleship, and spiritual formation through outdoor adventure. People today are eager for more experiential approaches to learning. This book re-asserts Jesus' experiential discipleship strategy by showing how to incorporate outdoor adventure into ministry the way he did. Few books on evangelism or discipleship probe the outdoor dimension of Jesus' apprenticeship methods, and this book fills that gap.

This book builds on Dr. Robert Coleman's classic *Master Plan of Evangelism* by addressing an element of Jesus' apprenticeship strategy that has been given too little attention: The outdoor *setting* and *timing* were often the crucial elements of his teaching that fueled radical change of heart. Jesus often coupled his teaching with adventurous outdoor experiences to facilitate experiential learning. This is exactly what many people are hungry for today. Let *Christian Outdoor Leadership: Theology, Theory, and Practice* introduce you to a new way of making disciples that is profoundly anchored in Jesus' ancient style of apprenticeship, utilizing experiential learning and outdoor adventure as a catalyst for transformation.

TABLE OF CONTENTS

TABLE OF CONTENTS

TABLE OF CONTENTS

TABLE OF CONTENTS

FOREWORD BY DR. ROBERT E. COLEMAN
(AUTHOR OF *MASTER PLAN OF EVANGELISM*)

Everyone knows that young men and women imbued with the Spirit of Christ embody the hope of the world. Yet the question remains: how do you reach them?

Ashley Denton, in this landmark volume, turns to Jesus for some answers. What soon arrests attention is the priority given to the training of a few chosen disciples. While he does not ignore the multitudes—crowds sometimes numbering into the thousands— clearly he concentrates upon developing the potential of his closest companions. For the better part of those years he pours his life into them, then before returning to heaven, he tells them to go into the world and replicate in their lives what they had learned with him: "Make disciples," Christ followers who will disciple others, teaching them to do the same, until through multiplication the nations will hear the gospel (see Matthew 28:19).

One of the obvious ways to pursue this mission, especially appealing to youth, is working out-of-doors, a terrain where Jesus often ministered. Alert to this example, Dr. Denton has set out to capture that dynamic. Away from the confines of traditional centers of instruction, the wilderness becomes his sanctuary and classroom. He unpacks a comprehensive vision for Christian camping that builds relationships through trust and encourages strong commitment to Jesus. It is experiential learning all the way, full of adventure and challenge. The book is also replete with resources for lifestyle teaching and leadership development in the way of Christ.

Giving the presentation a ring of authenticity is the author's own experience in this work. He speaks, not as a bystander, but as a practitioner. For more than twenty years, discipling young people in the world has been his ministry, and what he writes has been forged on that anvil. We can learn from such a teacher.

This is a refreshing study. It is relevant. It is spiritually motivating. One looking for some new ways to fulfill the Great Commission will find it here. With joy, I commend it to you.

—Dr. Robert E. Coleman

ACKNOWLEDGEMENTS

Family

Jesus tells a parable about the importance of counting the cost before building a tower (see Luke 14:27-29). The point is that he wants us to finish what we start. My family has played an integral role in helping me finish the marathon of completing this book. It was difficult to truly count the cost when I set out on the journey to write this one. As my friend Howard so wisely said (after I finished the book): "If a new author knew what it actually took to finish a book, there would be a lot less books in the world." So I owe a huge thank you to my bride, Becky, and my children, Will, Claire, Daniel, Hannah, and Stephen, for not letting me stop at the half-marathon water station. I could not have made it to the finish line without you cheering me on.

I also want to thank my parents for giving me the freedom to roam the Rocky Mountains at a very young age. Those days and nights exploring the wonder of God's creation marked my soul from a young age. And thank you to my siblings, Jay, Kevin, and Kelly, for your constant encouragement to pursue a dream to help young people around the world experience Christ through outdoor adventure. And to my grandparents, Edward and Zita Hayden, I owe an eternal thank you for how you have prayed for me daily—I can only imagine how much of my life has been impacted by your prayers.

Mentors

By the grace of God, I have been blessed with some unbelievably gracious and wise mentors. I want to thank each of you for the unique ways you have marked my soul: Doug Self, Ron Henderson, Louis McBurney, Mike Ferguson, Don Hardenbrook, Mark Whitney, Bill Hamilton, Dave Gater, Skeet Tingle, Bill Maston, Howard Baker,

Rick Funk, Tom Harcus, Bob Reeverts, Tim Tennent, Peter Kuzmič, and Robert Coleman.

Community

I am surrounded by an incredible team of staff who consistently display to me the winsomeness of Christ, as we work together to advance the gospel. To the staff at Nexus International, Wilderness Ministry Institute, and the Center for International Youth Ministry, thank you! I want to especially thank Jon Hoppin, Patrick Crossland, Thomas Haines, Janet Wulf, and Todd Hunsicker for their help with research, administration, editing, photography, and website development. Another hearty "thank you" goes out to the faculty at both Fuller Theological Seminary and Gordon Conwell Theological Seminary for the ways you helped me learn to think theologically by seeking to ask the right questions. I also want to thank the students and faculty at Denver Theological Seminary for helping me refine my thinking and presentation of outdoor leadership theology, theory, and practice. And thank you to Mountain View Community Church in Fort Collins, Colorado, for your wholehearted support of our family and ministry.

International Friends

One of the exciting things about theological inquiry is that it provides a forum for us to openly express some of our most heartfelt and sincere questions about God and how he works in the world. Having friends from a variety of cultures has shown me that we all grapple with some of the same questions, yet some of our questions are culturally unique. I am continually humbled by what I learn from brothers and sisters who have grown up in different cultures than me. Learning theology in the context of international relationships has only deepened my awe of God. His Word is living and active and relevant to all people at all times.

ACKNOWLEDGEMENTS

With that being said, I thank each of my friends from the following countries/regions: Australia, Bosnia-Herzegovina, Canada, Central Asia, China, Costa Rica, Croatia, Czech Republic, Denmark, England, France, India, Indonesia, Japan, Lebanon, Malaysia, Mexico, Mongolia, Nepal, New Zealand, the Philippines, Romania, Samoa, Singapore, South Africa, Sweden, Thailand, Turkey, and Uganda. Each of you has deeply enriched my life by showing me the ways God expresses his beauty through cultures—and each of you has helped me grow in my worship and love for God. Even the way I have approached writing this book from a theological perspective has been influenced by my friendships with you. More and more I am realizing that the best way we can help build up one another in the Body of Christ around the world is to tenaciously anchor our relationships and our conversations in the timeless bedrock of God's Word, the Bible. For these reasons it is my hope and prayer that the theological perspectives offered in this book will span cultures and offer encouragement to leaders from a variety of traditions.

PREFACE

"Jesus did many other things as well. If every one of them were written down, I suppose that even the whole world would not have room for the books that would be written."
—the apostle John (John 21:25)

Jesus promoted experiential learning by doing much of his teaching outdoors. Did you know that more than half of Jesus' teachings recorded in the Bible occurred in an outdoor setting? The New Testament Gospels contain roughly 366 coherent units of teaching.[1] Called *pericopes*, these units are sets of verses that form a unit of thought used for public teaching. Often the English Bible has a heading before these blocks of teaching to help you follow the beginning and end of that particular passage. For example, if you look at Matthew 5 in many English translations it will say, "The Beatitudes," which denotes a unit of Jesus' teaching. If you look at every block of Jesus' teaching in the New Testament, you'll discover that more than 50 percent of them occurred in the outdoors, whereas 16 percent occurred indoors. The particular indoor or outdoor setting of the remaining 33 percent of Jesus' teaching is unknown but, from the context, the majority of these passages may also have occurred in the outdoors.[2] In stark contrast, most of today's preaching and teaching happens indoors where there are few natural creation analogies from which to draw.

Some might be inclined to say, "Who cares where we teach? The content is what matters, not the setting." I have used the outdoors extensively to teach Scripture over the past twenty years, and the Scriptures show us that Jesus highly valued experiential learning in the outdoors. Many evangelists and Bible teachers will *talk* about the outdoor or wilderness context in which Jesus taught, but few of us *practice* teaching the way Jesus did—*in the outdoors*.

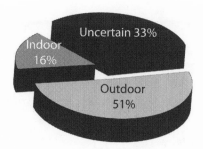

Over the past twenty years, I have been trying to apply the principles of Robert Coleman's *Master Plan of Evangelism* to my ministry among youth, college students, and adults. Coleman's idea of patterning ministry like Jesus is incredibly simple, yet deeply profound. By focusing on equipping a *few* people in Christ, your ministry is multiplied when those in whom you've invested are transformed and go do the same with a small group of others. Over many years, this can expand your ministry a hundredfold. This was the profound genius of Jesus choosing just twelve disciples in whom to invest most of his time. Yes, he interacted with the masses, but he focused his effort on just a few.

Soon after I made a decision to follow Christ in high school, I had the incredible blessing of having several men pour their lives into me, teaching me through their example what it looked like to follow Jesus. I didn't realize it at the time, but they were modeling for me this pattern of discipleship that Coleman discovered in the early 1960s. And now, twenty years into my own ministry, by God's grace I continue to invest in others the way those men did in me. They demonstrated for me what making a disciple is about. Through experiencing it firsthand, it got into my blood, so to speak.

This book is meant to be a companion to *The Master Plan of Evangelism* with one simple development. This book expands on Coleman's chapter on "Demonstration," to highlight in detail the significance of the *outdoor setting and the adventurous context* in which Jesus conducted much of his ministry training. Jesus used his creation so often as the backdrop for his teaching that I believe we can view the outdoors as his *primary classroom*. Colossians 1:15-20 tells us Jesus made all of creation, so it should come as no surprise that he would use what he made as the theater to demonstrate the character of the Trinity and the ways of the Kingdom. In an increasingly urbanized world, there is a heightened need to go out into the wilderness, to places where creation is untrammeled and awaiting to teach us through its pristine palette of God's colors. People today are busy, out of rhythm, and unable to experience the peace of Christ. Even in the church, we are tempted to expand programs instead of enlarge souls.

The rhythm of Jesus' life was rest and work. He labored hard to meet people's needs and accomplish the work the Heavenly Father gave him to do. But he regularly retreated to the outdoors for renewal and conversation with the Father. He routinely took his disciples into the wilderness to restore and prepare them to go back into civilization to transform it. As we look at this theme of wilderness in the New Testament, not surprisingly we see the same pattern emerging in the Old Testament, which was Jesus' prayer book and leadership training manual. We see in the Hebrew Scriptures that God took his people into the wilderness to prepare them to be a family of his very own, through whom he would bless all of civilization. Their trials and struggles produced character and community, which would make them salt and light to the people of the world. Because Jesus modeled this Old Testament pattern of regular retreat to the wilderness, we, too, should sit up and take notice. Combating busyness with more programs is not going to transform the souls of people. *Developing Jesus' rhythm of retreat will.*

Even though for Christians, outdoor leadership or wilderness ministry seems like a fairly new field of ministry, it has actually been around for a *very long time*. Hiding from the masses for a few centuries, like a diamond in the rough, it's simply a style of ministry that mirrors the way God apprenticed his people throughout ancient history. As I write today, there are still very few written resources that provide a theological rationale and biblical philosophy of outdoor leadership. I anticipate this changing, as interest in this field is growing rapidly with more people becoming environmentally aware and hungry for experiential learning.

Honestly, I questioned whether there was a need for this book. There are numerous secular books, articles, and journals supporting the viability of outdoor leadership and experiential education as useful disciplines for developing creative, courageous leaders equipped with exceptional decision-making skills. Yet these readily available secular resources only point back about one hundred years to a few great leaders considered to be the founders of outdoor leadership. I quote some of these excellent resources throughout the book. Yet without taking anything away from the amazingly daring approach to experiential education that these "founding fathers of modern day outdoor leadership" have made, I'm offering a theological rationale for outdoor leadership from a more ancient perspective. We want to get back to its real roots. I think Kurt Hahn of Outward Bound and Paul Petzoldt of National Outdoor Leadership School would approve of my critical inquiry into the origins of this dearly loved field.

Jesus Christ never referred to himself as an "outdoor leader." But by studying carefully how he produced such catalytic leaders as the twelve disciples, we find that much of his methodology employed outdoor adventure and experiential learning. Although God did not refer to himself as an "experiential educator", we find a rich and vibrant catalogue of teachable moments where he facilitated and debriefed with some of the world's most renowned and influential leaders; men and women like Moses, Abraham, Sarah, Jacob, and Joseph, just to name a few. Each was dramatically transformed through God-facilitated adventures and wilderness experiences. Experiential learning aims to achieve transformational outcomes that

24

make a long-term difference in one's life. Not surprisingly, God's stated *outcomes* are always achieved. His objective was to form a following of loyal families who would glorify him and make him known to the rest of the world. That outcome is *still unfolding today* even in places where people are persecuted for their loyalty to Jesus Christ! God's stated *outcomes* are always achieved, and experiential learning is one of the ways he accomplishes such radical commitment.

Many Christian outdoor leaders in a myriad of cultures have asked me why there are so few books and articles written on outdoor leadership and experiential learning from a biblical perspective. Not having any good answers for them, I decided to embark on this journey to expose the roots of outdoor leadership from a theological, theoretical, and practical perspective. In my humble quest, I found that most of the principles employed today by our world's best outdoor leaders and their representative organizations find their origins in principles gleaned from God's creation. So with the Bible as our textbook, I have set out to provide a solid rationale and some practical steps to deepen our understanding of this field and its origins that reach much further back than the great outdoor enthusiasts of this century.

A Concrete Problem: Young People Must be Prioritized

To lay the groundwork for understanding why wilderness adventure ministries and outdoor leaders are needed today, I want to first look at the needs and opportunities to reach *young people*, who are generally (but not exclusively) the ones most captivated by the invitation of a great adventure. To be clear, I am not overlooking more mature people who need wilderness experiences for rest, reflection, and spiritual formation as well. But young people are our future. Those of us who are a bit older and further along in the journey are called to serve as stepping stones for these young pioneers to make them ready to set sail into our communities and the rest of the world with fresh ideas and vision. For them to do this, however, they need the confidence and competence to meet the pressing needs of our hurting world. So, without apology, I am dedicating this book to young people. I will emphasize the need to raise up, equip, and send out younger leaders into the Great Commission by providing spiritual formation experiences in the wilderness much like Jesus did with his young disciples.

To begin, let's consider a snapshot of where youth ministry has come from historically and where it is presently. From this vantage point it will be easier to connect the dots and see why outdoor adventure ministries are particularly relevant for reaching young people *today in our global and postmodern youth culture*. So grab your journal and let's hit the trail!

Young people have often been the catalyst for sparking revival and renewal in society: "In the 1840s Bennet Tyler wrote a book analyzing twenty-four revivals during the period from 1797-1814. In his opinion fifteen of those started among youth."[3] In the early 1900s, Edwin Starbuck noted, "This much we can say with certainty, that spontaneous awakenings are distinctly adolescent phenomena."[4] A friend of mine and youth ministry expert, Dean Borgman, asserts that both Tyler's and Starbuck's conclusions apply to the Great Awakening and Second Great Awakening from about 1790 to 1840.

One afternoon in 1806, having been forced to take shelter from a pounding thunderstorm, a freshman at Williams College in Massachusetts challenged his prayer group with a vision to see more students leave the comfort of their homes to advance the gospel in other cultures. That "Haystack Prayer Meeting" formed a well-remembered mission group called the Society of the Brethren at Williams College and Andover Theological Seminary.[5]

These events were the precursor to a unique period of mission activity that came to be called the "Student Volunteer Movement." Driving this movement was a passionate leader named John Mott. He was convinced that there was, "no more important work on earth than influencing students."[6] In the summer of 1886, two hundred and fifty-one students from several dozen colleges gathered at the

Mount Hermon Conference in Massachusetts to learn about the need for a renewed commitment to missions. Dwight Moody called this the first national intercollegiate Bible study in America. After being challenged to answer the call, one hundred students pledged to go wherever they were needed to bring the light of the gospel to unreached people![7]

As with most movements, some apathy among students began to slow the progress of the Student Volunteer Movement. Noticing this, Francis Clark, who founded the Christian Endeavor Movement, felt young people were not challenged enough. As a result, he began to cast new vision to students with the profound perspective that, "the life of Christ and his teachings appeal especially to the young: how natural, almost inevitable, it is for a young person to be drawn to Christ and to accept him as Pattern and Guide when he is winsomely presented."[8]

Jim Rayburn, the founder of Young Life drew upon this lofty and compelling vision of Francis Clark. One of Rayburn's most famous sayings was, "It is a sin to bore a kid with the gospel." It is likely that his belief in the importance of a winsome proclamation of the gospel came from Clark's socio-theological assertion that young people were particularly open to the gospel because of their simplicity, zeal, adventurous spirit, and admiration of the humble personal qualities of Jesus Christ. Clark wrote in *Christ and the Young People*:

> As inevitable it is that the young should be attracted to Christ as that the magnet should draw the iron, as that the needle should point to the pole. It is only the perverted, blunted, or preoccupied nature that in youth can resist this attraction... To become a Christian is no unusual, abnormal development. It is as natural as for a flower to open under the genial rays of the April sun, or for a bird to sing at mating-time. It would be a tremendous gain if this truth were fully understood: that it is the natural, normal, to-be-expected development that a young person should become a Christian before he is (we will say) eighteen years of age.[9]

This was one of Clark's most poignant statements. It contributed significantly to the development of youth ministry as a viable focus for the church especially in western countries where his writing was available. Clark was impassioned by the apathy he saw poisoning the once catalytic YMCA movement. As a result, he hardened his resolve to convince local churches and ministries to take more seriously the responsibility to introduce young people to Jesus and help them grow in their faith. He wrote:

> I believe that parents, Sunday-school teachers, pastors, should expect those for whom they are responsible to become Christ's willing and avowed followers before they reach the legal age of manhood. It should be considered a strange, abnormal, almost an inexplicable, thing if a boy or girl should grow up in our Christian families, in our Sunday-schools, within the sound of church bells, and not become a Christian. This does not do away with the idea of conversion, or substitute confirmation for regeneration; but it does show that there is a harvest-time in the spiritual realm, and that harvest-time is not at the end of the season, when the grain is matured, and, like a shock of corn fully ripe, man is waiting to be gathered to his fathers, but that is nearer to the other end of life, when the generous, alert young soul is eager to ask the question, "Lord what wilt thou have me to do?" and, when he hears the Master speak, to say, "Here, Lord, am I; send me."[10]

Percy Crawford was another uniquely gifted young leader who had a razor sharp focus on reaching young people with the gospel. He pioneered the art of contextualizing the message of the gospel for the youth culture of his day. Probably the most profound contribution Crawford made to the contemporary development of youth ministry was his use of current and popular music.[11] He believed that secular music could be redeemed for sacred purposes. Young people listen to and sing secular music and this inevitably affects their worldview. So he sought to redeem it for God's glory rather than fight against it.

I remember many a day hiking along with groups of kids singing songs to take the focus off the grind of a climb. As I reflect on the secular songs kids like to sing, it is amazing how many current songs have an element of spiritual value. In his day, Crawford challenged youth workers to reclaim secular music as a sacred tool for pointing young people to Christ—the ultimate fulfillment of their longings. In addition to his novel perspective on the importance of music, he also revolutionized how to preach to young people using a lively and personable style with clear and simple language.[12] I emphasize this style of teaching in later chapters as we discuss "teachable moments" and "opportunity-teaching" in the outdoors.

In the 1930s, a young engineering student named Jim Rayburn began to sense a call to pursue young people as his primary ministry in the Presbyterian church:

> ...the advice of a Dallas pastor challenged him to a revolutionary kind of ministry. That challenge involved a moratorium on developing youth programs and on inviting teenagers to church or youth group. It demanded that one go from the church to where youths were. There one was to meet and listen and laugh and learn. Out of relationships formed, a whole new kind of program might emerge.[13]

In the wake of Mott, Clark, and Crawford, Rayburn trained each of his youth evangelists to, "Earn the right to be heard by a ministry of presence. Rayburn and those around him developed singing, humor, and telling the gospel in stories to a fine art."[14] Soon after Rayburn's radical shift from program-based ministry to turf-based youth work, Billy Graham helped develop a similar model called Campus Life. They also aimed at going after kids on their turf—the school campus.

Concern for Youth Today

Jumping ahead to youth culture today, we need to consider some trends among youth in both the developed and developing world. In Chap Clark's book, *Hurt: Inside the World of Today's Teenagers*, he sites some very important contemporary research on adolescents. He claims that teenagers, particularly in western cultures, are growing up with an increasing sense of *abandonment and hurt*. As a result, he suggests that any youth ministry approach today would do well to focus on three goals: 1) Develop nurturing environments for young people; 2) Provide stable and secure relationships where young people truly feel loved; and 3) Help young people experience authentic and intimate relationships with loving adults.[15]

As we step into considering *why outdoor adventure is particularly relevant today*, Chap Clark's findings provide a good foundation by showing us the *felt needs* of many young people. This book illustrates how outdoor adventure ministries directly address those needs.

A unique demographic shift is also under way in the rest of the world. Youth populations are bulging at the seams. As I have worked with, interviewed, and learned from youth workers in more than twenty-five countries, I have become more convinced of the necessity for the church to re-assert its commitment to young people. We must focus on making disciples of young people so they can become the social entrepreneurs and spiritual leaders their communities desperately need.

For example, as we have listened to Christian leaders throughout Asia over the past several years, it is commonly agreed that one of the most pressing needs today is a strategy to address the *vacuum of leadership* within the church in Asia. Hwa Yung, a mission leader in Singapore, described the problem of leadership in Asia: "There is almost a total vacuum here...Because there is a dearth of older and wiser leaders in this part of the world, there is insufficient modeling and mentoring of younger leaders."[16]

Consider this shocking statistic: The church in North America spends 94 percent of its resources on its own ministries and only gives away 6 percent to missions. Yet only 5 percent of the world's population is in North America![17] That means that roughly 95 percent of the world's young people live outside of North America, and only 6 percent of the North American church's financial resources are being invested in the majority of the world!

This is a big challenge, but I'm not a doomsayer. Following Jesus' lead, we take heart that the best way to move forward is to *start small*. Jesus started by apprenticing twelve disciples. We can do the same today. If we are to develop a new wave of young leaders who will engage in global missions (as in the radical days of the "Student Volunteer Movement" more than one hundred years ago), we must renew our commitment to Jesus' way of apprenticeship as the means for preparing and sustaining them in missions. So where do we start? By modeling the Master's way of personal evangelism. Through the rest of this book we embark on a journey to rediscover Jesus' uncanny preference for equipping his disciples through outdoor experiential learning. In his day, he tapped into creation— *the tangible antique version of YouTube*—to show them clip after clip of what it meant to live a radically transformed life. Not having YouTube to toy around with or an Internet connection to illustrate the ways of the Kingdom, he decided that the technicolor theater of creation itself, with all of its pithy object lessons, would suffice. That's much better than a flat screen.

New Wineskins

One might say, "Yeah, but Jesus lived in an agrarian society. Would he still do the same thing today in our ever-changing urban communities?" I'd respond, "Yes, *especially* in the midst of an increasingly urban world where people are largely out of touch with creation, Jesus' strategy for changing people's lives needs to still be emulated." Given the theological rationale I will present throughout this book, I believe he would likely do much of the same today. I think he'd be outside a lot, looking for ways to get people's attention through experiences that could scrape the plaque off their jaded souls.

We don't have any reason to believe his vision or methodology has changed. Unfortunately, what has seemed to change is our lack of commitment to making disciples like he did through *apprenticeship*. Yes, I'm making a generalization, but it sure seems to me that we have become fascinated with programs. For some reason, we have a tendency to still invest most of our time, energy, and money in *attractional* models of evangelism and discipleship. It's a "build it and they will come" strategy rather than a "they will come if we go out and pursue them" strategy. The church needs to consistently resist this shift and instead imitate Jesus' model of apprenticeship.

Jesus Didn't Come to Rubber Stamp the Status Quo

After four hundred years of silence following Malachi's prophetic ministry, Jesus came into history with a bang—to radically shift the prevailing *inward* posture of Israel to a more outward missional way of life. The Jews, living under the pressure of the Roman government, were marginalized and the fruit of that oppression turned them away from the trajectory God had set for them to be an outwardly mission-focused people of God. This was their original commission through Abraham (see Genesis 12:1-3). Through the wearing down pain of being an occupied nation, they became inwardly focused and, rather than engaging the world, they withdrew from God's mission to "be a light to the nations."

Because of fear and selfishness, we all have this tendency toward inwardness. Yet Jesus inaugurated his ministry with a new wineskin full of life-giving vision to transform lives, communities, tribes, clans, cities, and nations to the very ends of the earth. His way of transforming lives was *incarnational (relational), rather than attractional.* In just three years, he had developed an estimated one hundred devoted disciples who carried on his ministry after his ascension. And they multiplied their number of followers after he was gone by mimicking his model for change.

A lesson from nature illustrates his strategy: Small, seemingly insignificant, and powerless grains of yeast can bloat and reshape a whole lump of crushed wheat dough. Similarly, Jesus chose a few young people probably in their late teens and twenties to fill the world with a gospel virus for which there is no vaccine. I believe Jesus' focus on young leaders was strategic. Here's why: after the ascension, because these leaders were so *young*, they were able to make more disciples through *three or four generations*! This solidified a movement that has now stretched to most of the people groups in the world. These young leaders who had been stamped by his presence had several generations to keep retelling the story until that fledgling movement had successfully carved a canyon of young churches, through which the stream of the gospel has continued to flow for all generations since. And apprenticing young people to make Christ one's all and all is still the church's feature film. This is not the time for a long winter's nap from evangelism. Is it tolerable that seven thousand people groups in our world still remain completely unreached with the gospel? The question is not "if," but "how" will we effectively develop more young leaders who will enthusiastically and courageously proclaim the good news message of Jesus Christ to the unreached?

Old Wineskins

In answering this question, we must first look at Jesus' intent for his followers to bring the gospel to *all* of creation (see Mark 16:15). There is no shortage of literature addressing the subjects of evangelism and discipleship and leadership. Leadership has become a *buzzword* for the twenty-first-century church. There are countless conferences, seminars, parachurch groups, motivational speakers, etc., who promise to help groups learn how to reach people with the gospel. Yet, Todd Johnson provides a very important perspective on the recent history of the church's mission efforts. If taken seriously, his research leaves us with few choices. If we are to truly advance the Kingdom by breaking new ground and renewing previously "reached" mission fields, we must radically prioritize missions to youth today. Johnson mentions several global plans attempted in the past hundred years. In 1900 it was, "The evangelization of the world in this generation"; in 1963 it was, "The master plan of evangelism"; and in 1986 it was, "One million native missionaries," just to name a few of the dozen or so recent global plans.

Yet, even with the significant fruit resulting from these plans, Johnson offers some startling observations about the state of missions today. His findings will filter back to our discussion regarding how to reach the young people of every city through developing leaders through outdoor adventure experiences. Johnson writes:

> There is a strong tendency to recreate plans without reference to previous plans. The most significant problem with this list of plans is the passage of time. One can see this in Samuel

Zwemer's *Unoccupied Mission Fields of Africa and Asia* (1911). He wrote this book in response to a request for a pithy survey on the unfinished task from the World Missionary Conference in Edinburgh in 1910. Much has stayed the same in the nearly 100 years since the book was published. His description of the unfinished task in 1911 stretching from Morocco to Indonesia is largely true today.[18]

He asserts that even with the notable success of many of these global mission plans, more than 90 percent of all Christian evangelism is still aimed at people groups with sizable Christian influence. It does not break new ground with non-Christian people groups. As long as this is the case, unreached people are not being reached.

I have observed that much of the material and training available to aid leaders in developing global evangelism and discipleship plans focuses on: 1) How Jesus taught (Method/Style); 2) What Jesus taught (Content); and 3) Why Jesus taught (Purpose). Two of the most widely embraced examples of this trend are: *The Purpose Driven Church*, and *40 Days of Purpose*. (There are many others, as well). We heartily agree that these three aspects of Jesus' teaching are important to understand in order to train disciples to be mission-focused.

Yet even with wide availability of such excellent resources, why are we still making such little headway globally among unreached young people? I contend one possible reason is a lack of emphasis on apprenticing young people the way Jesus did. We sometimes rely on programs or events rather than emphasizing long-term relationships. In building relationships with young people we can't just focus on *what* we are teaching them but we also have to give attention to the *context* (setting and timing). In preparing his disciples to follow him for a lifetime, Jesus seemed to be as much concerned with the *timing* and *setting* (when and where) of his teaching, as he was with the "*what* and *why*" of his teaching. In other words, Jesus' teaching and training methods were relational and experiential in nature: He was the Master of *utilizing novel settings and well-timed instruction to create a need-to-know* among those who were following him. This fostered trust in his relationships and created a platform for radical transformation because people knew that he cared about them. Theodore Roosevelt coined a phrase that youth workers know is true among young people: "People don't care what you know unless they know that you care." Jesus seemed to operate in his relationships this way.

Jesus wasn't just trying to get good content out there because good content doesn't change the world. He was trying to change lives through apprenticeship, which is intensely experiential in nature. He was about making disciples not just preaching. To enhance disciple-making today, we need to look not only at *what* he taught, but *when and where* he taught, which was often in the context of the outdoors.

Life-Changing Experiential Learning

Over the past twenty years, my wife and I have worked primarily with university and high school students. We have taken hundreds of young people and their leaders to evangelism-focused camps, and facilitated opportunities for them to hear the gospel and grow in their faith through large and small groups. Yet as we look at the fruit of this ministry (by the grace of God), many of the young people whose faith has become most rooted and fruitful are those who have participated in a wilderness and/or short-term missions trip. Why is this? A common denominator is that these young people who participated in wilderness or mission trips encountered Christ in an environment of experiential teaching and modeling. What contributed largely to their transformation was the *setting in which they learned*, e.g., the wilderness, or in the context of serving others in community.

I have led more than thirty-five groups of young people (group sizes averaging between ten and fifteen) on weeklong wilderness journeys, encompassing more than three hundred and sixty-five days of leading and equipping in the context of outdoor adventure. These trips have spanned North America and ten other countries, and that number continues to grow. We have observed that *timing* and *environment* are critical elements in the learning process. Yet most contemporary paradigms of teaching focus only on *style of communication*. The emphasis in training Christian leaders is on acquiring speaking skills to effectively capture people's imagination through intelligent rhetoric. The weakness in this paradigm is that most teaching today happens in *contrived settings*, e.g., a church building, Sunday school class, through television or video programs, etc.

When Jesus taught his disciples he did so mostly in *real* dynamic settings that were in a constant state of flux. From what we can tell, his stories and illustrations were not usually contrived to just make a point, but rather he crafted his teaching to sow seeds of life into people's hearts in the context of a real experience the audience was either currently experiencing, or had recently experienced. Their frame of reference was genuine and fresh.

I am particularly fascinated with how often Jesus took his disciples on *journeys* in order to facilitate teachable moments from situations that occurred. He taught along roads, in fields, in boats, in the Temple court, and while resting in gardens. I believe that if you look at the setting of his teaching and try to discern the impact of the experiential aspect of the learning process, you might discover fresher ways to reach the hearts of people today.

When Jesus taught, he was not interested in giving people information. Rather he gave them *himself*. Information is passive, whereas a *message* evokes and calls for a response. Jesus masterfully made people respond. It is widely accepted today that learning increases as stress and tension increase. In other words, *our senses are more keenly involved in the learning process as we're pushed out of our comfort zone.* Jesus was the master of applying just enough stress to observers (especially his band of followers) so they would begin to ask questions rooted in the core of their being. Yet, he did not push them over the edge. There is a point where, if people are over-stressed, the learning curve goes down because survival becomes the focus. A recent study on the value of stress experiences supports this view:

> [There is] encouraging empirical support for the philosophy of stress-inoculation training as implemented in an Outward Bound program. The cutting edge of challenge, it seems, can and does make people stronger, particularly when the salve of social support is applied.[19]

Jesus strategically took his disciples on "stress-inoculating" journeys during his ministry in order to deepen their faith. *Jesus' pattern of teaching coupled compelling rhetoric with authentic experiences.* Research indicates people forget 55 percent of the words they've heard within six hours of hearing them, and they forget 80 percent of what they have heard within three days.[20] I think most would agree that folks rarely walk away forever changed even by the greatest of sermons: This was even true among the crowds that followed Jesus. They listened, were amazed, walked away, and after a while forgot what Jesus had said and done. So, in contrast, Jesus connected object lessons and learning experiences with what he was teaching. *The outdoors was an anvil he chose to shape his apprentices.* Today, we must renew this ancient style of apprenticeship if we are going to raise up young leaders with a missionary spirit to once again turn the world upside down with the good news.

CHRISTIAN OUTDOOR LEADERSHIP

Introduction: Five Smooth Stones of Wilderness Theology

Awakened in the Wilderness

As a landscape architecture student at the University of Arizona, I gained an appreciation for the desert. In trying to excel in my design projects I would spend countless hours looking at outdoor landscapes and working in the studio to design spaces that would provide rest and renewal for people. (While seeking to design restful spaces I'd sometimes be in the studio for a couple of days at a time without sleep, trying to perfect my drawings—how ironic that I was getting no sleep while designing spaces for rest and renewal! I admit, at the time it was a bit of an obsession.)

Having grown up in the mountains of Colorado, I had a real appreciation for the natural art of God's creation, so I tried to make all of my architectural designs reflect the creativity I saw in God's creation. The closer I could make my work resemble something I had seen in nature, the more appealing it seemed to be to my audience of critiquing students and professors. Maybe you have experienced this walking through a beautifully designed park or enjoying a well-landscaped back yard. The closer these spaces parallel the creativity we see in the natural world, the more restful these spaces seem to be. Well, after four years of being trained in the design studio, as I was about to graduate and take a job in a landscape architectural firm, Jesus got through to me that, although I knew a lot *about* him from observing his qualities in creation, I still did not *know* him personally. So in God's sovereignty, grace, and perfect timing, he turned my world upside down to finally orient me to himself and save me from my pride and rebellion. Appreciating his beauty was not enough—he wanted me to belong to him.

One of the most significant changes that occurred after committing my life to Christ was a vocational shift. Although I absolutely loved architecture, Jesus had other plans and called me to start pursuing high school kids in the community with the gospel. The Lord called me to walk away from what was looking like a promising career and invited me into the ministry of Young Life to make disciples of young people—starting with a subculture of *Goth* kids who hung out at the local Wienerschnitzel.

While working with kids in Tucson, Arizona, I began to develop a desire to take them out into the wilderness to experience the beauty and perspective the wilderness offers. I applied for an outdoor guide position at Wilderness Ranch, in Creede, Colorado, and was accepted. The first week of the summer, I led a trip with Becky. We became fast friends and got married a couple years later. That was the best decision I ever made!

After moving to Aurora, Colorado, to direct an urban and suburban youth ministry at Aurora Central, Eaglecrest, and Smoky Hill high schools, we continued to take young people out into the wilderness every summer. At the time, Wilderness Ranch was full to the gills with summer campers, so we began to pray about a way to get more young people from the Denver area out into the wilderness. Soon, we began to sense the Lord giving us a vision, so we stepped out in faith and started a backcountry ministry to serve kids in the area. We started small, but by the second summer more than three hundred kids and leaders experienced guided wilderness adventures throughout Colorado! This was obviously the Lord's idea. After several more years our vision continued to grow, and I began traveling to help expose youth workers in other countries to the benefits of taking young people on outdoor adventures. And the journey continues...

Serendipitous Discoveries

In doing research for this book the past five years, I tripped over a few unexpected discoveries. Not surprisingly, wonderful discoveries usually happen when we start mining down deeper into something. Maybe it's one of God's small rewards for the effort of inquiry. For example, in the closing moments of writing this book, I came across the apostle John's words at the end of his gospel: "Jesus did many other things as well. If every one of them were written down, I suppose that even the whole world would not have room for the books that would be written" (John 21:25). I sat in complete silence and awe with tears welling up in my eyes, realizing I had been feebly trying to write a book these past five years *to make a point John summed up in thirty-three words*. For the three years John walked side by side with Jesus, he saw him constantly using experiences and object lessons to demonstrate the secrets of the Kingdom of God both in word and deed. In fact, there were so many examples for John to draw from when he sat down to write his account of the gospel that even the whole world would not have had room for all the books that could have been written.

This little book is one to add to that never-ending library. These pages are simply an attempt to send out a smoke signal to Christian leaders today, that we can't forget Jesus' style of teaching was mostly experiential. At the risk of being a little dramatic, in writing this book I feel a little bit like the character Pippin in *The Lord of the Rings* trilogy, who lit the signal fire above Minas Tirith to call for help from the warriors of Rohan at a desperate hour. As signal fires were lit across the whole mountain range toward Rohan in response to Pippin's alarm, I'm inviting leaders on every continent who see the decreasing effects of outmoded programmatic approaches to ministry, to light with me a string of signal fires stretching across both hemispheres to begin a massive return to Jesus' shoulder to shoulder style of experiential, adventurous, and relational evangelism.

In *The Ring of Truth: A Translator's Testimony*, J.B. Phillips retells several of his own serendipitous discoveries in the process of writing his modern-day student version of the New Testament. *He also found there are rewards for deeper inquiry*. Have you ever been studying something that is really familiar to you, or walked a path that you've walked before, and for some reason you slowed down and looked deeper at the details? When we do this, we sometimes see secret treasures of truth that are only visible to those who are courageous enough to pause. One of Phillips' friends, C.S. Lewis, described a memory when he, as a boy, looked intently into his brother's homemade terrarium and was immediately struck with a realization that he had within his soul a desire to know the One who knew the mysteries of the life bursting forth in his miniature garden. Lewis writes:

> On a summer day there suddenly arose in me without warning, and as if from a depth not of years but of centuries, the memory of that earlier morning at the Old House when my brother had brought his toy garden into the nursery. It is difficult to find words strong enough for the sensation which came over me; Milton's "enormous bliss" of Eden...comes somewhere near it. It was a sensation of course, of desire; but desire for what? Not, certainly, for a biscuit tin filled with moss...It has taken only a moment of time; and in a certain sense everything else that had ever happened to me was insignificant in comparison. [21]

Phillips, while translating familiar passages of the Bible had a serendipitous discovery of his own. As simple as it sounds, he says that it finally hit him that *God cares for us personally*. The apostle Peter wrote, "Cast all of your anxiety upon him; for he cares for you" (1 Peter 5:7). What a delightful, breathtaking surprise it is to realize that the Heavenly Father does care for you and me, and that he is ready and willing to take all of our burdens onto himself. That is a relief, a breath of fresh air. *Familiar paths can reveal deep and transforming surprises if we stop long enough to gaze into the details.*

When I was in college, I too was surprised by God's mercy when I was awakened to the reality of my sin that not only affected me, but really hurt others as well. As I sat piled in a heap of guilt, a married couple picked me up and began spending time with me to pick up the pieces of my broken life. They were busy people but they invited me to join them on each of their date nights for a year! During that time, they showed me through their actions, and through the honesty of their own testimonies, that I was not a helpless cause. That maybe, just maybe, God had a plan for my life beyond my failures, and the hurt I had caused others. Phillips states, "We are in no position to judge ourselves; we simply must leave that to God who is our Father and who 'is greater than our heart and knows all things.'"[22] That was a serendipitous discovery that changed my life. Now, in a similar way that J.B. Phillips had a few serendipitous discoveries in translating the New Testament for students, I'd like to share a few discoveries that I stumbled upon in preparing this little book.

Discovery #1: Jesus' First Disciples Were Young

It is fascinating to consider the education system of the ancient Hebrews. At the time Jesus was born, the Jewish nation was in essence a nation within a nation. They had their own laws, their own education system, their own grocery stores, and their own calendar. A typical Jewish child would start their education at home. They would learn the *Shema* (see Deuteronomy 6:4-9; 11:13-21 and Numbers 15:37-41), various other Bible stories and proverbs, as well as prayers and hymns.[23] Then, at age six, they would start attending a Jewish elementary school called *Beit Torah*. Their *Hazzan* (teacher) would teach them portions of the Hebrew Scriptures (Genesis-Malachi), but especially the Pentateuch (first five books of the Bible).

By age twelve or thirteen they would have the Pentateuch memorized. Then most students would graduate to become an apprentice in a family trade. This is probably what Jesus did in taking after his carpenter father. Some kids who really excelled in school would get the opportunity to learn from a *Soferim* (scribe) at a Scribe's school that was called *Beit Talmud*. These kids would spend about three years continuing to study and memorize the rest of the Hebrew Scriptures. They would also receive training in advanced religious and theological literature, both written and oral.[24] The final season of education for the most elite students would be to apprentice a rabbi for the next 15 years or so until they could become a rabbi themselves.

This season of their education was called *Beit Midrash*. In this rigorously academic environment, a student would become intimately acquainted with their rabbi's interpretation of the Scriptures and would, in essence, promote and carry the baton of their rabbi's teachings and interpretations. The term rabbi simply means "my master." During the time of Jesus, "rabbi" was a title applied to the head of any trade. For example, certain religious teachers were called rabbi, as was the head of the weaver's guild. Even the head of the gladiators was called a "rabbi".[25] This form of address was commonly applied to teachers, but not used exclusively as a teacher's title until after the time of Jesus Christ.[26] One common characteristic among all types of rabbis, though, was having a group of apprentices diligently seeking to learn and master their trade.

When Jesus became a rabbi around age thirty, he, too, followed the model of apprenticing young students (disciples), yet with one significant contrast from other "religious" rabbis. Other religious rabbis followed the *Beit Midrash* model and would choose only *elite students* who had completed the strictest education available in the Jewish community. Yet, apparently, none of Jesus' first disciples had been given the privilege of this elite education. They were far from elite—they were tradesmen. This is where Jesus broke from the mold in a very distinct way. Instead of choosing the valedictorian and salutatorian from the most prestigious *Beit Talmud* schools, Jesus went out to a beach and chose some minimally schooled fishermen to be his first group of apprentices. Another *radical break from the system* was that *he chose* his disciples; they didn't choose him. He went to them, chose them, told them to leave their nets and vocations, and start following. They didn't go to him and ask to be his pupils. Nor did they go through some sort of grilling process...they just became his chosen ones by the authority of his call.

Choosing Adolescents?

In the time of Jesus, the Jewish community recognized adolescence as a special period in one's life. It was set aside as a special time for assuming political and religious responsibilities, and was ushered in with special ceremonies. B.A. Hindsdale writes:

> Many a Jewish tradition and legend represents the hero as having made his first great decision in life at the opening of adolescence. According to legend, it was at twelve that Moses left Pharaoh's daughter's house, and that the boy Samuel heard the voice of God in the night.[27]

Jesus began his public ministry when he was around thirty years old. His disciples would have been younger than he, and it is likely that Peter would have been the oldest among the disciples since he was designated as their peer leader. Although we don't know each of their specific ages, we can assume they were young, and chomping at the bit to make their lives count.

Young people today are also yearning for a meaningful vision for their future. The world of video games and reality TV has only deepened their starvation for experiences that cause true transformation and cast compelling vision for their ultimate purpose. Thankfully, first century Palestine was absent of addicting games like "Grand Theft Auto IV" and "Soul Calibur," but, in reality, it did not lack distractions and burdens that were equally concerning. There were distractions of wealth, poverty, and religion. There were weighty burdens of Pharisaical laws and bitter Roman occupation. As Jesus looked into the culture of his day, he settled on a surprising strategy to reach them: *He chose a group of young people to turn the world upside down, he used the wilderness as his primary classroom, and he employed adventure to produce radical commitment toward his mission.*

Young people have always needed time away from distractions so they can rest their soul and learn to think clearly. Observing how Jesus invested in his young disciples, we can see that their basic needs were the same as young people today. Chap Clark's recent research encourages youth workers to focus on: 1) Developing nurturing environments for young people; 2) Providing stable and secure relationships where young people truly feel loved; and 3) Helping young people experience authentic and intimate relationships with loving adults.[28] This was what Jesus did. Apparently, time *journeying in the outdoors* with the twelve was one of the main ways he accomplished this goal. Experiential learning accomplishes these goals by offering natural decision-making scenarios that teach young people how to avoid trivial emotional distractions that can consume them. Wilderness journeys draw out the best in people by confronting their fears and exposing the traps of entitlement. We'll see throughout this book that the wilderness helps sever the entanglements that strangle away God's epoch vision for our lives.

Discovery #2: Jesus Led Wilderness Adventures

Jesus taught along roads, atop mountains, in fields, in boats, while resting in gardens. He used adventure to produce faith. Jesus' aim was to develop salty leaders who would be resilient to the temptations of the world. God often allowed fearful circumstances to test belief in his followers to show them nothing was too difficult for him to do on their behalf. *Copying an Old Testament pattern, Jesus often arranged for his disciples to experience fearful wilderness experiences in order to grow their faith.* For example, after a long and tiring day of ministry Jesus instructed his disciples to go over to the other side of the lake for some rest:

> And there arose a fierce gale of wind, and the waves were breaking over the boat so much that the boat was already filling up. Jesus himself was in the stern, asleep on the cushion; and they woke him and said to him, 'Teacher, do you not care that we are perishing?" And he got up and rebuked the wind and said to the sea, "Hush, be still." And the wind died down and it became perfectly calm. And he said to them, "Why are you afraid? How is it that you have no faith?" They became very much afraid and said to one another, "Who then is this, that even the wind and the sea obey him?" (Mark 4:37-41)

The treachery of a furious squall tested their strength to the point where they thought they were going to die. Waking up in the stern of the boat, Jesus spoke to the wind, commanding it to halt its fury. The waves calmed. What an eerie experience it must have been to witness a conversation between Christ and his creation! Jesus intentionally crafted this wilderness experience to show them that, although they had every reason to trust him, they still lacked faith. Could they have learned the same lesson from a lecture hall in the Temple? Or in this case, was the classroom of the sea and the timing of a raging tempest necessary to transform their hearts? The Scriptures seem to indicate the latter to be true.

Jesus shows us that the wilderness is a place where God gets our attention. If Jesus chose the wilderness as a favorite setting to shape his disciples into dynamic leaders, then is it not equally critical in our increasingly urban world for young people to encounter him through wilderness adventure? Today we must rediscover this ancient apprenticing method, which produced leaders such as Noah, Abraham, Sarah, Moses, Jacob, David, Peter, James, John, and Paul. Each of them was profoundly called and shaped by God in the wilderness.

Discovery #3: Five Smooth Stones of Wilderness Theology

Developing an adequate theological rationale for Christian outdoor leadership and adventure camping requires more than pointing to a few verses of Scripture that seem to support this type of ministry. The process of turning over scriptural stones to chart the theme of wilderness journey through the Bible was laborious, yet exciting. The first step was to identify all verses in Scripture that *explicitly illustrated change or personal transformation taking place as a result of a wilderness experience*. From this we developed a theological grid through which to filter all of the passages. We looked at *who* was involved in the passage. Was it an individual, a small group or a massive crowd? Next we looked at *where* the account took place. Was it on land or on the sea? Was it in the desert, along a river, in a cave or in a garden? Did the transformation happen as they walked along the road or through the desert canyons and valleys, or did it take place in a stationary setting: a camp, settlement, or a destination of some kind?[29]

Timing and Physical Conditions Present

Then we explored the timing of the transformational events. Was the transformation occurring during a non-stressful moment in the individual or community? Or was there a change that occurred due to some sort of *stressful pressure* applied to them? For example, what *environmental conditions* contributed to their change of heart or perspective? Was it during a storm, on a mountain, or in a harsh desert? We then looked more specifically to determine what *physical conditions* were present during this transforming event. Were they hot, cold, wet, thirsty, hungry, or tired?

Emotional Conditions

In addition to the physical conditions at hand, it soon became obvious there were a myriad of *emotional conditions* present among the individuals that may have contributed to the transformation. For example, we evaluated whether fear, grief, confusion, or relational/ interpersonal conflict contributed to the learning experience during the adventure.

Intellectual Stress

We also noted in several cases a type of *intellectual stress* present during the journey that may have contributed to the radical change of heart. For example, were the people *learning something new* or were they *reminded of something they had already known* and had subsequently forgotten to their peril?

State of Being

As we analyzed the importance of *timing* in God's transforming work, we discovered three states of being that commonly occurred during wilderness journeys. Following a line of theological study employed by Walter Brueggemann in *The Message of the Psalms*, we looked to see if the individual or group was in a comfortable state of being where they were seemingly *oriented* and "doing well" in their situation. Or were they experiencing a sense of *disorientation* where they were being stretched out of their comfort zone? Lastly, was it plainly evident in the passage that the individual or group had *come through* a disorienting experience and was now resting in a place of *new orientation* where growth and maturity had taken place because of the journey?

The Message

Next, we dug further to consider the *message* being taught during these wilderness journeys. What was God teaching the people? We discovered common themes such as the Kingdom of God, the Fatherhood of God, ethics, and Christology. Why was God teaching them this lesson at this particular time? What was the purpose or desired outcome of the lesson? The three most common purposes behind what God taught his people on wilderness journeys were 1) Changing their spiritual direction; 2) Leading them to gain a new perspective; and 3) To meet current felt needs. Regarding changes of direction, it appears God often taught a message in the wilderness to change people's view of God, to change their view of themselves, to change their view of community, and to change their view of the nations (Gentile world). Changing their view of the nations often led to the self-discovery that their identity as God's children came with a responsibility to pursue missions—to call the nations who were estranged from God back into a relationship with him.

As God sought to provide a new perspective for those in the wilderness, the essence of his message scraped beneath the surface of the soul to reveal either 1) Where the people had come from historically; 2) An honest appraisal of where they were currently in their orientation to God; or 3) A reminder of where they were headed in the future if they didn't respond obediently to him. When I take people on an adventure in the outdoors, it is easy to illustrate these lessons with a topographical map or from an elevated vista where we can see our progress on the journey. Every outdoor expedition has a starting point and a destination: each requires a keen sense of awareness of where you are, where you've come from, and where you are going. Later in the book we'll look in more detail at how to facilitate teachable moments through these kinds of wilderness object lessons.

As we developed this theological grid to understand the main categories of transformation going on in the wilderness journey passages, we discovered five main overarching principles that are the framework for our *theology of wilderness journey*. In a general sense, all of the biblical wilderness journeys that explicitly state or indicate transformation because of a coinciding desert experience fall into the following five themes, which we'll call the "Five Smooth Stones of Wilderness Theology."

When young David picked up five smooth stones to put in his pocket before facing Goliath, he knew he had the skill to defeat the giant because he had practiced throwing stones his whole life. *It wasn't the stones that would win the battle, but his skill with the stones and the favor of God.* He had confidence that the battle was the Lord's. My vision for Christian outdoor leaders is that we would also have this same level of skill to effectively lead people on spiritual journeys in the wilderness. And, like David, who only carried five little stones to carry out his objective, by learning these five main themes of wilderness theology I'm hoping outdoor leaders will be able to more effectively focus on becoming excellent in their skill as spiritual leaders without having to rely on a lot of gear or props. Like David, we need to practice the basics over and over again so that we are skilled and confident to handle even unexpected challenges.

So without further ado, what are these five smooth stones of wilderness transformation that occur in the Bible? We'll call the first stone TEMPO: The rhythm or tempo to Jesus' ministry began with retreat, which launched him into doing the work the Father had prepared for him. Jesus highly valued *retreat,* for reflection, perspective, strategy, and changing wrong views. The second stone is TERRAIN and TIMING: *The physical setting of the wilderness and the timing in which teaching occurs* are vitally important aspects of God's call upon individuals and groups. Thirdly, we see a regular occurrence of TRIALS: Trials have a purpose...*the wilderness was a special place for testing and establishing character*. Fourth, the desert was used as a *platform for establishing* TRUST. *Jesus' identity and his people's identities were established on the basis of an unconditional trust toward God*. And lastly, the wilderness was often used as a laboratory for leadership TRAINING. These five themes are the bone structure of this book.

Discovery #4: The Great Commission Setting

The most startling serendipitous discovery of all in carrying out this study was finding a "mother lode" passage in the Bible that contains all five of these themes concisely packed into it. Are you ready to hear what that passage is? *It's the Great Commission!* The Great Commission account in the Gospel of Matthew provides succinct usage of all five of these themes categorized in our study toward a theology of wilderness journey.

These themes will be woven throughout, but certain chapters will focus more directly on each one. For now, here is a brief overview of how these themes are packed into the Great Commission: First, Matthew 28:16 says, "Then the eleven disciples went to Galilee, to the mountain...where Jesus had told them to go." In other words, they *retreated* (TEMPO) to gain perspective on their mission, and to hear Jesus' strategy for carrying out their commission.

Secondly, we see the elements of *the physical setting and timing* (TERRAIN and TIMING) at work in that Jesus sent them *to the mountain*. This was an actual place, a mountain in the wilderness they had probably climbed with Jesus before. The passage continues: "When they saw him, they worshiped him; but some doubted." Here we see a pithy example of Jesus *testing and establishing character among his disciples* (TRIALS) in the context of this mountain-wilderness setting. Similarly, God tested Moses up on the mountain, transforming his heart and countenance to go down into the valley with forged character to lead the people of Israel regardless of their rebellious tendencies.

Matthew's account continues: *"Then Jesus came to them and said, 'All authority in heaven and on earth has been given to me.'"* In typical style, Jesus gets to the point straight away, clearly re-establishing his own *identity* (TRUST) and asserting unforgettably that their identity is now based on a foundation of trust in the One who has all authority in heaven and earth! Their identity is secure in him. Jesus concludes his Great Commission with these words: *"Therefore go and make disciples of all nations...and surely I am with you always, to the very end of the age."* This text has served the church as perhaps the most classic leadership (TRAINING) maxim throughout history.

Jesus had a *tempo* to his life—a rhythm of retreat. And he used the outdoor *terrain* and the *timing* of teachable moments to instruct his disciples in the secrets of the Kingdom. Through testing and *trials* in the wilderness he established an abiding *trust* in his followers. He was *training* them to be loyal and resilient so they could faithfully carry out his Great Commission. The Scripture reveals that the wilderness was central to his strategy.

PROLOGUE

The Wilderness Story...

Scrambling over rocks, zigzagging between bear grass and other scraggly desert shrubs, his feet testing each step to make sure it was solid—finally he reached the summit. Wind howling in minor diminished chords, the storm sounded like the opening music to an eerie mystery movie. He sat quietly for what seemed like hours watching with eagle eye a small rowboat pinned by the wind in the middle of the lake while his best friends strained at the oars. Waiting. Waiting. More waiting. "Father, shall I go to them now?" he asked. "Not yet" was the quiet answer, which agonized him further... not enjoying watching his friends suffer, but in the deeper wisdom of the Father, he knew they must if they were to snap out of their faithless rut.

Finally, wind-whipped and facing the darkness, Jesus stood up and retightened his sandals for the descent to the water's edge. Climbing down was a relief. He knew his friends would soon be released from the painful predicament with which they had been struggling. Sand sinking and oozing between his toes, he walked into the foaming waves. Then, with only a thought, he stepped onto the shimmering glaze of the waves and ambled the rest of the way to the tossing boat. Standing atop the very waves that threatened to capsize this little vessel full of terrified men, he pretended to walk by them as they fought against their perishing. One of them saw a shadow and screamed, "'It's a ghost...' and cried out in fear. But Jesus immediately said to them: 'Take courage! It is I. Don't be afraid'" (Matthew 14:26-27). God used the wilderness of this wild water to strip away facades and reveal the core of who they really were. These men were in great need of faith. Their foggy human-sightedness was getting in the way of liberating belief. Now from the stress of the adventure, Jesus had them in the palm of his hand. He came out to them like a potter to his wheel. God is about shaping his disciples into vessels for a noble purpose. Like sheep that tremble when the shepherd holds them tight to shear their wool...God uses the wilderness and all of its adventure and fearful circumstances to still us into faith and trust. Jesus loved them enough to wait on the mountain long enough for them to reach a point of desperation. Then he came to their rescue, and their formidable faithlessness met its match...the loving face and embrace of their Master who has authority over all creation.

When Jesus created the world in perfect community with the Trinity, he made some of it to be deserts, wilderness, and solitary places. Many of these landscapes have been settled and heavily populated, but still there remain places that offer uninterrupted quiet to connect with God and be still. The earth is no longer a ball of wild uninhabited spaces; it is also a globe full of megacities and urban sprawl. But in most places around the world solitary places can still be found. We need those places.

What is Wilderness?

With such a variety of outdoor settings in our world, how are we to compare our local outdoor environment with a biblical definition of wilderness? If I live near a rainforest in Brazil, do my wilderness encounters parallel the experiences of biblical characters that wandered around in the bone-dry desert? Does tramping through the lush wilderness landscapes of the Fiordlands in New Zealand compare at all to the wilderness sojourns of ancient Hebrews who wandered through barren lands? Is the term "wilderness" describing aloneness or does it refer specifically to geography, climate, flora and fauna, etc.? These are important questions. To have a credible theological rationale for wilderness adventure ministries, we need a working definition of wilderness so we can relate our experiences to the transformational wilderness encounters that instruct us from the Bible.

The biblical writers used various terms for wilderness that describe desert or desolate lands uninhabited by man. Robert Funk, in his article, "The Wilderness," provides a geographical definition of the term "wilderness" as it appears throughout the Hebrew Scriptures and New Testament:

> On the basis of annual rainfall...the lower half of the Rift Valley merits the description desert. This desert-dry area, moreover, covers the lower half of the valley in the shape of an inverted-U, climbing the slope on the west until it rises nearly to Jerusalem; it embraces the whole of south Judah and east of the central ridge...Apart from a few settlements supported by elaborate water systems and military outposts, there has never been extensive occupation in the wilderness of Judah. It is significant to note that this area is still dominated by Bedouin today.[30]

Defining Wilderness

Parameters are needed for using the term "wilderness," otherwise we might name any natural setting "wilderness." The danger in this approach is that if everything outdoors is wilderness, then nothing will be wilderness. Conversely, I believe the Bible uses the term wilderness to describe places with several unique qualities. *Therefore, we will define wilderness primarily in terms of its remote proximity to civilization and its limited habitation.* The wilderness is any place where the natural creation dominates the landscape, thus distant enough from civilization where one's senses ascertain he or she is more influenced by the forces of nature rather than the comforts of civilization. For practical purposes, we will use three standards to describe where wilderness might be; all of which, to the best of our knowledge, parallel the biblical definition of wilderness: 1) Biblical references to wilderness refer to desert or desolate lands *uninhabited* by man; 2) The standards of the United States Wilderness Act of 1964, authored by Howard Zahniser, describe wilderness in terms of *pristine* landscapes; "untrammeled by man"[31]; and 3) The standards of the National Outdoor Leadership School (NOLS) Wilderness Medicine Institute specify that if a person is more than one hour from medical help, this is considered "wilderness," thus the person administering first aid has other priorities to consider in providing treatment because of the risks of exposure and weather. This is a more practical definition but it is useful because it is measurable.

"Wilderness" in the New Testament refers to the wilderness of Sinai or the wilderness of Judea (not just Judah), including the lower Jordan Valley and most likely the eastern slopes of the valley as well. This description is important for our theology of wilderness because we must understand that "wilderness," as it is mentioned in the Old and New Testament, is a *specific place not just a metaphor*. This distinction has enormous theological implications. Ultimately, we desire to see more Christian leaders changing the way they approach spiritual formation and apprenticeship by employing more experiential learning and adventure in the outdoors. So this chapter is very important in order to strengthen our argument that focusing primarily on the *metaphor* of wilderness and "our own personal wilderness experiences" is insufficient if we are committed to modeling Jesus' way of apprenticeship. He rarely alluded to personal "spiritual wilderness experiences" with his disciples. Rather he *took* them *into the actual physical wilderness* to stretch their spiritual muscles and increase their leadership capacity.

Scripturally, the term wilderness is most often used to describe a specific place rather than as a generic term. However, the "wilderness" is also used from time to time in the Bible as a metaphor. In Near Eastern thought the wilderness does carry at times a non-local connotation, but this is rare in the biblical text.[32]

From a global perspective, McCloskey and Spalding provide a contemporary perspective on the way wilderness is understood cross-culturally:

> The term "wilderness" is used primarily in North America, Australia, New Zealand, and South Africa. Elsewhere, the term "wildland" may be used more commonly for the kind of land identified in this inventory, but there are no accepted definitions of that term. In some places, wildland includes land with low-standard roads and limited levels of resource exploitation.[33]

They also provide further insight regarding the intrinsic value of wilderness and its importance in environmental terms. And they give us a description of how the international community describes its concern and affinity for wild places:

The term "wilderness" in contrast enjoys a settled definition in the places where it is used and a growing body of literature elaborating on its values. Its values fall largely into four broad categories: (i) biological: as a gene pool and benchmark against which to measure change; (ii) geophysical: to buffer climactic change and to enhance watershed function; (iii) recreational: as a place of refreshment, adventure, and rediscovery; and (iv) moral: as a place where other forces and creatures can seek their destiny free of human domination; and in some cases, it is the homeland for truly indigenous peoples.

Old Testament Terms for "Wilderness"

There are four main words in the Hebrew language used in the Old Testament to describe the wilderness. These words are: *midhbar, arabah, chorbah,* and *jeshimon.* There are two primary Greek words (with the same root) used in the New Testament: *eremia* and *eremos.* In the remaining pages of this chapter, we will look at each of these terms for desert or wilderness to gain a clearer understanding of how to use the term "wilderness" today.

Midhbar (mid-bawr')

"Therefore, behold, I will allure her, Bring her into the wilderness and speak kindly to her." —Hosea 2:14

Midhbar is a special name for the wilderness, which is applied to the deep valley of the Jordan extending from Lake Tiberias to the Gulf of Aqabah. This word is particularly associated with sunken valley north and south of the Salt Sea also known as the Rift Valley. *Midhbar* is the most commonly used word for "desert" in the Bible. It describes a landscape primarily used for driving or pasturing flocks. It means, "to drive," as in driving flocks of sheep. These *midhbar* regions were often near cities, but were clearly uninhabited lands. *Midhbar* also describes the location of the desert wanderings of Israel in the northern part of the Sinai Peninsula.

So what did it look like? For those who have not spent much time in the desert, one might imagine a vast wasteland of sand like the Sahara Desert. But for the people of Israel, the nearest desert like that would have been several days' journey away in Arabia. Instead, the backdrop for Israel's wilderness wanderings was rocky terrain, with small hardy plants, and very limited supplies of water. Rain was scarce, but when it fell the desert sprang to life. Plants, grasses, and flowers patiently waiting for the rain would gleefully sprout up almost overnight. Isaiah's vision of the renewal of Israel was an analogy drawn from what he would have seen in the desert after a rain: "The wilderness and the desert will be glad, and the Arabah will rejoice and blossom; like the crocus" (Isaiah 35:1).

Considering the scarcity of desert plants in this region, it was truly a forty-year miracle that millions of Israelites survived as they wandered through the wilderness. The fact that there was enough food for their livestock to survive is possibly the greatest miracle of all, given the limited rain and vegetation in this region of the world. Where the Hebrews had come from near the delta of the Nile there was plenty of good farmland to support millions of people, but now in the deserts of Sinai, no such farmland was available. They had to depend on the Lord to provide every meal, every rainstorm, and every spring from which they and their livestock could drink.

Midhbar is also used to describe mountains, valleys, and grassy plains surrounding the cities of Palestine where Israel eventually settled after the death of Moses when they crossed the Jordan River into the Promised Land. Jesus would eventually travel with his disciples through desert lands like this. This landscape, where nomadic shepherds could graze their flocks freely, provided Jesus with many opportunities for drawing shepherd-sheep analogies. Describing these regions, Alfred Ely Day writes:

> To obtain water, the shepherds with their flocks traverse long distances to the wells, springs or streams, usually arranging to reach the water about the middle of the day and rest about it for an hour or so, taking shelter from the sun in the shadows of the rocks, perhaps under some overhanging ledge.[34]

After escaping Egypt, it was in this landscape Moses pastured the flock of Jethro, his father-in-law. He led his flock to the west side of the wilderness until he came to Horeb, the mountain of God (see Exodus 3:1). Then, after God's commission to call for the release of

Israel from her captivity in Egypt, Moses and Aaron went to Pharaoh. Being responsible for shepherding the Hebrews they pronounced the ever-remembered oracle: "Thus says the LORD, the God of Israel, 'Let my people go that they may celebrate a feast to me in the wilderness'" (Exodus 5:1). God was releasing Israel into the wilderness to begin experiencing the freedom and security that would come through serving him alone (Exodus 7:16). This would not be a "party" in the sense that we think of a party, but it would be a lengthy celebration of dependence on God alone. The wilderness would be harsh and uninviting, but the Lord was leading them into this journey to refine their trust in him. I, too, view extended-day wilderness adventures much like this. They aren't a party in the sense of merriment all the time (because trials are inevitable in the wilderness), but they are a type of *extended celebration*. It's a gala without masks, where participants get to experience the dawning of true freedom in their soul through the transformational experiences of learning to depend on God for the basics of life.

The Lord had them safely in the palm of his hand on this desert sojourn, but their faith would be tested when they found no water for days at a time (see Exodus 15:22). After much grumbling and complaining which revealed the immaturity of their newfound faith, "they looked toward the wilderness, and behold, the glory of the LORD appeared in the cloud" (Exodus 16:10). It is important to pause and really grasp the significance that, during their time of slavery in Egypt, the Hebrews had been drawn into polytheism— away from their loyalty to just one God. Now returning to the monotheism (worshipping one God) of their ancestors, Adam, Abraham, Isaac, Jacob, and Joseph was a novel experience for them because just like the Egyptians at the time, they had digressed into polytheism. We see, in hindsight, this extended desert experience was largely ordained by God to severely test their commitment to him alone, so that, one day through them, all future people groups would be blessed because of what they learned from the One True God, Yahweh. Our adventure-loving God pulled out all the stops to ensure the Hebrew people would have forever ingrained into their community the knowledge of him and the path to eternal salvation through him alone. When the stakes were high, the wilderness was one of God's favorite instruments to ensure that permanent community transformation took place. There is no reason to think this is not still true today.

Through trials and testing, Israel wandered for countless years in *total dependence* on God for their basic needs. With sighs of relief, just before entering into a land flowing with milk and honey (see Joshua 5:6), Moses unveiled the distinct purpose God had in mind for those years of wandering:

> You shall remember all the ways which the LORD your God has led you in the wilderness these forty years, that he might humble you, testing you, to know what was in your heart, whether you would keep his commandments or not. (Deuteronomy 8:2)

This reminds me of what it's like coming back to the comforts of civilization after an intense adventure with a group. It's a relief to have comforts again, but quite often something has shifted in my soul as a result of the time of solitude with God in his creation. Being stretched out of our comfort zones helps us see what's truly in our hearts so we can orient ourselves back to fidelity with God.

Many years after this wilderness event, the twelve tribes of Jacob eventually settled the Promised Land. They had settled Palestine, but their trials were not completely over. In one of their ongoing skirmishes with the Philistines, we are introduced to a young shepherd who lived in the *midhbar* (wilderness) tending sheep for his father Jesse (see 1 Samuel 17:28). When Jesse sends David to the battle lines, we observe that God has shaped this young warrior through his wilderness experiences to have the courage and faith to be the future leader of Israel.

This wilderness-worn shepherd, David, wrote most of the Psalms. Interestingly, the words "wilderness" and "desert" in the Psalms are most often translations from the word *midhbar*—this lonely desolate land for driving flocks with which David was so familiar. For the past three thousand years, the Psalms have served as the main prayer book for people to worship and draw near to God. It's interesting to note the main shepherd-author of this prayer book spent most of his young years wandering through these barren *midhbar* landscapes driving sheep. He would have spent many of his nights warming by a fire under starry night skies. A few examples of David's (and Asaph's) wilderness psalms show us how this waterless terrain of rocks and wild animals was instrumental in producing a people of faith:

> How often they rebelled against him in the wilderness and grieved him in the desert! (Psalm 78:40)

> The voice of the LORD shakes the wilderness; The LORD shakes the wilderness of Kadesh. (Psalm 29:8)

> He split the rocks in the wilderness and gave them abundant drink like the ocean depths. (Psalm 78:15)

> The pastures of the wilderness drip, and the hills gird themselves with rejoicing. (Psalm 65:12)

> He changes a wilderness into a pool of water and a dry land into springs of water... (Psalm 107:35)

Foreseeing the Day of the Lord and the return of Christ, Isaiah also prophesied how his redemption would be like transforming a harsh barren desert into a new Eden:

> Indeed, the LORD will comfort Zion; He will comfort all her waste places. And her wilderness he will make like Eden, and her desert like the garden of the LORD; Joy and gladness will be found in her, thanksgiving and sound of a melody. (Isaiah 51:3)

God is about transforming people's souls. And the wilderness is one of his preferred instruments to produce the kind of change that puts his people back in equilibrium with his intended design. The wilderness can be a harsh and desolate place, but it produces peaceful trust in those trained by it.

Arabah (ar-aw-baw')

Besides learning a new word you can amaze your friends with when playing Scrabble, there is another term commonly used for "wilderness" in the Bible. *Arabah* refers to a very depressed and enclosed region, a sunken valley north and south of the Dead Sea. It is the deepest and the hottest chasm in the world. *Arabah*, a term referring to the specific location of the Jordan Valley, is translated by the word "desert" only in Ezekiel 47:8. It has a connotation of sterility because of the harshness of this climate. It is usually translated "desert," "plains," or "steppe" in our English translations. For example, there are several references to the "plains of Moab," which was the location of the camp of Israel on the eastern side of the Jordan River just opposite Jericho.

Before commissioning Joshua to cross over with the people into the Promised Land, Moses died at Mount Nebo, which is located in this region called *arabah*: "Now Moses went up from the plains of Moab to Mount Nebo, to the top of Pisgah, which is opposite Jericho. And the LORD showed him all the land, Gilead as far as Dan" (Deuteronomy 34:1). Interestingly, the "Dead Sea," as we refer to it today, was also called the Sea of Arabah (Joshua 3:16).

The well-known prophecy of Isaiah that John the Baptist quoted just before the baptism of Jesus uses this Hebrew word *arabah* for wilderness: "A voice is calling, 'Clear the way for the LORD in the wilderness; Make smooth in the desert a highway for our God'" (Isaiah 40:3). It is an important distinction that this word *arabah* was used here because John the Baptist's ministry actually occurred in this very place, along the Jordan in the distinctly dry and harsh desert region referred to as *arabah* throughout the Old Testament. This prophecy, foretold roughly seven hundred years before the birth of John the Baptist, was not only specific to John the Baptist's paving the way of Jesus' ministry, but also gave a *specific regional location in which this prophecy would take place.* And Jesus fulfilled this prophecy through his baptism in the Jordan in the *arabah* region, just as Isaiah said he would. The fulfillment of that prophecy couldn't be more specific!

Chorbah (khor-baw')

Chorbah is a less commonly used word, but appears to have the force of dryness and desolation. It is commonly translated as "waste places," "desolation," and "desert." For example, Isaiah reminds Israel, "They did not thirst when he led them through the deserts. He made the water flow out of the rock for them; He split the rock and the water gushed forth" (Isaiah 48:21). Isaiah later portrays a vision of seemingly impossible renewal and restoration that will resemble a desert instantly splashed with life and color so magnificent, it will resemble Eden.

This is also what God does when he makes a new creation—when a person crosses over from death to life through faith in his Son Jesus. It's like being ushered in from a desolate and parched land into an Eden, teeming with sights, sounds, and life, which awaken our senses to their original design. At last, we're saved from the arid desolation of living alone in rebellion against God. According to Isaiah's prophetic vision, *to be reconciled with God is more dramatic and miraculous than a lifeless desert turning into a Garden of Eden!*

> Indeed, the LORD will comfort Zion; He will comfort all her waste places. And her wilderness he will make like Eden, and her desert like the garden of the LORD; Joy and gladness will be found in her, thanksgiving and sound of a melody. (Isaiah 51:3)

Jeshimon (yesh-ee-mone')

Another lesser-used but important word is *jeshimon*, which literally means, "to be empty." Most often rendered "desert" in English, it denotes the wasteland tracts on the eastern and western shores of the Dead Sea (Salt Sea). It especially applies to the peninsula of Arabia, the most dreadful and remote of all the deserts (of which the Israelites were well acquainted), and is a proper name for this region. In addition, *jeshimon* without the article occurs in a few passages of biblical poetry in which it's rendered, "desert."[35] Another notable occurrence of this word is in Numbers 23:28: "So Balak took Balaam to the top of Peor which overlooks the wasteland." This reminds me of how impactful it is to take a group of people to the top of a peak to offer a little perspective. Balaam gave Balak some serious perspective.

Describing God's loving protection of Jacob in the desert (*jeshimon*), Moses recited a song that would become a familiar song of remembrance passed down through the generations: "He found him in a desert land, and in the howling waste of a wilderness; He encircled him, he cared for him, he guarded him as the pupil of his eye" (Deuteronomy 32:10). Similarly David used this word in remembrance of how God went out in front of his people: "O God, when you went forth before your people, When you marched through the wilderness, Selah" (Psalm 68:7).

Two things that desert sojourners understandably have a craving for are *water* and a *smoother path* to walk on. Rocky terrain gets a little old after a while as ankles turn and muscles ache from the constant climbing and slipping. Two passages use *jeshimon* to describe this context really well. Psalm 106:14 describes Israel's unmet thirst in the wilderness: "In the desert they gave in to their craving; in the wilderness they put God to the test." And Isaiah 43:19 offers a vision of hope for eventual reprieve: "Behold, I will do something new, Now it will spring forth; Will you not be aware of it? I will even make a roadway in the wilderness, Rivers in the desert." Through challenging trials, wilderness experiences show us what we are yearning for most. A cool drink of water or a nicely maintained "roadway in the wilderness" would certainly be a welcome sight on a difficult day of bushwhacking up a mountain, but the Lord has an even greater gift for those who belong to him. He sent his Son, who laid down his life to be that very water and that straightened path in the desert for us to walk upon. Christ sacrificially lying down on that wooden cross was not just an act of heroic martyrdom. No, it changed reality in heaven and on earth for eternity.

James also reminds us that, as inconvenient as they are, trials are not all that bad because they actually increase our endurance and refine our desires to be aligned with what the Spirit of God desires (see James 1:2-3; Galatians 5:17-18). Wilderness experiences teach us what we ought to desire—God.

For those who will put their faith and loyalty in Jesus, a narrow path suddenly appears beneath our feet to show us the Way. Different from worldly religions that promote good works to earn access to life after death, Jesus of Nazareth pointed to a different Way. Ironically, there are no *ways or means* to earn our entry into Jesus' favor. Instead, we are surprised to find that he himself is the Way, not any of our good works! Hopefully, wilderness experiences make us crave for a *drink* from the Source that never ceases to satisfy and they make us long for the *level* path (Christ) to walk on through this dangerous journey called life. A skillful Christian outdoor leader can use these moments of awakened awareness to teach her participants that the Level Path and the Living Water is Jesus: "I have given waters in the wilderness and rivers in the desert, to give drink to my chosen people" (Isaiah 43:20).

New Testament Terms for "Wilderness"

Eremia (er-ay-mee'-ah) and *Eremos* (er'-ay-mos)

Much like David, and a myriad of other desert-formed leaders in the Old Testament, a couple of New Testament figures were also profoundly impacted by their ministry in the wilderness. John the Baptist's setting for ministry was in the wilderness. Speaking of John, Luke writes, "And the child grew and became strong in spirit; and he lived in the desert until he appeared publicly to Israel" (Luke 1:80). Later, the apostle Paul would restart his ministry in the desert of Arabia so God could establish him on new footing—with crystal clear comprehension of the gospel and how Jesus fulfilled the Messianic prophecies (see Galatians 1:16-18). Time and again, solitude with God in the wilderness seems to be an instrument of spiritual strengthening for some of our faith's most renowned leaders.

Throughout the New Testament two words, *eremia* and *eremos,* are used to describe wilderness or desert. They focus primarily on the lack of population in a region rather than upon sparse vegetation or topographical descriptions. This is important for us to know if we are to answer some of those questions posed at the beginning of this chapter, e.g., can a lush jungle be interpreted as "wilderness" or does the Bible not leave room for that application?

Because *eremia* and *eremos* generally denote a place where few people live, we can clearly make that exegetical parallel. Writers in the New Testament use these terms to describe deserted places, lonely regions, and untilled, uninhabited land fit for pasturing flocks. Interestingly, when these words are personified in the New Testament they describe persons who are deserted by others or deprived of help or protection, especially of friends and family. For example, these words describe a flock deserted by its shepherd or, in a more rare case, a woman neglected or abandoned by her husband.[36] In all of these cases, the primary meaning of *eremia* and *eremos* describes deserted places, barren regions, and loneliness (see Matthew 12:43; Luke 11:24).[37]

The gospel writer, Mark, uses these words when he records: "But he went out and began to proclaim it freely and to spread the news around, to such an extent that Jesus could no longer publicly enter a city, but stayed out in unpopulated areas; and they were coming to him from everywhere" (Mark 1:45). And Matthew records: "When it was evening, the disciples came to him and said, 'This place is desolate and the hour is already late; so send the crowds away, that they may go into the villages and buy food for themselves'" (Matthew 14:15). The common thread of these places is a natural outdoor environment relatively untrammeled and uninhabited by man.

So what are the key theological conclusions we can draw from these word studies? Louw and Nida offer a very helpful and concise explanation of how to interpret the New Testament words for "wilderness" and "desert" with biblical integrity and relevant contemporary application:

Throughout the NT eremia and eremos focus primarily upon the lack of population rather than upon sparse vegetation, though the two features are closely related ecologically in the Middle East. In most languages, the most satisfactory equivalent of eremia and eremos is a word or phrase suggesting a place where few if any people live. Such expressions are generally far better than a word meaning "a bare place" or "a place of sand," since in some languages such expressions could mean only a clearing in the forest or a sandy beach along a river bank. In the case of translations being made for people living in jungle areas, it may, however, be necessary to describe in a footnote the nature of an eremia in NT times.[38]

So, for those who live in a place that has access to beautiful wilderness areas full of wildflowers and gushing waterfalls, it's completely appropriate to connect your wilderness experience with those of your desert-wandering forefathers in the Bible. These are lonely regions. And for those who are able to access jungles for wilderness adventure experiences, the same is true. Even water-based wilderness experiences like sea kayaking, sailing, or rafting can fit this definition as they provide opportunities for solitude away from civilization in a distinctly natural landscape. Matthew records that when Jesus needed to grieve and process the death of John the Baptist, "He withdrew from there in a boat to a secluded place by himself; and when the people heard of this, they followed him on foot from the cities" (Matthew 14:13). We *all* need a secluded place from time to time.

SECTION I: THEOLOGY

CHAPTER 1
TEMPO

A Rhythm of Engagement and Retreat

My fifth-grade band teacher taught me the importance of tempo. I wanted to be a rock band drummer and beating sticks on a cowhide seemed easy enough. Boy was I wrong. I first had to learn how to keep a beat. I had to learn how to set the tempo and stick to it through the whole number so that the rest of the band could orchestrate all of the various strands of the music. When the drummers got off tempo, the conductor would stop everybody and reiterate the importance of our role to keep the rhythm. We had to learn how to focus on the beat rather than listen to all of the other instruments tooting, tweeting, and blasting away. Keeping the tempo requires you to ignore distractions. I think by the 7th grade I finally got it, and what a difference it made. I was elated at the Christmas concert after we had played all of our songs to the best of our ability. The final applause brought a sigh of relief and a big grin on my face.

If we don't establish some kind of tempo or rhythm to our spiritual life, it is going to throw off everything. One of the more striking patterns of Jesus' life was his rhythm. The tempo he modeled for his disciples was remarkably simple. The movement of his ministry song was composed of two basic strands. He began with rest, reflection, and *retreat* with the Father. Then from this peaceful garden of communion with the Heavenly Father, he launched out like a cup overflowing into the Palestinian cities, towns, and villages with incredible capacity for the hard *work* to which he was called. In the most rudimentary terms, *his tempo was a pattern of retreating to the wilderness to be with God, and then engaging civilization with the message and the ministry of the gospel.*

Retreat away from the city for rest and reflection

Engaging ministry in the towns, villages, and cities

Jesus of Nazareth's rhythm of ministry typically involved engaging the masses and retreating into the wilderness with a small band of followers for rest and renewal. He retreated to reflect and remember, to gain perspective, and to form strategy. He clearly modeled this rhythm for his disciples to carry on after he was gone, and for good reason: This rhythm was sustainable and promoted health and longevity in his followers. Jesus knew how to be a marathon runner—the pace in which he trained his disciples to "run" was sustainable. Jesus' rhythm of labor and retreat models a vital principle for us today, that the right *starting place* for ministering to others is *rest*, not busyness.

God Enables a Different Way of Life

Jesus engaged the masses as a shepherd gathering lost sheep, and then he retreated for renewing fellowship with the Father. He didn't burn himself or others out in ministry. We also see this pattern in the Old Testament as God apprenticed his people to *be a people of rest*. In Exodus 16:22-36, the Lord provides extra manna for Sabbath observance to teach his people this principle. In this account, God tested the people in the wilderness to establish them in obedience to Sabbath rest and to teach them this tempo: "Then the Lord said to Moses, 'Behold, I will rain bread from heaven for you; and the people shall go out and gather a day's portion every day, that I may test them, whether or not they will walk in my instruction'" (Exodus 16:4).

Moses taught the people in the wilderness that the Sabbath was not a regular day—it was a day for retreat—for rest: "Moses said, 'Eat it today, for today is a Sabbath to the Lord; today you will not find it in the field. Six days you shall gather it, but on the seventh day, the Sabbath, there will be none'" (Exodus 16:25-26). Yet some people went out to gather on the seventh day, against the Lord's command. They got off tempo like I did with my fifth grade drum beat. And the conductor (God) stopped the music to rebuke them as well: In his response to their disobedience, we discover how seriously the Lord wants us to be *a people of rest and retreat*. His rebuke beautifully accomplished *transformation* in the people for a period of time:

> Then the Lord said to Moses, "How long do you refuse to keep my commandments and my instructions? See, the Lord has given you the Sabbath; therefore he gives you bread for two days on the sixth day. Remain every man in his place; let no man go out of his place on the seventh day." So the people rested on the seventh day. (Exodus 16:28-29)

Nahum Sarna comments:

> Not all the people were enjoying the Sabbath. Some were out hunting for manna. Once again, the theme of God testing the obedience of the people recurs. "How long will you refuse to keep my commandments?" God gives them a double portion of bread, but he demands a different way of life.[39]

Limitation

Now we will explore several sub-principles related to this rhythm throughout the Bible. Early in biblical history, God used the wilderness as a special place to teach his people that *limitations and personal boundaries are good and necessary because of pride and sin*. Through rest and retreat, we learn to respect our human limitations. God is serious about his people embracing their constraints rather than trying to be like God who has *no* limits. We see the consequence of man trying to live without limits and his abuses of power and pride early in the city of Babel (see Genesis 11:1-9). With one universal language, the potential for disaster was inevitable because of man's hunger for power and propensity toward pride. So God instituted the limitation of language (many languages instead of a universal one) upon humanity and then dispersed them into the wilderness to protect them from the power of their sinful nature. Sarna notes:

> Humankind has abused the benefactions of kinship and ready communication for unworthy, vainglorious ends in defiance of God's will that the entire earth be populated. Unless preventative measures are taken, there will be no limit to man's arrogant schemes.[40]

Again, in the wilderness at Sinai, God in his love and mercy, instituted good and necessary limitations for Israel through his servant Moses. The Ten Commandments (see Exodus 20) teach us to rejoice in limitations instituted within community for *protection and freedom* as we live in a sinful world. The Psalmist declares, "Open my eyes, that I may behold wonderful things from thy law" (Psalm 119:18). People clearly learn this principle of limitation in the context of wilderness experiences. As people experience physical limitation and fatigue, they're often more able to understand their dependence on God, and thus, more receptive to his grace. Robert Coleman agrees: "Times of human weakness afford opportunity for learning deeper spiritual truths. Usually people in physical distress are more aware of their own limitations, and hence have greater receptivity to divine grace."[41]

Wilderness experiences naturally teach us about limitations and boundaries. One can only carry so much weight on his back, paddle so long each day, and live without food and water for a limited time. One should respect the boundary of a cliff's edge if standing on a peak with 80 mph winds at his back, and probably remain at camp on the beach if the waves are too intense to navigate safe passage in a sea kayak. Thus, the wilderness is an ideal place for people to grasp the goodness of God's loving boundaries and limitations. For example, one camper shared his reflections on what he learned about the principle of limitation: "The whole experience was fantastic! Through the entire trip I was learning how to relate to people and God, learning about myself, my limits, my possibilities."[42]

Remembrance

Another principle of retreat Jesus modeled for his disciples was remembrance. We need to be reminded of timeless truths often, and probably because of its lack of distractions, the wilderness was a favorite place for Jesus to forge remembrance. In Genesis 15:1-21, the LORD made a covenant with Abraham and *reminded* him of his blessing. Another significant moment in Israel's history came after Moses appointed Joshua to succeed him in leadership. After miraculously passing through the Jordan River on dry land, God instructed Joshua to set up a memorial of stones at the edge of the Jordan River to remind succeeding generations of the Lord's faithfulness in providing safe passage into the Promised Land (see Joshua 4:6-7). It was also at this memorial ceremony by the Jordan River that God reminded Israel of *Missio Dei* (his mission to reach all the people of the world through Israel):

> For the Lord your God dried up the waters of the Jordan before you until you had crossed, just as the Lord your God had done to the Red Sea, which he dried up before us until we had crossed; that all the peoples of the earth may know that the hand of the Lord is mighty, so that you may fear the Lord your God forever. (Joshua 4:23-24)

In the most exhaustive Old Testament restatement of Israel's historic wilderness wanderings, Joshua models this principle of *remembrance* by reminding Israel of the lessons they learned through their wilderness journeys (see Joshua 24:1-28). He outlines Abraham's journey to Canaan, Jacob and Esau's journey to Egypt, and Moses' mission to lead the Hebrews out of Egypt even as Pharaoh's chariots pursued them to the Red Sea. They journeyed through the Red Sea, into the wilderness, and across the Jordan where the Lord gave Jericho into their hands—driving many people out of the land before them. After Joshua's remembrance speech in the wilderness, the people gave glory to God saying, "We will serve the LORD our God and we will obey his voice" (Joshua 24:25). After *reminding* Israel of God's faithfulness to them, Joshua dismissed each family— each to his inheritance.

In the New Testament, John the Baptist stands out as the prophet preparing the way of the Lord in the wilderness by calling the people to *remember* God's holiness and man's sinfulness (see Matthew 3:1-6). The message of repentance he preached in the wilderness rekindled distant memories for people because his preaching was similar to the prophets of antiquity. His message contrasted the other wandering prophets of his day whose false messages did not parallel the major and minor prophets of the Hebrew Scriptures. He stood out for two reasons: 1) Because he preached a message of *transformation, and* 2) The *desert-place* from which he preached contrasted the routine and comfort people were experiencing in their normal urban lives. As people traveled out of the cities to hear John the Baptist preach and receive the baptism of repentance in the Jordan River, his message stood out from the false prophets of the day because he called for *repentance and heart transformation*, and because he shouted his rebuke from the wilderness rather than from the comforts of the city. His message was different. He was different. And the wilderness-place from which he taught *reminded* people of their obstinate forefathers' journey through the wilderness. He shouted: "And do not suppose that you can say to yourselves, 'We have Abraham for our father'; for I say to you that God is able from these stones to raise up children to Abraham" (Matthew 3:9). John the Baptist's method and message wreaked havoc on the complacent attitudes that arose from comfortable cosmopolitan life. Similarly, spending time in the wilderness today can have the same freeing effect on our soul.

A theme of *remembering* the wilderness wanderings threads its way through the whole book of Hebrews. Just a brief look at the first six chapters of Hebrews establishes the following principle: *Man's continuance in following Christ is the test of the reality of his faith.* Speaking of Israel's hardened forefathers during the time of the wilderness wanderings, the writer says, "For indeed we have had good news preached to us, just as they also; but the word they heard did not profit them, because it was not united by faith in those who heard" (Hebrews 4:2). Israel often began well, but did not finish well. Ouch! Sometimes I see that pattern in my life as well—how about you? Wilderness adventures are a sure way to challenge one's propensity to give up when the going gets rough. Yet in the encouraging environment of community we persevere and endure what we started, learning that the rewards for perseverance are always worth it in God's economy.

The writer of Hebrews directly connects the Old Testament leader Joshua as an archetype of Jesus. Both Joshua and Jesus are prime examples of those who finished what they began. Continuance and perseverance in their lives was hard evidence of their faithfulness to God and his mission for each of them. As Joshua courageously led them out of desolation into the Promised Land, Jesus leads people out of lonely desolate sin into the eternal security of Paradise with God. F.F. Bruce notes:

> The reader of the Greek Bible had (and still has) an advantage over the reader of the English Bible because to him "Joshua" and "Jesus" are not two names but one; he could distinguish between our Lord and his most illustrious namesake of Old Testament days, and at the same time appreciate some of the implications of the fact that they are namesakes. The parallel between the Old Testament "Jesus", who led his followers into the earthly Canaan, and Jesus the Son of God, who leads the heirs of the new covenant into their heavenly inheritance, is a prominent theme of early Christian typology.[43]

Temporary Community

The Festival of Booths (*Hagha-Sukkot*) is a celebration to remember Israel's dependence on God as they traveled through the wilderness for forty years, living in relatively meager tents. Josiah Derby provides a helpful study on the Festival of Booths, which supports our assertion of the significance of the memory-forging benefit of wilderness experiences. He writes:

> The rationale for building a sukkah and living in it during the seven days of Hagha-Sukkot (Festival of Booths or Tabernacles) is set forth in Leviticus 23:43: "In order that future generations may know that I made the Israelite people to live in sukkot when I brought them out of the land of Egypt." The question comes to mind: What is so remarkable or significant about the manner in which the Israelites were housed during their forty-year sojourn in the wilderness that it is necessary to hold a special observance every year, generation after generation, as a reminder? Moreover, why must it be celebrated for seven days, beginning on the fifteenth day of the seventh month (Tishri); that is, at the end of summer (Leviticus 23:33)? Furthermore, why does the text say [I caused to dwell] rather than simply [they dwelt]?[44]

He continues with a description of their tents and travel garments, and their theological significance:

> The sukkah, it is argued, is a fragile hut and could not have given the Israelites much protection in the wilderness were it not for the presence of God in their midst, the real source of their protection. Hence, the sukkah is a reminder of our complete dependence upon God, since life is so fragile...The Torah is telling us that the entire sojourn of the Israelites in the wilderness was a miraculous one, under the care of the Almighty. And this phenomenon is worth remembering and celebrating with a... festival. Since we cannot replicate the manna, nor the well-preserved garments of the wilderness, we built the sukkah as a symbol of that miraculous survival.[45]

When we lead groups of people in the wilderness, we typically live in tents for several days, and sometimes a whole week. There are practical and theological reasons for doing this, such as remembering our dependence on God in every way. It is significant for the Jews that the Festival of Booths is annual and lasts for a *week*. One would not have the same experience at a *Hagha-Sukkot* festival if he were sleeping in the comforts of his home at night and just playing games in his tent during the day. And the same is true for people enjoying the wilderness. There is something special about having extended time in makeshift accommodations that forges trust in God. I say this tongue in cheek, but think about this: It's actually *a biblical idea* to plan an *annual* weeklong camping trip with your family or friends! Don't feel guilty for taking time off to make this happen—it's biblical!

On the anvil of temporary community in the wilderness, Israel learned that when God speaks, he does not change what he says. In the wilderness through regular times of reflection and journaling, we are often reminded of what *God has spoken to us personally* in the recent and distant past. The practice of regular quiet times along the journey creates space for people to think and remember ways they have seen God work or heard him speak to them in the past. His Word is living and active, shaping us like clay in the Potter's hand.

Three other passages give us further understanding that the *wilderness is a special place where God speaks to us*. In speaking of Moses' life-changing experiences in the wilderness with God on Mount Sinai, the first-century disciple, Stephen, preaches of the *living* character of God's word: "This is the one who was in the congregation in the wilderness together with the angel who was speaking to him on Mount Sinai, and *who was* with our fathers; and he received living oracles to pass on to you" (Acts 7:38). The apostle Peter asserts, "For you have been born again not of seed which is perishable but imperishable, *that is,* through the living and enduring word of God" (1 Peter 1:23). And the prophet Isaiah preaches: "So will my word be which goes forth from my mouth; It will not return to me empty, without accomplishing what I desire, and without succeeding *in the matter* for which I sent it" (Isaiah 55:11).

If he has spoken to you, his word has not changed. Because our flesh is weak, we can often become deceived by our feelings so we easily change our minds or forget what God has spoken. While leading an adventure, once your group has had adequate time to settle their souls to a position of listening in the outdoors some-where, you might ask them to consider, "Has God spoken clearly to you on some issue with which you are currently struggling? Have you, over time, fallen into unbelief even though God has already spoken to you on this issue?" We need regular wilderness ex-periences to *remind* us of what God has spoken.

Kingdom Strategies Revealed

Another principle we glean from Jesus' excursions with the disciples is that the wilderness setting is a unique and special place where new concepts of the Kingdom are often communicated and where Kingdom strategy is revealed. One of the qualities each of us is given as image bearers of God is that we are able to think and plan for the purpose of creating and producing something good and fruitful through our efforts. Humans naturally plan and develop strategies for growth. Adam was given the task of naming each animal God created and initiating a strategy for ruling and subduing the earth. In Genesis 4, we see *ingenuity and strategy* first becoming prominent among Lamech's sons. Jabal became "the father of those who live in tents and raise livestock" (Genesis 4:20). His brother Jubal became, "the father of all who play the harp and flute" (Genesis 4:21). And Tubal-Cain became the father of metal work, forging "all kinds of tools out of bronze and iron" (Genesis 4:22). The vocations of agriculture, worship leading, musical entertainment, and metal craft all originated from this family. Strategy and creativity are a part of our framework as we are created in God's image. Yet, because of our sin and pride, mankind often uses this capability for self-promotion or vain ambition rather than submitting to the purposes of God. *In contrast, Jesus modeled through his wilderness retreats a dependence upon prayer and communion with the Heavenly Father to develop his strategy for Kingdom growth.*

In the miracle of the large catch of fish where Jesus called Peter to follow him, this principle is illustrated. Peter had used *his* skill and ingenuity all night, working to bring in a catch of fish to provide for his family, his business, and his fellow workers. This particular night was exhausting and unsuccessful. Then Jesus came to Peter and his friends while they were cleaning and putting away the nets. He climbed into Peter's boat and instructed him to put out into deep water (another unique wilderness setting) for a catch. Peter reluctantly obeyed because he was tired, but nevertheless trusted Jesus and submitted to him. After rowing out into deep water, they brought in such a colossal catch of fish that both boats were about to sink.

Peter realized that the only difference between this moment and the night before (when he had been in charge using his ingenuity and strength yet caught no fish) was that Jesus was in his boat now, and it was *he* who *told* him where to drop the nets. Moreover, Peter realized Jesus had actually crafted this whole experience to show him that no longer would he rely on *his own ingenuity and strategy*, but at this moment, Jesus was making a claim on his *whole life*. Peter repented in complete humility. Now during this richly teachable moment Jesus *revealed his strategy for Kingdom growth*: "Then Jesus said to Simon, 'Don't be afraid; from now on you will catch men'" (Luke 5:10). That's the Kingdom strategy revealed through this wilderness experience: we are called to be fishers of men. Luke records Peter and his friend's life-changing response: "So they pulled their boats up on shore, left everything and followed him" (Luke 5:11). The massive catch of fish was not the issue. It was probably worth a lot of money, but Peter left it and his family business to become (like one of Lamech's sons) *the father of those who catch men—the* pillar of the first church! After confessing that Jesus was the Christ, Jesus replied,

> Blessed are you, Simon son of Jonah, for this was not revealed to you by man, but by my Father in heaven. And I tell you that you are Peter, and on this rock I will build my church, and the gates of Hades will not overcome it. I will give you the keys of the kingdom of heaven; whatever you bind on earth will be bound in heaven, and whatever you loose on earth will be loosed in heaven. (Matthew 16:17-20)

God reveals Kingdom strategy in the wilderness. Let's consider another poignant example. After climbing up a mountain, Jesus "summoned those whom he himself wanted, and they came to him. And he appointed twelve, so that they would be with him and that he *could* send them out to preach, and to have authority to cast out the demons" (Mark 3:13-15). Here we see *Jesus retreating to the moun-tain* to prayerfully select those disciples in whom he would invest most of his time. Then after choosing them, he gave the twelve a simple strategy for how to grow the Kingdom of God in their earthly ministry.

Here was the strategy he revealed to them up on that mountain regarding what it means to be a disciple: First, Jesus called them to *be with him*. Second, he appointed them to go out and *be openly verbal with what they knew of the gospel, i.e., preach*, and third, they were to *engage in conflict with the enemy* by casting out demons with his authority. Jesus, in this brief wilderness experience *on a mountain* both chose the disciples the Father told him to focus on, and gave them a simple yet timeless strategy for anyone who would come and follow him in the future.

Again, the Gospel of Mark shows how Jesus often went away to solitary places in the outdoors to receive guidance and strategy from his Father through prayer. Although doors for ministry were wide open in a certain region, Jesus chose to go to other towns and villages. During his wilderness retreat the Father spoke and reminded him that although things looked like he should stay in this town where people were readily responding to the message, the other towns and villages needed him as well. It was time to go, contrary to the disciples pleading with him to stay there to capitalize on the success he was having. We need time away to pray and listen so our strategy is formed in the *spiritual realm* rather than in the realm in which we can only *see*:

> In the early morning, while it was still dark, Jesus got up, left the house, and went away to a secluded place, and was praying there. Simon and his companions searched for him; they found him, and said to him, "Everyone is looking for you." He said to them, "Let us go somewhere else to the towns nearby, so that I may preach there also; for that is what I came for." (Mark 1:35-38)

This strategy was revealed while Jesus was on his knees in the fresh air of *retreat and prayer*. Is that how we discern our strategies for building relationships, running our businesses, or leading our ministries? I'm convicted. My knees are not calloused enough.

From a brief perusal of mission history, there are a wide variety of strategies one could use at different times and in various situations to introduce people to Jesus Christ. From these examples above, we learn that when one decides on a strategy to use, he must not be exclusively pragmatic. It's not a good idea to default to using something that has worked before somewhere else. Rather one needs to seek the Holy Spirit and ask him to reveal the strategy most appropriate in that time and place. The key principle in all these strategies is that *prayer is the way to discern which strategy to employ*. No strategy is all-sufficient. This is why Karl Barth was known to teach his students that the most important theological exercise is prayer. Jesus *models for us a routine of retreat in the wilderness to pray and discern the most appropriate strategy for the mission context we are called to engage*. Do we need a new strategy for reaching people around us? If so, a good starting place for discerning new strategies is to pull away and be alone with Christ in prayer, and see what the Lord might reveal through our time alone with him.

Kingdom Perspectives Perceived

The wilderness is also a place to gain Kingdom *perspective*. Jesus' encounter with the woman at the well is perhaps one of the most instructive passages dealing with this principle. When standing on a mountain, one has a wonderful perspective of her surroundings. With this perspective, one can see for 360 degrees and observe *where she has come from, where she is,* and *where she is going*. In this encounter, making use of the vantage point from a mountain (see John 4:20-21), Jesus first reveals to the Samaritan woman where she had come from by revealing her sinful past and her misunderstanding of worship. Then Jesus showed her where she currently *was* (in relation to the spiritual realm). He said to her, "Woman, believe me, an hour is coming when neither in this mountain nor in Jerusalem will you worship the Father. You worship what you do not know; we worship what we know, for salvation is from the Jews" (John 4:21-22). Finally, Jesus gave her perspective on where he was leading her, i.e., *where she was going*: "But an hour is coming, and now is, when the true worshipers will worship the

Father in spirit and truth; for such people the Father seeks to be his worshipers. God is spirit, and those who worship him must worship in spirit and truth" (John 4:23-24).

As we highlighted in the introduction, even the Great Commission scene exemplifies this point. The disciples proceeded to the *mountain* he designated, and from that mountain perched above the city; the apostles were able to hear his word from a vantage point, which gave them a unique *perspective on their surroundings*. Sitting on a mountain top, in a physical sense, the apostles were able to gain perspective on *where they had come from* (i.e., the path leading up the mountain which they had followed), *where they were* at the moment (on top of a mountain with Jesus having received the revelation and understanding of Jesus' position as the Son of Man), *and where they were going* (back down the mountain into the cities to engage the lost). From this *setting* on the mountain, they received a *spiritual perspective*. And, most importantly, on this special day, Jesus would point them to a path ahead which would lead them to places where they didn't often want to go, but where in the power of the Holy Spirit they would each choose to go joyfully in submission to Christ. We know from the evangelists who wrote the four gospel accounts, that each of these apostles would remember this moment and draw on its significance for the rest of their lives. *His words were not forgotten perhaps in part due to the fact that he coupled them with an unforgettable setting and experience on which to hang his words.*

I too have found *mountain-top experiences* in the wilderness to have a similar effect. Through these experiences, I can remember the climb and the view with great clarity. I need to remember these moments when I walk through some of the more difficult ravines of my normal daily routine—*in the valley below*. Hardly anything lives on the mountaintop because the environment is too harsh for creatures to thrive. Life is lived in the valley, *but times of perspective on the mountain are designed to carve landmarks of perspective into our memory, which can fuel new hope as we journey in the valleys below.*

Standing upon a peak is often a breathtaking experience. So, too, when the Lord gives us a Kingdom perspective, it lifts us from the valley of minute details that may bog us down and it gives us a fresh vision that is bigger than us. This is a healthy routine Jesus employed with his disciples. It's also a healthy practice for us to climb mountains with those we're leading in order to help them gain a renewed sense of the larger landscape of God's purposes in our world, our city, and our neighborhood—beyond our own limited personal perspective from the valley floor. May we recognize our need for this kind of routine so we don't get stuck in a rut that will sap our joy.

CHAPTER 2
TIMING & TERRAIN

The Judea Triangle

Much like the Bermuda Triangle, which has an eerie reputation for mysterious disappearances and shipwrecks, this chapter explores the desert as a mysterious place that provides the backdrop for some of history's most spectacular supernatural events. Moreover, the wilderness has been a setting for orienting some of the world's most important leaders toward God. The Bible chronicles radical events in this part of the world that make the Bermuda Triangle look like the *Pirates of the Caribbean* ride at Disney World. The "Judea Triangle" is a tongue-in-cheek term I'm using for the geographical *setting* around Judea that Jesus used for breaking and remaking his disciples. Some truly astonishing things have happened in the Judea Triangle—and in contrast to the mysterious legends of the Bermuda Triangle, we have reliable and detailed records of these supernatural events in the Scriptures.

The wilderness was a mysterious terrain for transformation throughout salvation history, and it remains so today. If we believe wilderness experiences in the text are only to be metaphorically applied, then we are missing what Jesus modeled. He took his disciples into the fresh air, on pebbled paths; he sat under trees, slept under the stars, and walked along the beach with his disciples. This was the habit of his ministry. What we see in the life of Christ is dusty feet, tired bones, and sweaty brows. He taught his disciples Kingdom truths in the midst of the physical environment (a terrain for transformation). To teach them the secrets of the Kingdom, he hardly needed to engage their imaginations at all because his audience was sitting in the "set" of the parables; all he had to do was point out the scene. Yes, learning from the wilderness metaphor teaches us something, but journeying *in* the wilderness *makes* us something. God is more interested in making and remaking, sanctifying and growing men and women.

Why Jesus Spoke in Parables

F.F. Bruce asserts the purpose of Jesus' teaching was often to shock his audience awake with the reality of their situation: "He comes to us in parables because we have a tendency to look without seeing and listen without hearing or catching on...Jesus draws us pictures—he stages little dramas for us—because he wants to make us well."[46] In most cases,

> Parables don't give us the specifics about what must be rejected, nor do they tell us the precise content of the new discovery. What they do tell us is that the discovery is so overwhelming that it shatters the routines that characterized our old way of living... Jesus is not talking about reform, but about transformation.[47]

In other words, parables can be viewed as a sort of literary "Trojan Horse"—the truth hidden inside them reveals our motives and wars against the status quo. Jesus' parables were like slow-moving glaciers marking the terrain of his audience's soul.

At first it may seem like a daunting challenge to have to discern the motives of our audience in order to speak or teach with words on target. Yet the apostle Paul tells us that if you know what *you* struggle with, chances are, other people are struggling with the same thing: "No temptation has seized you except what is common to man" (1 Corinthians 10:13). By knowing the deceitfulness and brokenness of our own lives, we can assume that our audience shares similar patterns of unbelief, temptation, and sin. By being personally vulnerable with our own common temptations, we're able to offer grace to others who share in the same brokenness. And our vulnerability invites others to be openly honest, which leads to transformation. This is a key principle for outdoor leaders to understand as they artfully guide participants through a spiritual adventure in the wilderness: although we can't perceive a person's specific motivations, we can generally know the motivations (holy and unholy) of our audience because there is no temptation that is uncommon to man. One of the keys to using Jesus' parables to foster experiential learning is recognizing that each of them speaks to the general temptations, conditions, and motivations of every person's soul. *Parables break through the most barricaded barriers of hardened human hearts.*

Anatomy of Parables

Robert Stein gives a brief history of parable interpretation over the past two hundred years to show the progress of research that has sought to understand the purpose of Jesus' parables. Toward the end of the twentieth century, Adolf Julicher's research on the parables of Jesus led him to a perspective that within each parable was *one main point*. He urged students of Scripture not to seek allegorical significance in the details of the parables unless it was absolutely necessary. Later in the early twenty-first century, C.H. Dodd and Joachim Jeremias focused their parable research on seeking to understand the *original setting (sitz en leben)* in which the parable was uttered. In the mid-1950s, Hans Conzelmann and Willi Marxsen conducted their parable research through the filter of the redaction criticism method, which was a popular technique at the time. They sought to understand *how the evangelist who wrote the parable would have interpreted it.*

Today's parable research can be understood in two main categories: 1) *Structural analysis* seeks to understand deep structures of meaning below the surface of the narrative, and 2) *Aesthetic analysis* is concerned with the larger units and surface level of the text. This method seeks to understand the text in light of literary forms and paradigms (humor, tragedy, analogy, simile, etc.). According to Stein, the prevailing view today is that parables are not limited to a single meaning or point as Julicher, Dodd, and Jeremias maintain: "Since the way in which parables became language events is different for each hearer or reader, the meaning of the same parable will of necessity also be different for each individual."[48] In other words, contemporary exegetes are encouraged to focus more holistically with special attention to what God is *saying to us* in the parable. I believe a careful and balanced perspective in our interpretation of the text will protect modern interpreters from missing the literary and historical context of the parables, while remaining open to the Holy Spirit as he translates the principles into one's contemporary context, where we can practically apply what God speaks to us.

Point of Parables

What is a parable? C.H. Dodd provides a concise definition in his classic work, *The Parables of the Kingdom*:

> At its simplest, the parable is a metaphor or simile drawn from nature or common life, arresting the hearer by its vividness or strangeness, and leaving the mind in sufficient doubt about its precise application to tease it into active thought.[49]

Richard Trench, whose *Notes on the Parables* may be the most widely cited work on the parables, illustrates, "Each one of the parables is like a casket, itself of exquisite workmanship, but in which jewels richer than itself are laid up; or like fruit, which, however lovely to look upon, is yet more delectable in its inner sweetness."[50] Trench provides commentary on each of the parables— describing the context, content, and application to their original audience.

It's also helpful to note what a parable is not. It differs from fable, myth, proverb, and allegory. Archbishop Trent clarifies:

> The parable differs from the fable, by moving in a spiritual world, and never transgressing the actual order of natural things—from the myth, because in that there is an unconscious blending of the deeper meaning with the outward symbol, the two remaining separate in the parable—from the proverb, inasmuch as it is longer carried out, and not merely accidentally but necessarily figurative—from the allegory, by comparing one thing with another, and not transferring, as the allegory, the properties of one to the other.[51]

There is a distinct difference between a parable and an allegory. The parable is more of a full-length story that usually illustrates a single point: "The details are not intended to have independent signific-ance. In an allegory, on the other hand, each detail is a separate metaphor, with a significance of its own."[52]

Jesus took great care in anchoring his parables to situations the audience commonly knew. We can do the same to be more effective. He began with what people knew from experience; then expanded the story to evoke understanding of a spiritual reality that was either dulled or unknown to the hearers. To be an effective teacher, one's language must be fresh, yet it must begin where the hearer can understand:

> For while all language is more or less figurative, yet long use has worn out the freshness of the stamp, so that, to create a powerful impression, language must be cast into novel forms, as was done by our Saviour.... He brought forth out of his treasure things new and old; by the help of the old, making intelligible the new. And thus in his own example he has given us the secret of all effectual teaching.[53]

Michael Knowles, in his article, "Challenge of Jesus' Parables," agrees with Trench's point:

> The compelling appeal of parables, however, derives from the fact that their familiarity—dealing with such common matters as farmers, rulers, seeds and weeds—is often confounded by unexpected reversals or outcomes. The listener (or reader) is drawn by the power of a good story, only then to discover that the narrative leads him or her in unexpected directions or to unanticipated conclusions.[54]

Familiarity is a key aspect of culture. Although generalizations are at best an approximation of truth, I can say from my own experience in cross-cultural missions that familiarity and tradition profoundly influence one's viewpoint. We learn from Jesus' example that: 1) Learning to speak of what's familiar is of primary importance for communication (especially cross-cultural), and 2) Understanding the Scriptures and having the ability to draw the audience into dialogue through what is familiar to them is a skill worth learning as a "fisher of men." As a teacher it is a good discipline to spend ample time prayerfully crafting ways to *use what is familiar to reveal the unexpected*. The next time you read a parable, look at how Jesus did this—it's truly amazing. He was the master of this skill.

Parables act as a *preservative for spiritual truth in an ever-changing world*. Cosmo Lang notes that parabolic teachings by design preserve truth because they're tethered to timeless, observable principles found in the natural realm: "...mere words are constantly changing their meaning, whereas the symbols of life and nature, such as our Lord used in his parables, are as abiding as Nature and Life themselves."[55]

Although parabolic teaching arouses thought, stirs affections, arrests and holds the attention of an audience, the ultimate fruit of a well-aimed parable is that they reveal true seekers. In Jesus' time those who were truly seeking were the ones who asked Jesus follow up questions after hearing his parables because they realized that the parable related to them. James Hastings remarks:

> Parables sometimes withdraw the light from those who love darkness. They protect the truth, which they enshrine from the mockery of the scoffer. They leave something with the careless, which may be interpreted and understood afterwards. They reveal, on the other hand, seekers after truth.[56]

Latitude of Parables

Parables cover an extensive span of human experience. Many have labored to understand Jesus' use of parables through categorizing them into patterns. A.B. Bruce systematically divides Jesus' parables into three categories: 1) Theoretical parables (discussing facts and principles that explain phenomena we see in the world); 2) Parables of grace; and 3) Parables of judgment. By looking at the broad topics addressed in the parables, we see that Jesus was familiar with his audience. We, too, need to make ourselves aware of the issues hindering others from following God. This requires studying the culture we're trying to reach. Jesus was able to draw from the surrounding context to provide visual or emotionally laden word pictures to illustrate life-changing principles the audience needed to hear.

As we practice looking into creation for ways to connect with our modern-day audience, there's one caution to consider as we interpret the parables. In our efforts to be relevant and practical, we must avoid focusing first on nature illustrations (which are copiously available in the outdoors) and then looking around for some way to apply it. In contrast, it appears that Jesus' usual starting point for crafting illustrations was his awareness of the needs of his audience. Prayer, conversation, asking questions, and being sensitive to the Spirit will help you discern the needs and issues of individuals and groups. Start there and then look around in creation to find an object lesson to illustrate the chosen scriptural principle. So if a fitting creation analogy for a spiritual principle presents itself as you are outdoors, be disciplined to consider the state of being of your audience before shooting from the hip to try to force an application for others—it may just be something that the Holy Spirit is teaching *you*.

Pay Attention to Setting

St. Irenaeus of Lyons (129-203) said, "For even creation reveals him who formed it, and the very work made suggests him Who made it, and the world manifests him Who ordered it."[57] St. Athanasius (297-203) stated, "About the 'Book of Creation,' the creatures are like letters proclaiming in loud voices to their Divine Master and Creator the harmony and order of things. For this reason, God gave creation such order as is found therein, so that while HE is by nature invisible, men might yet be able to know him through his works."[58] St. Augustine (354-430) put it this way:

> Some people, in order to discover God, read books. But there is a great book: the very appearance of created things. Look above you! Look below you! Note it. Read it. God, whom you want to discover, never wrote that book with ink. Instead he set before your eyes the things that he had made. Can you ask for a louder voice than that?[59]

It is obvious from Jesus' teaching that he spent a good bit of time formulating ways he could use the creation to instruct people in the secrets of the Kingdom of God. This is also true of the writers of the Psalms. Probably the largest body of evangelistic sermons, poems, and songs related to the awe-inspiring setting of creation is found in the Psalms. David was profoundly shaped by his wilderness experiences. In Psalm 8, he writes, "When I consider your heavens, the work of your fingers, The moon and the stars, which you have ordained; What is man that you take thought of him, And the son of man that you care for him?" (Psalm 8:3-4). In the wilderness (through thoughtful observation of creation), we learn that neither man nor any other created being could have created what is visible. This points us to the existence of God: "The heavens are telling of the glory of God; and their expanse is declaring the work of his hands. Day after day they pour forth speech, and night after night they display knowledge. There is no speech or language where their voice is not heard" (Psalm 19:1-3).

In the wilderness, David learned to listen to the Word of the Lord. His confidence grew through the fear of God. "By the word of the Lord the heavens were made, and by the breath of his mouth all their host. He gathers the waters of the sea together as a heap; He lays up the deeps in storehouses. Let all the earth fear the Lord; let all the inhabitants of the world stand in awe of him" (Psalm 33:6-8). Through times of solitude in the wilderness, David's heart (expressed in Psalm 139:7-14) was transformed and strengthened by the presence of the Lord:

> Where can I go from your Spirit? Or where can I flee from your presence? If I ascend to heaven, you are there; If I make my bed in Sheol, behold, you are there. If I take the wings of the dawn, If I dwell in the remotest part of the sea, even there your hand will lead me, And your right hand will lay hold of me. If I say, "Surely the darkness will overwhelm me, And the light around me will be night," Even the darkness is not dark to you, And the night is as bright as the day. Darkness and light are alike to you. For you formed my inward parts; you wove me in my mother's womb. I will give thanks to you, for I am fearfully and wonderfully made; Wonderful are your works, And my soul knows it very well.

He was able to spend much of his early life in the wilderness, learning the ways of a shepherd and the awareness of God's presence, which elicited songs of praise. I find *awareness* and *attentiveness* are often the marks of someone who spends adequate time in rest and reflection with the Lord. David was so caught up with paying attention to God that in Psalm 148 he invokes the whole of creation to praise God in awareness of his glory:

> Praise the Lord from the earth, Sea monsters and all deeps; Fire and hail, snow and clouds; Stormy wind, fulfilling his word; Mountains and all hills; Fruit trees and all cedars; Beasts and all cattle; Creeping things and winged fowl; Kings of the earth and all peoples; Princes and all judges of the earth; Both young men and virgins; Old men and children. Let them praise the name of the Lord, For his name alone is exalted; his glory is above earth and heaven. (Psalm 148:7-13)

If you are looking for it, it is hard to miss the parallel pedagogy of how the psalmists and prophets used creation analogies and how Jesus crafted creation parables as a tool to communicate sweeping truths that are illustrated in God's created order. In a similar way that Jesus used creation parables, several Hebrew prophets wrote creation psalms to invoke awareness and worship of God. Amos wrote: "For behold, he who forms mountains and creates the wind and declares to man what are his thoughts, he who makes dawn into darkness and treads on the high places of the earth, The Lord God of hosts is his name" (Amos 4:13). Again, he points to the wonders of creation as he is attentive to the Lord's sustaining hand: "He who made the Pleiades and Orion and changes deep darkness into morning, Who also darkens day into night, Who calls for the waters of the sea and pours them out on the surface of the earth, The Lord is his name" (Amos 5:8). Isaiah marvels at the Lord's greatness evidenced in his creation:

> Who has measured the waters in the hollow of his hand, and marked off the heavens by the span, and calculated the dust of the earth by the measure, and weighed the mountains in a balance and the hills in a pair of scales? Who has directed the Spirit of the Lord, or as his counselor has informed him? (Isaiah 40:12-13)

The wilderness is a special *place* for transformation, not just a metaphor for life. It has always been a special locale for men and women of God to walk and freshly enjoy their relationship with God. We can know God more fully and intimately as we walk in the outdoors...quietly allowing our senses and spirit to be attentive to his voice speaking directly to us. Although the distraction-less setting of the wilderness is a vital conduit for hearing God, the writer of Hebrews asserts that this kind of intimate communication with God is ultimately only possible through faith: "By faith we understand that the worlds were prepared by the word of God, so that what is seen was not made out of things which are visible" (Hebrews 11:3).

Sea and River Crossings

There is ample evidence in Scripture to show how God used the special *setting* of the wilderness and the unique elements of *timing* to profoundly shape his people. One cannot imagine how the Israelites must have felt after having escaped Egypt successfully, only to find themselves trapped with the Red Sea in front of them and Pharaoh's chariots closing in behind. The setting appeared to be hopeless. Was it a mistake that Moses led them to a beach by the Red Sea? It may have appeared that way to them because they did not know what God had up his sleeve next. Although the situation seemed scary and hopeless, God had actually led them to the edge of this seemingly impassable obstacle for a purpose. Moses and the people may have felt hemmed in, but God was not going to abandon them at their time of need. He brought them to the edge of their comfort zone to teach them something. Through this fearful circumstance in the wilderness, God would again show Israel he had chosen them for a divine purpose and that he could be trusted: Nothing is too difficult for him.

As we read on in Exodus, we see the unfolding of his perfect plan. See if you can observe both elements of setting and timing in this passage:

> The angel of God, who had been going before the camp of Israel, moved and went behind them; and the pillar of cloud moved from before them and stood behind them.... Then Moses stretched out his hand over the sea; and the Lord swept the sea back by a strong east wind all night and turned the sea into dry land, so the waters were divided. The sons of Israel went through the

midst of the sea on the dry land, and the waters were like a wall to them on their right hand and on their left. (Exodus 14:19-22)

The setting was fearful, the timing was designed to leave a lasting impression, and the result was transformation of his people: "When Israel saw the great power which the Lord had used against the Egyptians, the people feared the Lord, and they believed in the Lord and in his servant Moses" (Exodus 14:31).

Similarly, in another case study we see God using the elements of timing and the terrain of the outdoors to bring transformation through the crossing of the Jordan River. Moses, having led the people through the wilderness for forty years, was now passing on the baton to Joshua who would lead the people across the Jordan River into the Promised Land. They were more than ready to experience the land filled with "milk and honey." They were tired of eating manna and quail, yet the reason they were in the wilderness in the first place was because of the unbelief of their fathers. Now it was this new generation's turn to be tested. To test them, God brought the people to the banks of the Jordan River at a very suboptimal time. Rather than bringing them to the river when it was low and easily passable, he brought them to its edge at flood stage.

During much of the year the Jordan River is a mere trickle of water, but at this time of the year melting snows from the northern mountains were causing the Jordan to overflow its banks. This was no little stream, and there was no bridge. Why didn't God choose the dry season to bring them across the river? The text explains he chose this setting and timing to amaze them—to transform them. Joshua said to the people, "Consecrate yourselves, for tomorrow the Lord will do *wonders among you*" (Joshua 3:5, emphasis added). And that's just what happened. The priests exercised their faith and walked into the Jordan holding the Ark of the Covenant on their shoulders, and the Lord amazed them by holding the river back in a heap to allow Israel to cross the swollen river. What was the outcome of this faith-testing event? They were deeply transformed and had a story to tell their children for generations. As a memorial they stacked a heap of stones at the water's edge as a way to remember this amazing teachable moment in the wilderness. Now with fortified faith from this event, they marched confidently toward Jericho to bring its powerful towers down with the simple weapon of trust in God.

Mountains, Awe, Authority, and Mission

Imagine sitting in a house church in the second century and hearing the apostle Peter's second letter to the churches read for the first time. As the elder slowly reads the opening of the letter your imagination is piqued at the authoritative tone in Peter's written words. These are firsthand experiences Peter is relaying to us. Into the second paragraph of the letter you nod your head and smile, feeling the security and peace, which comes to those who listen with unwavering faith. Although the world outside of this little home fellowship is chaotic and critical of Christians, you rest in the truth of Peter's words:

> We did not follow cleverly invented stories when we told you about the power and coming of our Lord Jesus Christ, but we were eyewitnesses of his majesty. For he received honor and glory from God the Father when the voice came to him from the Majestic Glory, saying, "This is my Son, whom I love; with him I am well pleased." We ourselves heard this voice that came from heaven when we were with him on the sacred mountain. (2 Peter 1:16-18)

Like Moses' encounters with Yahweh atop a mountain, Peter also had several mountaintop experiences with Christ. This passage in Peter's letter alludes to an awe-inspiring moment in the clouds with James, John, Jesus, Moses, and Elijah atop the Mount of Transfiguration. In classic form, just as God had established his authority in and through Moses on Mount Sinai, the Heavenly Father displayed his glory and demonstrated the depth of Jesus' authority over all of creation atop another mountain. Jesus had been climbing with Peter, James, and John, when, after reaching the top, he paused to pray. Then without warning, he started to glow! Transfigured before them he began speaking with Moses and Elijah about his mission that was about to culminate in Jerusalem (see Luke 9:31). Then:

While he was saying this, a cloud formed and began to overshadow them; and they were afraid as they entered the cloud. Then a voice came out of the cloud, saying, "This is my Son, my Chosen One; listen to him!" And when the voice had spoken, Jesus was found alone. And they kept silent, and reported to no one in those days any of the things which they had seen. (Luke 9:34-36)

Mountains have always been a special terrain for God encounters. When the Israelites finally arrived at Sinai, God called Moses to climb the mountain to meet with him: "Moses went up to God, and the Lord called to him from the mountain, saying, 'Thus you shall say to the house of Jacob and tell the sons of Israel'" (Exodus 19:3). God gave Moses authoritative and clear instructions to pass on to the people. Then,

The LORD descended to the top of Mount Sinai and called Moses to the top of the mountain. So Moses went up and the LORD said to him, "Go down and warn the people so they do not force their way through to see the LORD and many of them perish. Even the priests, who approach the LORD, must consecrate themselves, or the LORD will break out against them." (Exodus 19:20-22)

Moses and the people humbled themselves before God and listened to his commandments. In this case, only Moses was allowed to ascend the mountain to meet with God, which set him apart as the leader of the people. God used this alpine ascent to transfer his authority to Moses as his ambassador. In case after case, mountains mentioned in the Bible provide awesome vistas for those who climbed them to see God more clearly for who he is. And climbing them today still affords a majestic setting for recognizing Christ's authority over all.

After the resurrection, Jesus sent the disciples on a hike up a mountain outside the city. This summit experience had a point in that Jesus was going to make it clear that although Moses had been given some authority to lead God's people, that authority was about to be transferred to them. In order to grasp the gravity of this leadership shift, Jesus had to make it clear to them that he was greater than their revered patriarch, Moses, and that as the Messiah, he had power and authority over everything in heaven and earth! The writer of Hebrews draws upon this theme to help us understand its significance: "For he has been counted worthy of more glory than Moses" (Hebrews 3:3). Oscar Seitz provides further insight into the rationale for Jesus' habit of climbing mountains: "Our first evangelist intended to present Jesus on the 'mountain' as the giver of a New Law...He went up on the mountain...as Moses did to receive the law."[60]

So, the One with all authority was now transferring it to these eleven apostles who would be called to go out as torches to light the wildfire of the gospel that would sweep across the whole world. Like God had done with Moses up on a mountain, Jesus transferred ambassadorial authority to the apostles on a peak: "All authority in heaven and on earth has been given to me. Therefore go and make disciples of all nations" (Matthew 28:18-19).

The apostle Paul later reiterates this point to the church at Corinth: "We are therefore Christ's ambassadors, as though God were making his appeal through us." From passages like Mark 3:13-19 and Matthew 28:16-20 we see that Jesus saw intrinsic value in mountain peaks as a setting to impart *his authority to his disciples as ambassadors*. Outdoor leaders can use peak experiences to remind believers that Christ has imparted his authority to *us* to spread the gospel. In some mysterious way, vistas can inspire renewed vision. And the vision that Jesus kept steering his disciples back to was one that involved going back down into the valley to be fishers of men—to penetrate their cities as ambassadors of the Great Commission.

CHAPTER 3
TRIALS

Trials Expose Unbelief

Plain and simple: trials expose unbelief and promote real belief. Time and again, belief is shown to be true or false in the wilderness, and trials are an instrument to expose whether we fear God or man. By removing familiarity, trials also have a way of expanding our comfort zones and keeping us humble. Following Jesus Christ is not a walk in the park all of the time. We all have rough edges that need to be rubbed off, and we all have sinful tendencies that are at odds with the desires of the Spirit. The spirit is willing, but the flesh is weak. As we look at the theme of trials or testing in the Scriptures, it becomes strikingly obvious that the wilderness is a favorite place for God to get our attention. The Father is after our fidelity to him, and through the trials of Israel in the wilderness of Sinai we learn that perseverance *is an indicator of covenant relationship.*

God intentionally tests us through various forms of resistance to establish our belief and integrity. Through the process we learn he is the One who sets the terms of discipleship, not us. When pushed, we might want to push back at God, but in his perfect wisdom he questions and stretches us in such a way that draws us nearer to him rather than causing us to run away. Job, Sarah, Abraham, Peter, and Paul are all prime examples of those who have learned obedience through suffering. Each went through a process of disorientation and re-orientation in the wilderness. As God adds the salve of grace to the struggle of our trials, he miraculously raises up servants who can transform nations.

The Spirit is Willing, the Flesh is Weak

Trials *expose the reality of our humanity and the inadequacy of our worship.* In the Garden of Gethsemane Jesus stated to the twelve, "The spirit is willing but the flesh is weak" (Mark 14:32-42). In the same way that squeezing a sponge reveals what's soaked inside of it, difficult trials squeeze out the truth about ourselves and make us honest about what's in our heart. This makes us more authentic and opens the door to experiencing abundant life through reliance on the Spirit rather than our own strength.

After the resurrection, Jesus decided it was time to squeeze the sponge. Now in his glorified body he went to meet the apostles on a mountain outside the city. Matthew records, "When they saw him, they worshiped *him;* but some were doubtful" (Matthew 28:16). The very appearance of the Risen Christ squeezed the apostles so that their true colors came oozing out. Some worshipped, but others doubted. Even after witnessing the events of the crucifixion, after hearing the reports of those who had seen Jesus arisen from the dead, and after seeing Jesus in the upper room when he appeared to them, some were still doubtful. Why do we doubt when given every reason to believe? The spirit is willing, but our flesh is weak. Wilderness experiences, therefore, have an essential purpose to make us more reliant on the Spirit of God and less on our flesh.

The temptation of Christ (see Luke 4:1-3) was also a form of flesh testing which deepened Jesus' dependence on the Father. The writer of Hebrews comments on the significance of Jesus' suffering during his life on earth:

> In the days of his flesh, he offered up both prayers and sup-plications with loud crying and tears to the One able to save him from death, and he was heard because of his piety. Although he was a Son, he learned obedience from the things which he suffered. And having been made perfect, he became to all those who obey him the source of eternal salvation, being designated by God as a high priest according to the order of Melchizedek. (Hebrews 5:7-10)

The temptation in the wilderness tested Jesus' humanity. We learn from this encounter that Jesus' arch enemy, the Devil, tried to appeal

100

to the *deity* and power of Christ, whereas Christ held firmly to his weakness and humanity. Rather than exercising his sovereign power over Satan, he chose to depend on the Heavenly Father in the face of trial. He embraced his humanity fully because he knew that God's plan was to defeat Satan through his humility, not his power: "He... did not count equality with God a thing to be grasped, but emptied himself" (Phil. 2:6). In a parallel argument, Paul indicates the same principle at work in Titus' life, as he encourages him to faithfully teach and exhort the church in Crete to continue in their belief, *denying the cravings of their flesh* to produce fruit of the Spirit (see Titus 2:11-15).

Wilderness Stress Tests

Like a stress test given in a cardiovascular clinic or one given to a failing bank to see if they pass muster, Israel had to regularly go through a series of true or false tests so they wouldn't fool themselves when the lab results turned up at their doorstep. It's so easy to think we are okay when in actuality our soul is not well. Israel's "true or false tests" in the desert either led them to repentance, or to a further hardening of the heart. They either responded to the test with a renewed trust, belief, and obedience, or they flatly ignored their prophets' warnings to their peril. The rebellion against Moses at Meribah is a prime example of a stress test that did not turn out well for Israel (see Exodus 17:1-7). Israel may have felt like they had a right to grumble against God because they were thirsty and tired in the Desert of Sin, but according to the commentary of this event in Psalm 95, this was a stress test that revealed their hardened hearts toward God:

> Today, if only you would hear his voice, do not harden your hearts as you did at Meribah, as you did that day at Massah in the wilderness, where your ancestors tested me; they tried me, though they had seen what I did. For forty years I was angry with that generation; I said, "They are a people whose hearts go astray, and they have not known my ways." So I declared on oath in my anger, "They shall never enter my rest" (Psalm 95:7-11).

As we turn to the New Testament, we have several instructive passages to consider. When Jesus stilled the storm in Mark 4:35-41, he *questioned* the twelve, "Why are you so afraid? Do you still have no faith?" Although we can empathize with their fears, as the storm was about to capsize their boat, apparently their lack of faith in Jesus as the Son of God was without excuse. This stress test brought their secret doubts out into the open. The twelve openly confessed their unresolved tension between belief and unbelief when they said, "Who is this? Even the wind and the waves obey him" (Mark 4:41). The wilderness is a place where *unbelief is exposed and confronted so belief becomes possible.*

Jesus also tests the twelve at the feeding of the five thousand, which occurred in a remote setting (see John 6:1-15). Here, Jesus asks Philip what they ought to do to satisfy the hunger of the masses. There were no bakeries around for miles, so he didn't know what to do. Philip's response revealed his (and the other disciples') lack of faith, to which Jesus responds by unfolding a pair of purposeful miracles that were designed to soften their hearts toward authentic belief. After feeding the crowds, there were twelve basketfuls left over—enough for *each* disciple to have more food than they even needed.

The object lesson was enough to make the point, but apparently they still did not fully understand the personal implications of this tutorial, so Jesus sent them on an adventurous wilderness experience across the lake (see Mark 6:45-52). Copying Christ's apprenticeship style, outdoor ministry uses adventure as a means to challenge stubborn unbelief. That is one of the main reasons why people need to take risks—we all need out of comfort zone experiences from time to time to expose our stubborn doubts and double-mindedness. Consider for a moment some of the major lessons that God has taught you in your walk with him, but how often it is that you forget the implications of that lesson to your daily life. It is easy for us to slip into doubt and faithless living. For this reason, God continues to

push us out of our comfort zone so that faith continues to be the fuel for our life rather than fear.

After the miracle of the five thousand being fed, there was obvious intentionality in the way Jesus sent his disciples immediately out on a wilderness-type experience on the lake. How was he intentional? First, Jesus sent the disciples on ahead of him. They were on their own. They were going to have to go through this storm *without* him. Outdoor leaders can simulate this by sending the group ahead without them to give a chance to feel the weight of responsibility. When they have to call the shots rather than rely on a knowledgeable guide, learning is piqued. Sometimes when people are plagued with pride or stiffened with stubborn skepticism, they need to be left to their own to fall apart: "That is why Scripture says: 'God opposes the proud but shows favor to the humble'" (James 4:6).

With another display of intentionality in facilitating this transforming wilderness experience for the disciples, after sending them out on the lake ahead of him, he went up on a mountainside to pray for them (see Mark 6:46). Mark notes that when evening came, the twelve were in the *middle* of the lake. Jesus was able to see the disciples straining at the oars from the mountaintop. He watched as the wind was against them. This was part of the plan—Jesus was watching the events of the evening unfold—waiting for the moment when he would step in to save them. Parents often have to do this with their children—letting them learn while they watch from a distance. Teachers do this with their students—giving them space to discover truth for themselves, which requires patience because it would be so easy to speed things up by stepping in to give them the answer. But a wise teacher knows that this will derail the learning process. Similar to the way Jesus watched from a distance, in the context of outdoor leadership, it is not uncommon for a pair of guides to let the group find their way for a few hours while they shadow them from a perch somewhere to make sure they don't get lost—that way they experience the stress of being in charge, but the guides are still ensuring their ultimate safety.

From his mountain watchtower, Jesus watched them strain at the oars awhile, surely praying that this night would become a pinnacle of heart transformation for them. Finally in the darkness of the night he went out to them. He was "about to pass by them" (Mark 6:48), when they saw him walking on the lake. They thought he was a ghost, so Jesus spoke to them saying, "Take courage! It is I. Don't be afraid" (Mark 6:50). Then he climbed in the boat and the wind died down. The gospel writer, Mark, provides a parenthetical comment to help the reader understand the reason why Jesus took them through this trial: "They were completely amazed, for they had not understood about the loaves; their hearts were hardened" (Mark 6:51-52). Here in this account we see how *Jesus intentionally crafted a wilderness experience to expose unbelief, in order to establish true belief.* He could have rebuked them after the miracle of the five thousand for not believing, but he chose instead to send them on an experience that would stretch them physically and emotionally to prove once again that there is no other One worthy of their faith.

Resistance for a Purpose

Scripture unabashedly presents a precedent that *God intentionally tests his disciples through various forms of resistance to establish relationship and trust.* From this account we see that Jesus advocates the use of "resistance training" (see Mark 6:45). In this passage he crafted resistance (winds against them) to get results. The weather and the wind were instruments of transformation because they offered a necessary challenge that would produce humility. Even as we disciple others in the normal everyday life of the city, it is important for leaders to craft challenging adventures to stretch people out of their comforts. Discussions at Starbucks are not always enough to really change one's heart. We need challenges to force us to grow.

In the Old Testament, there are many examples of God's personal initiative in resisting persons to produce life change. Jacob's wrestling with God is one of the most vivid examples:

Then Jacob was left alone, and a man wrestled with him until daybreak. When he saw that he had not prevailed against him, he touched the socket of his thigh; so the socket of Jacob's thigh was dislocated while he wrestled with him. Then he said, "Let me go, for the dawn is breaking." But he said, "I will not let you go unless you bless me." (Genesis 32:24-26)

His transformation is symbolized in the Lord giving Jacob a *new name*. The One who wrestled with Jacob all night said, "Your name shall no longer be Jacob, but Israel; for you have striven with God and with men and have prevailed" (Genesis 32:28).

One indicator of authentic transformation is a willingness to come under the authority of the Heavenly Father. Again, because of our sinful nature this does not happen naturally. So we find that *the wilderness was a place where people learned obedience through suffering*. Throughout the Old Testament we see Israel grumbling because of suffering. Whether it was because of a lack of food (see Exodus 16:1-7, Exodus 16:8-21), lack of water (see Exodus 15:22-27), or because of suffering under captivity, Israel learned obedience through suffering. The writer of Hebrews reminds us Jesus also humbled himself to learn obedience through suffering: "For it was fitting for him, for whom are all things, and through whom are all things, in bringing many sons to glory, to perfect the author of their salvation through sufferings" (Hebrews 2:10). If you suffer, be comforted—God disciplines those he loves (see Hebrews 12:7-11).

The temptations of Christ in the desert (see Luke 4:1-3) modeled for his disciples a common-sense principle that if he had to learn obedience through suffering, it is also fitting that they will also learn obedience through suffering. If the Holy Spirit apprenticed Jesus this way, then it makes sense that Jesus would choose this mode of training with his apprentices. This goes for us too. Athletes know that some strenuous suffering is a prerequisite for performance, so they endure a disciplined exercise regime to achieve excellence. Since we learn obedience most adequately through stress, suffering, and discipline, when discipling others we need to find ways to push them to encourage growth. Like a good coach, effective leaders know how to put those they are discipling in situations where perseverance is required so that endurance is produced.

The wilderness is a place of *physical testing to produce transformation for God's glory*. The connection between physical challenge and spiritual growth is a very broad topic in which we cannot provide adequate space to explore its complexities. But the physical body has a part to play in the fulfillment of the spiritual life. Wilderness experiences are often remembered by the physical challenges they provide. Dallas Willard offers a summary of the relevance of this principle to our topic:

> The physical human frame as created was designed for interaction with the spiritual realm and this interaction can be resumed at the initiative of God. Then, through the disciplines for the spiritual life, that interaction can be developed by joint efforts of both God and the person alive in the dynamism of the Spirit.[61]

We all have responsibility to take initiative in disciplining and training our bodies in submission to God for his glory. Richard Foster calls the spiritual disciplines the "Door to Liberation" in that: "The purpose of the disciplines is liberation from the stifling slavery to self-interest and fear."[62] Jesus modeled a commitment to the spiritual disciplines of meditation, prayer, fasting, study, simplicity, solitude, submission, service, worship, and celebration. And the early church carried on these and other corporate disciplines like confession and spiritual guidance. Wilderness encounters with God are a physical *and* spiritual experience. Through exercise, solitude, silence, prayer, etc., we feel invigorated and often experience a sense of joy as we use our bodies to bring glory to God. For example, I am reminded of Mildred and Sylvio's comments about what they learned during a wilderness experience through the element of physical challenge:

> Mildred explained how she was "absolutely loving being completely knackered at the end of the day." Sylvio has a similar opinion: "You do feel better at the end of the day, when you walked back to your camp and you were tired—it does something." These quotes demonstrate how the expedition would not have held the same meanings for the venturers if it had not been physically challenging.[63]

Weaned from Fearing Man

We have looked at many forms of testing the Lord used in the wilderness. One final test we observe in our analysis reveals the wilderness as a place where the Heavenly Father tested his people to expose whether they feared God or man. After the twelve spies returned from their reconnaissance trip into the land of Canaan, the people rose up in rebellion against Moses because their fear of the giant powerful people living there was greater than their fear of their giant powerful God (see Numbers 13:1-33).

Dietrich Bonhoeffer explored this topic in his book *The Cost of Discipleship*. He paraphrases several passages of Scripture pertaining to the fear of God versus the fear of man:

> Think not that I came to send peace on the earth: I came not to send peace, but a sword. For I came to set a man at variance with his father, and the daughter against her mother, and the daughter-in-law against her mother-in-law. He that loveth father or mother more than me is not worthy of me; and he that loveth son or daughter more than me is not worthy of me. And he that doth not take up his cross and follow after me, is not worthy of me. He that findeth his life shall lose it; and he that loseth his life for my sake shall find it.[64]

Then he urges men to fear God rather than fear man:

> Men can do them no harm, for the power of men ceases with the death of the body. But they must overcome the fear of death with the fear of God. The danger lies not in the judgment of men, but in the judgment of God, not in the death of the body, but in the eternal destruction of body and soul. Those who are still afraid of men have no fear of God, and those who have fear of God have ceased to be afraid of men.[65]

The whole Hebrew congregation heard the testimony of the twelve spies in the wilderness and was confronted with the question, "Do we fear God or man?" They chose to fear men, and the consequence weighed heavily on their generation. By contrast, Joshua and Caleb were models of belief; they chose to fear God rather than the giants. As a result of his faithfulness and trust in God, Joshua was later selected to be the leader of Israel who would lead them into the Promised Land.

I have observed countless times in the context of outdoor adventure, through physical, emotional, intellectual, and spiritual challenges, that it is relevant and timely to ask people who they fear more in their daily lives: God or man? Do they blindly follow their peers even if their behavior is offensive to God? What indicators reveal where our fears truly lie? Over the years I've observed what we prioritize often reveals what we fear. We can help people see that the well-worn paths or *patterns* in their life actually point to whom they fear.

Anvil of Hunger

I've heard people make some pretty extreme statements when they get really hungry and tired and don't have the security blanket of home to coddle them. Food fantasies abound after a few days of eating simple backpacking food. As much as a backcountry trip can push someone out of their culinary comfort zone, the Israelites had it much worse. As a guide you may have had to bear the brunt of some snide remarks about your cooking skills or the palatability of your provisions. But to put this in perspective, consider the complaint of Israel toward their guides Moses and Aaron at the beginning of their forty-year sojourn.

Moses and the Israelites learned that a little hunger could be useful in forging character and belief. Just before God's provision of manna and quail was introduced, the people grumbled to Moses without reservation: "The sons of Israel said to them, 'Would that we had died by the LORD'S hand in the land of Egypt, when we sat by the pots of meat, when we ate bread to the full; for you have brought us out into this wilderness to kill this whole assembly with hunger'" (Exodus 16:3). In every culture, *one of our most dear comfort zones is our diet.* We become accustomed to certain foods, tastes, textures, and smells. And when that's taken away or altered significantly we get rubbed the wrong way. You may have experienced this yourself while traveling to another culture for a significant period of time. It takes a while to adjust your palette. Our snooty taste buds may tempt us to ungratefully grumble in our heart or fantasize for our favorite restaurant back home. The same thing happens like clockwork in outdoor adventures. When people get hungry and don't get food that necessarily fits their ideal menu, they get a little bit testy. This is a great opportunity to talk about entitlement and ungratefulness— ouch! *Grumbling is a great window to the soul.*

A passage that illustrates how God uses hunger in the wilderness to forge character and belief is 1 Kings 19:1-21. Here we observe Elijah fasting for forty days and forty nights before encountering God in a cave. The timing of his encounter occurred in the midst of great hunger and need. Similarly, in Matthew 4 we see Jesus fasting forty days and nights in preparation to inaugurate his ministry in conflict with Satan. These events forged strong character for future spiritual battle. The writer of Hebrews notes Jesus had to learn obedience through the instrument of suffering, of which hunger is one of the more distressing experiences to bear. Although the value of hunger, fasting, and suffering is certainly a mystery, the Scriptures teach that Jesus did not bypass this law of humanity that obedience is learned through adversity (see Hebrews 5:8).

After an exhausting day of ministry, the disciples urged Jesus to eat something. He must have been famished, but responded, "I have food to eat that you know nothing about...My food...is to do the will of him who sent me and to finish his work" (John 4:31-34). This is one of the more instructive and profound hunger accounts in the New Testament because it shows how often we are living by sight and not by faith. Physical hunger, especially through a controlled fast, can be transforming because it shows us we can say "no" to our cravings—we don't need as much as our eyes and bodies say we do.

Peter Scaer reflects on the test placed before Adam and Eve to *not* eat a certain kind of fruit even though it was incredibly appealing:

> This link between obedience and food is intriguing on any number of levels. It takes us back to the initial creation, where God issued one, and only one, command. Then the food of disobedience led to eternal death and separation from God. As

God began to create a new people for himself, he also used food as both a gift and a test of obedience.[66]

One simple takeaway as an outdoor leader is to capitalize on moments on your adventure when people are feeling hunger pangs. The cramps in our stomach can be a great experiential way to learn what Jesus meant when he said *his food was to do the will of God and finish his work*. What does that really mean?

Mourning and Prayer

The wilderness was also a place for encountering God through mourning and prayer. Daniel typifies this principle while out in the wilderness during a time of focused intercessory prayer. Daniel 10 describes an immense war going on in the spiritual realm while he was living in Babylon. We see Daniel mourning and praying—battling in the spiritual realm for a breakthrough in his ministry. Then to bless and reassure him, an angel appears to him while in solitude by the Tigris River. The angel Gabriel had been fighting an evil principality called the "Prince of Persia" for more than three weeks in order to break through to minister to Daniel in his time of need. Through the Archangel Michael's help, Gabriel was finally able to pass through the Prince of Persia's dark kingdom and give Daniel assurance his prayers were being answered. Soon princes of other lands would be defeated in the realm of the spirit and Daniel would be equipped and anointed to lead and make specific advances for God's glory.

Discouragements Illuminate True Success

Jesus often chose to initiate and teach his disciples in times when they were tired, discouraged, confused, or when they had failed. In Luke 5, we see Jesus calling Peter when he was exhausted and discouraged from failure. Similarly, when Jesus himself was tired, the Father instructed him to press on and reach out to the woman at the well. The example Jesus set for his disciples through his response to the woman (even while thirsty and fatigued) made a strong impresssion on them. As a guide you will encounter many moments when you are tired beyond what you thought you could handle. Then something will arise that pushes you way beyond your natural abilities. It is in these moments we need to lean heavily on the Holy Spirit because it may be a prime opportunity to reach out and minister to someone in need—even if we think we have nothing to offer. That's the point.

At the end of his earthly ministry, Jesus renewed his call to the disciples when they were sad, confused, and unsuccessful after a night of fishing on the Sea of Tiberias (see John 21: 1-14). And on the road to Emmaus, Jesus revealed himself to two men who were depressed and confused about Jesus' crucifixion, because they thought he was going to be the Messiah King who would free Israel. As they walked, Jesus asked questions and wisely concealed his identity, in order to discern what the two sojourners thought about the meaning of these events. Then, as they rested and broke bread together, their eyes were open to see him (see Luke 24:31). Wilderness or outdoor experiences provide many opportunities for challenge and adventure that inevitably afford moments of fatigue and discouragement. The perceptive outdoor leader can make the most of these opportunities by pointing people to their Comforter, Jesus Christ.

Perhaps one of the more potent passages where Jesus clearly redefines true success for his disciples is found in Luke's record of the Sermon on the Mount (see Luke 6:17-26). David Tiede writes:

> The problem, however, comes when the argument from success becomes self-justifying for the achievers, when those who have received benefits view them as unequivocal signs of divine favor...Jesus the Messiah assures his disciples that their suffering and apparent lack of benefits which others regard as signs of God's rejection are rather indications of their participation in God's reign which is at odds with the ways of the world in the present time.[67]

The world tends to define success in pragmatic, measurable terms. This leads more often than not to ungodly competition, rather than mutual benefit and cooperation for the glory of God. The wilderness is an effective setting for redefining success. Young people often comment at the end of a journey that it was the best week of their lives, regardless of the fact they had to live peaceably in community and put their wants aside at times to serve others. This, coupled with the fact they may have eaten different food, bathed very little, shared common gear, and seen each other at their worst (especially in terms of hygiene), helps young people realize what success truly looks like in the Kingdom of God.

When journeying together toward a common goal in the wilderness, the absence of competition is almost palatable compared to the emphasis on "winning" we normally experience in our world back at home. A Kingdom model of community looks more like a win-win for everybody rather than a gold, silver, and bronze medal for an individual. There is a place for this type of competition as it pushes us to excel to their highest level, but if our philosophy of life is always about winning, then we'll likely turn out the loser in what's most important: relationships. I know this from experience because that was my life before I started truly walking with Christ.

CHAPTER 4
TRUST

Trust is the foundation of all relationships. And *embracing the trustworthiness of God is the basis for a renewed identity*. Unfortunately, because of the sin and brokenness of our world, our lives can become defined by the distrust we carry around because of the ways others have hurt us. This radically distorts our identity away from God's design and completely saps us from the abundance of joy that he intends for us to have. One of the central aims of God's redemptive work is to unbend our identity back to its original design (see 2 Corinthians 5:17). Through conversion our identity changes from being a rebellious sinner to a saint who sins.

If you have put your trust in Christ you are in a royal family. You have become a son or daughter of the King! This chapter will take a deeper look at one of the most crucial elements of our sanctification process, which is our need to continually re-assert our trust in God. Because we have been sinned against, we may have a tendency not to trust others, even God. But this false perception of God has very damaging consequences. The wilderness experiences of the Bible show us that God uses trust-building experiences to teach people that there is *absolutely no risk in trusting him fully*. Although a common human experience, any *perceived risk* you might have about trusting God is false. He is fully trustworthy.

It is absolutely crucial that God's children begin to learn that just because they perceive a risk in following God does not mean that there is any *actual* risk. Those are two completely different things. God humbles us as only God can do to teach us that our perceptions are wrong and even though we may feel at times like God has abandoned us, he hasn't, and he can always be trusted. He will never change. It is we who are tossed around like the waves by our false perceptions and wounded emotions. It is crucial for the child of God to get anchored by trusting God or a shipwreck is certain.

God publicly established Jesus' identity in the wilderness by the Jordan River: "As Jesus came up out of the water, he saw heaven being torn open and the Spirit descending on him like a dove. And a voice came from heaven, 'This is my Son whom I love, with him I am well pleased'" (Matthew 3:17). We see similar concrete identity-establishing events in the Hebrew Scriptures. For example, Abraham was chosen and sent off with his family into the wilderness as a blessing to all peoples. Abraham became an icon of Hebrew identity because of his faith-living during those years of desert sojourn (see Hebrews 11). Jacob's identity-shaping event occurred in the wilderness at the well-known ford of the Jabbok River. Stories are still told of him thousands of years later about how he came to be identified by a wrestling match with God that took place on the banks of this brook. There, rolling in the sand and pebbles struggling for his identity, he received his blessing—and a limp.

The Lord established his identity by giving him a wound of love. And taking it a step even further he gave him a new name, Israel, which means "he that strives with God" (Gen. 32:28). Another Hebrew pillar of faith, Daniel was standing in solitude by the river Tigris when he experienced a stamp of identity on the curing concrete of his soul. After seeking the Lord in prayer, the angel Gabriel appeared to him with a personal message from God, "You are highly esteemed," Gabriel announced. Daniel was reminded that God had chosen him and favored him because he was his son. Daniel deepened his trust through this season of prayer once again as God proved his trustworthiness to him: *God is fully aware of what is going on and listens to our cry for help.*

Jesus followed the Old Testament choosing-model we see in Abraham, Jacob, and Daniel when he began to single out and *select* his disciples in the wilderness. For example, Jesus called and identified the twelve in a wilderness setting: "And he went up on the mountain and summoned those whom he himself wanted, and they

114

came to him" (Mark 3:13). At the close of Jesus' ministry on earth, after his resurrection, he once again established the identity of his disciples in a creation setting beside the Sea of Tiberias. In this account, Jesus showed a vital concern that Peter's identity be anchored securely in Christ through simple trust.

Over a morning meal of freshly cooked fish and bread on the hot coals of a beach lit fire, Jesus establishes Peter's identity on solid faith. He confronts him one on one and asks him some really hard questions about where his loyalties lie: "Simon son of John, do you truly love me more than these" (John 21:15)? Like Peter who failed Jesus by outright betrayal only a few nights before this encounter, if you or I fail Jesus somehow in our walk with Christ we too might be tempted to just give up in disgrace and go back to some of our old patterns of unfaithfulness and sin. But in the same way that Jesus said lovingly but firmly to Peter, "Feed my sheep," with overwhelming love Christ calls us to put our failures and unfaithfulness in the past, accept his grace, and recommit to a single-minded loyalty to Christ. The apostle Paul interpreted this same principle of Christ's teaching when he wrote to the young church at Philippi:

> Not that I have already obtained all this, or have already arrived at my goal, but I press on to take hold of that for which Christ Jesus took hold of me. Brothers and sisters, I do not consider myself yet to have taken hold of it. But one thing I do: Forgetting what is behind and straining toward what is ahead. (Phil. 3:12-13)

The Trust Distinctive

How did God set out to establish a culture of trust? When the Lord visited Abraham and Sarah to give them the good news of the birth of their son Isaac, Abraham recognized the Lord and *ran* to him. This is an illustration of the proper response one is to have when introduced to the Lord: Run to him! Trust him! Abraham then brought water and washed his feet (see Genesis 18:1-33) as a symbol of humble service to God. He knew his place. Now flash forward hundreds of years from this desert camping scene in the single room of Abraham and Sarah's tent to the upper room where Jesus served his last supper. In one of the most stunning scenes of the New Testament, Jesus intentionally *reverses this act of service modeled by Abraham in the Old Testament and instead of having his disciples rightfully wash his feet, the Master stoops down to wash theirs! This timeless symbol of his humility and humanity is the basis for servant leadership* (see John 13). After shocking them with this symbolic act, he flipped their leadership paradigm on its head by telling them, "Now that I, your Lord and Teacher, have washed your feet, you also should wash one another's feet" (John 13:14).

Talk about a seismic identity event. Yet this act was in line with the corpus of Jesus' teaching in the three years he had spent with them up to this point: "For he who is least among you all—he is the greatest" (Luke 9:48). I have found that washing one another's feet in the wilderness is a powerful way to teach this principle of trust and servanthood. With weathered stinky feet from the trail, each person is severely humbled when another person washes their feet for them. Foot washing is a very effective object lesson to tangibly illustrate the concept that our true identity in Christ is one of a servant. He came to serve, not to be served. And when we follow his model for the Kingdom and serve others, then we find that our whole identity starts coming together like missing pieces of a jigsaw puzzle. Ah ha, there's the missing piece! What Jesus is saying here is: *those who are willing to stoop down and pick up the basin and towel like Jesus did will discover secrets of the Kingdom of God and receive its rewards.*

As far as we know, Jesus' first ministry action was to go out to the wilderness to be baptized by John. Then, in this remarkable moment, *God established his identity* through baptism by blessing him as the only begotten Son in whom he took great pleasure. Sometime after this, Jesus asked his ring of disciples who the people were saying he was. After hearing their responses, in a more personal and direct tone, he asked *them* who *they* thought he was. He wanted them to take a stab at articulating his true identity. Then to the utter amazement of everyone, Peter confessed that Jesus was clearly the Messiah. This time it wasn't the Father from heaven announcing

Jesus' identity; it was one of the disciples to whom the Father had revealed his identity as the Anointed One (see Mark 8:27-30). Peter decided to fully put his weight down on the fact that Jesus was the Messiah. Soon after on the Mount of Transfiguration, the Father confirmed to Jesus' inner circle (Peter, James, and John) that Jesus of Nazareth was truly his Chosen One and that they were to listen to him (see Luke 9:28-36).

One additional example of how Jesus taught the disciples about his identity and theirs is found in the Great Commission: "And Jesus came up and spoke to them, saying, 'All authority has been given to me in heaven and on earth'" (Matthew 28:18). We see here Jesus began his commissioning words with the assurance that he had the authority to commission them because of his identity: he is the Son of God. There is no higher authority than he. And his life is so perfectly consistent that he gives no man any reason not to trust him.

Obviously the wilderness is not the only setting to effectively reveal the identity of Christ, but it is profound that Jesus commonly utilized remote settings to teach his disciples about his identity as the Messiah. It begs the question that if we haven't used outdoor adventure as a part of identity formation and imparting wisdom and guidance to those whom we are apprenticing, wouldn't it be worth a try since Jesus modeled this?

Inescapable Interruptions

The wilderness blesses us by interrupting our nicely compartmentalized life. I don't like to be interrupted. How about you? Honestly, interruptions really annoy me. Yet as grating as they are, have you ever looked at interruptions as a God ordained opportunity to grow up and mature in Christ-likeness? This principle comes to light as we survey the fruit of some of the more famous interruptions in Scripture. At the Tower of Babel, God interrupted his people to shape them according to his will (see Genesis 11:1-9). First God came to see what they were doing—he took initiative (see Genesis 11:5). Then, seeing how their pride had poisoned the whole community, he acted to preserve their future by confusing their languages and sending them into the wilderness to effectively make them depend on him again. When the angels announced the birth of Jesus Christ to the shepherds, they *interrupted* them in the middle of the night with an out of the box message that must have literally rocked their world:

> In the same region there were some shepherds staying out in the fields and keeping watch over their flock by night. And an angel of the Lord suddenly stood before them, and the glory of the Lord shone around them; and they were terribly frightened. But the angel said to them, "Do not be afraid; for behold, I bring you good news of great joy which will be for all the people; for today in the city of David there has been born for you a Savior, who is Christ the Lord." (Luke 2:8-11)

Saul was radically interrupted on the road to Damascus with a disturbing message that all of his zealous persecution in the name of God was actually blasphemous and offensive to the Heavenly Father because every time he persecuted a follower of the Way he was persecuting the Messiah himself! It is interesting and perhaps symbolic that Saul's encounter with Christ on the road to Damascus occurred near the same area in centuries past where Elijah was interrupted by God in a lonely cave. It was somewhere in this same region (the Damascus wilderness) where Saul was interrupted and commissioned as a missionary to the Gentiles. And it was somewhere in this same desert region that God, after whispering to him in the cave, sent Elijah on a history making mission to anoint Hazael king over Aram (see 1 Kings 19:9b-15). Similar to this interruption in a desert cave on Mount Horeb (see 1 Kings 19:8), Jesus interrupts Saul on a lonely desert road to bring color back into his ethnic and religious color-blindness: "As he was traveling, it happened that he was approaching Damascus, and suddenly a light from heaven flashed around him; and he fell to the ground and heard a voice saying to him, 'Saul, Saul, why are you persecuting me?' And he said, 'Who are you, Lord?' And he *said*, 'I am Jesus whom you are persecuting, but get up and enter the city, and it will be told you what you must do'" (Acts 9:3-6). From these and other examples, we have observed a similar pattern of interruption at work:

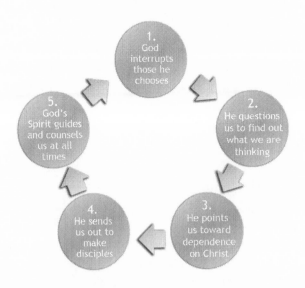

A Theological Model for Interruptions

As a case study similar to Saul's interruption in the wilderness of Damascus, we can also follow this basic model as it unfolds in Philip's wilderness encounter with the Ethiopian eunuch on a lonely desert road:

1. Philip interrupts the man in his chariot.
2. He questions him.
3. He introduces him to Jesus Christ and baptizes him.
4. He sends the man on his way; on a new mission.
5. He leaves, entrusting him to the Holy Spirit's counsel.

D.T. Niles (1908-1970), an indigenous mission leader in Sri Lanka, once said, "In our part of the world, the preacher, the evangelist, is engaged in the work of disrupting people's lives."[68] As we seek to share the gospel with people through outdoor adventure, a strategy that involves setting up learning environments to interrupt their lives is both necessary and highly effective. For example, by facilitating wilderness experiences that provide ample opportunities for people to be still and listen to God, we can trust that God will interrupt those whom he wants to interrupt (see Psalm 46:10). This is a good exhortation for Christian outdoor leaders: if we try to cover too much ground and forget to prioritize rest, free time, and directed reflection time, our participants may have a fun week of adventurous activities, but they might not connect much with Christ. By thoughtfully organizing your outdoor adventure with ample room for reflection you are making space for sacred interruptions.

Grace

U2 sings a song called "Grace": "She takes the blame; she covers the shame; removes the stain..." As we look honestly at the ways God allows trials of many kinds in our lives to grow us in Christ-likeness, it would not be possible without his grace. God does not get enjoyment out of watching us suffer, but he loves us so intensely that he allows us to go through trials because of our pride and sin. Paul discovered this in the midst of bearing a great nuisance: "But he said to me, 'My grace is sufficient for you, for my power is made perfect in weakness.' Therefore I will boast all the more gladly about my weaknesses, so that Christ's power may rest on me" (2 Corinthians 12:9).

In developing a theology of identity, we inevitably must develop our understanding of the relationship between grace and action. Jesus is God's beloved Son: the Father spoke his favor over Jesus but he also assigned work for him to do. We too as disciples of Jesus are favored as sons and daughters but we are given work to do. Our works do not save us, but we are given work to do for God's glory. *God is not against works; he is just against works as a means of earning favor.* Our identity as sons and daughters of God is that we are ones empowered by grace *and* we are created for good works.

In the wilderness just across from Jericho by the Jordan River, Joshua reminded Israel of their identity as children of God in that the gift of the Promised Land they were about to receive was given to them based only on God's grace, not because they earned it. Inheritance is a gift. It is given by grace not merit. In Joshua's magnificent speech to Israel before dividing and distributing the land as an inheritance to each tribe, he reminded them what the Lord had said: "I gave you a land on which you had not labored, and cities which you had not built, and you have lived in them; you are eating of vineyards and olive groves which you did not plant" (Joshua 24:13). In this climactic wilderness speech where Israel finally receives her promised inheritance, they're reminded that their new homeland was a gift. It has not been earned. The forty years of wandering in the desert had been orchestrated to drive this point home forever—"Every good and perfect gift is from above, coming down from the Father of the heavenly lights, who does not change like shifting shadows" (James 1:17). These are timeless identity principles that Israel learned specifically through her wilderness experiences.

We have found that this lesson of unearned grace is demonstrated beautifully through outdoor adventures. In the comfort of our daily routines we often take for granted the provision of the Lord, but in the wilderness, living in tents, eating basic food, drinking water rather than energy drinks and caramel macchiatos, etc., people are better able to recognize how much they have been given. They learn that what they have is theirs by grace, not because of merit. In an experiential and memorable way, the wilderness can be a place to teach the foundational truth that our *salvation* (not only the possessions we have been given) is by grace alone, and not by works.

As people have had time to listen to God throughout their relatively quiet week in the wilderness, you might want to ask a few relevant questions to push this concept from theory to action. We might say: "Jesus was favored and loved by the Heavenly Father, but the Father also gave him some important work to do for his Kingdom. We are in the same boat if we belong to him. What is an area of your life where you sense God calling you to *act* when you get home?" Or, "What is something you feel our *group* needs to act on when we get home?" These questions bring belief and action together as one, as they are meant to be.

How Questions Forge Integrity

Job, a man who typifies a life of faith, was tested severely by a direct line of *questioning* in order to forge a deeper foundation of trust in his relationship with God: "Brace yourself like a man; I will question you, and you shall answer me" (Job 38:3). In order to humble him and further establish his fear of God, Job is asked about the nature of *creation and its beings*:

> Do you know the time the mountain goats give birth? Do you observe the calving of the deer? Can you count the months they fulfill, Or do you know the time they give birth? They kneel down, they bring forth their young, They get rid of their labor pains. Their offspring become strong, they grow up in the open field; They leave and do not return to them. Who sent out the wild donkey free? And who loosed the bonds of the swift donkey, To whom I gave the wilderness for a home and the salt land for his dwelling place? (Job 39:1-6)

God continues this line of questioning in regard to his power shown in his *creatures*:

> Behold now, Behemoth, which I made as well as you; he eats grass like an ox. Behold now, his strength in his loins and his power in the muscles of his belly. He bends his tail like a cedar; The sinews of his thighs are knit together. His bones are tubes of bronze; His limbs are like bars of iron. He is the first of the ways of God; Let his maker bring near his sword. Surely the mountains bring him food, And all the beasts of the field play there. Under the lotus plants he lies down, In the covert of the reeds and the marsh. The lotus plants cover him with shade; The willows of the brook surround him. If a river rages, he is not alarmed; He is confident, though the Jordan rushes to his mouth. Can anyone capture him when he is on watch, With barbs can anyone pierce his nose? (Job 40:15-24)

> Can you draw out Leviathan with a fishhook? Or press down his tongue with a cord? Can you put a rope in his nose Or pierce his jaw with a hook? Will he make many supplications to you, Or will he speak to you soft words? Will he make a covenant with you? Will you take him for a servant forever? Will you play with him as with a bird, Or will you bind him for your maidens? Will the traders bargain over him? Will they divide him among the merchants? Can you fill his skin with harpoons, Or his head with fishing spears? Lay your hand on him; Remember the battle; you will not do it again! Behold, your expectation is false; Will you be

laid low even at the sight of him? No one is so fierce that he dares to arouse him; Who then is he that can stand before me? Who has given to me that I should repay him? Whatever is under the whole heaven is mine. (Job 41:1-11)

At long last, through Job's confession we see the transforming power of God's questioning. The result is trust and belief of the highest quality, which is what we find, brings glory to God. *Our single-minded belief is his aim*:

Then Job answered the Lord and said, "I know that you can do all things, And that no purpose of yours can be thwarted. Who is this that hides counsel without knowledge? Therefore I have declared that which I did not understand, Things too wonderful for me, which I did not know. Hear, now, and I will speak; I will ask you, and you instruct me. I have heard of you by the hearing of the ear; But now my eye sees you; Therefore I retract, And I repent in dust and ashes." (Job 42:1-6)

Ultimately, God is concerned about the integrity of his children. Because he loves us so much, he is continually at work to align us with his Word. Just as an architect is concerned about the integrity of the foundation and cornerstone before he begins to build, the Heavenly Father works in our heart to prepare us as his Temple. When we walk humbly before God we put him on display and bring glory to him in our sphere of influence: "He has shown you, O mortal, what is good. And what does the LORD require of you? To act justly and to love mercy and to walk humbly with your God" (Micah 6:8). Job's testing experience paralleled the integrity-building event of Israel's forty-year wilderness wandering: "Remember how the LORD your God led you all the way in the desert these forty years, to humble you and to test you in order to know what was in your heart, whether or not you would keep his commands" (Deut. 8:2). Job submitted to God's testing without testing God in return. That takes humility, but it is the only response that builds integrity.

Our Soul's Sole Provider

Thus far we have looked at how God uses wilderness experiences to lead his chosen people into situations where their comfort zones are expanded, resulting in transformation. God also breaks down barriers between himself and us by removing our spiritual blinders through prayer. This results in a community of people who know the thoughts of God and walk with him in singleness of heart and devotion. Another theme of God's testing is whether we trust in him as our sole Provider. In Genesis 22:1-19, God tests Abraham by asking him to sacrifice what is most dear to him—his son Isaac. From the most lonely of deserts, Abraham perseveres with radical trust and proves his faith genuine:

> By faith Abraham, when he was tested, offered up Isaac, and he who had received the promises was offering up his only begotten son; it was he to whom it was said, "In Isaac your descendants shall be called." He considered that God is able to raise people even from the dead, from which he also received him back as a type. (Hebrews 11:17-19)

Further examples illustrate how God established trust as his people's sole Provider throughout the Old Testament. In Exodus 15:22-27 (a parallel record of this account is Numbers 20:8-14, where the Israelites grumble and rebel against God at *Meribah*) we see him providing water for the people from a rock. In Exodus 16:1-7 he provides manna, and in Exodus 16:8-21, he provides meat in the form of quail. Even despite grumbling, God provides. Jesus illustrates the same principle of *undeserved provision* in his Parable of the Prodigal Son (see Luke 15:11-32).

Commenting on the Parable of the Laborers in the Vineyard (Matthew 20:1-16), Michael Knowles identifies a similar theme. The grumblers in the parable have missed the point that God is Provider and that he is fair. Knowles writes: "When the grumblers accuse the owner of unfairness, the only injustice in the situation is their own selfishness."[69] Thus, the only injustice of *our complaints* to God for unfair treatment is our own selfishness.

Perhaps one of the most instructive New Testament passages regarding this principle of provision is John 6:1-15. After looking around to see the crowd coming toward him, Jesus tests Philip by saying, "Where shall we buy bread for these people to eat?" (John 6:5). John parenthetically comments: "He asked this only to test him, for he already had in mind what he was going to do" (John 6:5).

Philip was confused and lacked the belief Jesus desired in him. So Jesus modeled this principle of provision before their very eyes. Even though the crowds were the beneficiaries of the miracle, *he was aiming the lesson of this teachable moment at the twelve* to transform their belief in him as Provider. As a true experiential teacher, Jesus instructs them to *gather up the pieces.* In the end, they gathered twelve basketfuls of scraps: enough for each to have his *own* basket. Point made.

Or was it? Unfortunately, their hearts were still hardened by unbelief. So, immediately Jesus sent the twelve on a wilderness experience across the lake to truly transform their hearts. After walking out to them in the middle of the storm and calming the waves, Jesus climbed in the boat to settle their fears. Mark notes, "They were completely amazed, for they had not understood about the loaves; their hearts were hardened" (Mark 6:51-52).

The main application for Christian outdoor leaders is to recognize that, when people are being pushed out of their comfort zones whether through rock climbing, hiking at night, paddling through some rough water, etc., there are going to be significant opportunities for debriefing. You may not know what is going on in people's souls while they're pushed to take a risk, but you can be assured that the Holy Spirit has used scenarios just like this in ages past to shake people to the core of their being. By facilitating a debrief that uses examples of others who were tested by God (like the ones mentioned above), you can open up opportunities for honest discussion regarding whether their human fears press them closer to God or drive them further away from him. If the latter is true it is because of pride, not because God hasn't proven himself as faithful Provider. He has done that time and again, the question is just whether or not we believe it.

Solus Adorate Deum

The wilderness is a place where God ushers his people to *worship him alone* (*solus adorate Deum*). Soon after Abram set out from his country to follow God into the wilderness, the Lord came to him in a vision to remind him of the covenant they had made. In this vision, God promises Abram a son through which salvation will come to all peoples. After the vision the writer of Genesis states, "Abram believed the LORD, and he credited it to him as righteousness" (Genesis 15:6). Nahum Sarna comments: "The scene that opens with fear and depression closes with a firm statement that Abram remains steadfast in his faith in God."[70]

Later in Abraham's desert journey, the Lord reveals that the time is at hand for his wife, Sarah, to become pregnant with the child he promised (see Genesis 18:1-33). In their old age, God tests their belief. Sarah laughs when she hears she will bear a child, to that the LORD replies, *"Is anything too difficult for God?"* (Genesis 18:14). It is interesting to note that the angel Gabriel utters the same phrase to Mary the mother of Jesus hundreds of years later, as she wonders out loud how it will be possible for her to bear a child as a virgin: *"For nothing is impossible with God!"* (Luke 1:37). As with Sarah and Mary, the Lord knows we too have a hard time believing sometimes. But we can't allow this to become a pattern because it will affect our worship. In those moments when we sense the Lord asking us to do something that we think is not possible, we have a choice to cling to Christ in unyielding worship. When we struggle with doubts, let us follow the humble model of the man who prayed, "I do believe; help me overcome my unbelief!" (Mark 9:24).

When Jesus paused on the mountain in Samaria to rest from his journey, he again takes advantage of a one-on-one opportunity to help a Samaritan woman find new freedom to *worship* the One true God in spirit and truth. From this solitary vista where she came to draw water at one of Jacob's wells, Jesus invited this broken woman to abandon her empty life of self-abasement and embrace instead a new life of satisfying worship:

> "Sir," the woman said, "I can see that you are a prophet. Our ancestors worshiped on this mountain, but you Jews claim that the place where we must worship is in Jerusalem." "Woman," Jesus replied, "believe me, a time is coming when you will

worship the Father neither on this mountain nor in Jerusalem. You Samaritans worship what you do not know; we worship what we do know, for salvation is from the Jews. Yet a time is coming and has now come when the true worshipers will worship the Father in the Spirit and in truth, for they are the kind of worshipers the Father seeks." (John 4:19-23)

This solitary setting provided the perfect backdrop for a long and personal conversation with Jesus who introduces himself as the mediator between her, her past, and the God who loves her so much that he sent his one and only Son to die for her. *She finally heard God's voice of love breaking through her baggage.* In response she ran into her village worshipping and praising God, inviting others to come worship him. Many did, and after spending two days with him, "They said to the woman, 'We no longer believe just because of what you said; now we have heard for ourselves, and we know that this man really is the Savior of the world'" (John 4:42).

CHAPTER 5
TRAINING

Where do we go to learn about leadership? It is overwhelming how many books, websites, seminars, and degree programs for leadership are available. The ancients did not have all of these resources at their disposal. But even with this seeming scarcity of resources, God was somehow able to develop catalytic leaders to shepherd, govern, and shape the norms of society. How did he do it without PowerPoint, YouTube, and motivational speakers? Interestingly, the way God chose to shape leaders quite often involved adventures and experiential learning in the outdoors. The experiences gained by many men and women in the Bible gives us a veritable textbook on leadership.

The way these leaders developed the heart and skills of leadership was through experiences with God and through hearing and obeying his Word. God sometimes used intense decision-making scenarios to draw out leaders in a group. From Moses' Red Sea predicament to Joshua's river-crossing scenario, to the three disciples' Mount of Transfiguration experience, God orchestrates situations where leaders must step out and lead. Outdoor adventures can set the stage for a superior leadership-learning environment. This does not take away from what can be accomplished in a classroom, but this generation is especially longing to get back to the ancient ways of learning leadership through observation and hands on experience. "Show me, don't tell me!" they say.

All we have to do to answer their call is familiarize ourselves with the leadership principles gleaned throughout biblical history, then go out into the fields, forests, and solitary landscapes surrounding our cities and tune our ears and hearts to what God can teach us through adventurous journeys. This may sound too simplistic to some, which is fair enough. But I challenge those who might think this is a simpleton's view of leadership to read the Scriptures with an eye for experiential education methodology in the Bible. It's hard to miss the simplicity of God's apprenticeship model if you are looking for it. The wilderness classroom was not the only venue he used, but it was an incredibly common one.

The Scriptures are full of leadership principles, from identifying one's natural leadership style to practical ways of compensating for one's weaknesses. Yet how do we become a better leader without being overwhelmed with all that there is to learn? In a nutshell, I believe this comes more from whom you are than what you know how to do. There is a spiritual perspective to guiding largely over-looked in secular outdoor leadership paradigms because it isn't a central priority for their programs. Yet for Christian outdoor leaders, the Bible shines a huge spotlight on the heart of the leader and his or her *spirituality as the prerequisite for influential leadership*.

Set Apart in the Wilderness

In the Great Commission, we see that wilderness is a special place for leadership training. A vital part of training is identifying who is actually a leader. God often identified and set apart leaders by placing them in situations where they could assert leadership. Three passages illustrate this principle. When the twelve spies returned from observing the land of Canaan, Joshua and Caleb were set apart as the true leaders. They stood out among the others as the authentic leaders who were willing to follow God and trust his Word (see Numbers 13:1-33). Wilderness experiences often cause true leaders to stand out as they rise to the occasion where leadership is needed. For the attentive guide, the elements of weather and other unpredict-able forces of nature provide a real-time observation theater to watch leadership develop among people in the group. Each person will generally gravitate toward a specific role in the group. It is very common for leaders to rise up instantly in times of stress or crisis.

According to the Scriptures, leaders were often identified through wilderness experiences (see Joshua 3:7, 4:14). The account of Moses appointing Joshua to lead Israel into the Promised Land is another example of how the Lord sets apart leaders in the wilderness. A third example is the apostle Paul. In Acts 27, we encounter Paul on a ship full of prisoners in the midst of a raging storm. Through the terror of the shipwreck, Paul's God-given leadership abilities stand out, and he is identified among the passengers as a leader who knew the true God.

Evangelists Identified and Trained in the Wilderness

Elijah was nurtured and exhorted as an evangelist to his culture after a cave encounter with God in the wilderness of Damascus. The shepherds tending their flocks in the wilderness near Bethlehem were transformed, as they adored the infant Jesus; and they immediately went out proclaiming the good news in the towns and countryside. Paul, after the Lord's rebuke on the road to Damascus, went into the Arabian Desert for a number of years. Then he emerges in the book of Acts as a radical evangelist!

John the Baptist was called into the wilderness by the Holy Spirit to prepare the way for the Lord—fulfilling prophecies in Isaiah 40:3, and Malachi 3:1. John the Baptist served as an evangelist calling people to repentance—pointing them to follow Jesus of Nazareth rather than himself. As we consider the need for developing young leaders to engage the mission fields of our cities today, we must give sincere attention to emerging leaders who have a gift in evangelism. It appears from the biblical text that often this spiritual gift was nurtured and drawn out of people through refining wilderness experiences, where clearly hearing the authority of Christ's call set the course for their ministry.

Character, Competency, and Double Standards

David was prepared for leadership in a desert classroom (see 1 Samuel 17). He grew in courage as he became more confident in God.

131

David displayed this confidence when, before standing up to Goliath, he told Saul the battle was the Lord's. Secondly, his courage and confidence came from skills he attained from being a shepherd in the hills of Judea. He was confident in his ability to kill lions and bears with his bare hands. He was sure of his aim with a stone and sling. He knew from daily practice that he was fiercely effective. He had proven it time and again. This was not pride; it was simply confidence from a lot of practice. Leaders can learn something from how he attained such remarkable skill through exposure to the challenges of the wild and the mastery of certain technical skills that enabled him to thrive in such a demanding environment.

Jonah was another man of God whose character was shaped in the wilderness. Regardless of how he felt about the Ninevites, three days in the belly of the whale certainly changed his perspective on unconditional obedience. Through his ocean ordeal God exposed Jonah's double standards: he was selfish—he was concerned for a desert plant that ceased to provide him shade, yet had no concern or compassion for the thousands of lost Ninevites whom God was calling to repent. From this we learn *God also uses the wilderness to expose one's double standards.*

As God shapes our character, we too struggle with double standards. For example, we might have fastidious taste in food— being irritated when something we want is not available. Yet we often disregard providing for the basic necessities for the poor in our city. Or we might desire superior intellect to climb the proverbial ladder in our career, yet we ignore opportunities to help provide education for the underprivileged in our society. We won't pass up opportunities to advance ourselves yet we conveniently overlook opportunities to increase the potential of the poor when we could do something to help them progress in developing their gifts and talents.

Or how about this double standard: when we are bored we can turn on the television for passive entertainment, yet we neglect opportunities to encourage and bring life to the lonely or elderly of our community whose boredom far exceeds anything we have to endure in our daily experience. Like Jonah's experience in the middle of the desert, *being alone with God in solitary reflection exposes the self-absorption that saps true joy.* It transforms our thinking, giving us the occasion to purify our heart so we can be more like the yeast and salt people in our sphere of influence greatly need. We all love to be around people who display godly character. As a leadership exercise, get in the habit of asking people whom you respect how God has shaped their character. Chances are it didn't come easily.

It's good to remember there are rewards that come with virtuous character. It is especially good for young people to hear that there truly are blessings and rewards for submitting to God. We can model this in outdoor adventures by providing some simple reward systems to encourage character development. For example, consider the wonderful reward of an hour of free time after setting up camp at the end of a long day of hiking or paddling. When we hike or paddle hard so we can arrive at our destination on schedule we can enjoy some needed rest and leisure time. At times when I've been able to do this as a guide, I've looked out over a hillside or along the beach and watched people walking, playing, or laying in the sun enjoying the reward for their hard work. This is so rewarding because I know they've learned something that has shaped their character, and now they get to smell the roses as a reward. The recompense is sweet and directly connected with the hard work it took to get to this stunningly beautiful place.

Scenarios that encourage character development abound in outdoor adventure. For example, showing people who may not naturally relate how to serve one another is a common situation. Simon Beames notes progress in this character trait among one of his wilderness participants:

> Rufus felt that "living in a tight community where there's no escape" was an important aspect of the experience. He explained to me that unlike the UK, where "if you don't like someone you can just walk away or not phone them again or stay out of their way," the circumstances of the physical setting demanded that people get along with each other. Rufus expanded on this point

by saying, "you have to get along with people, you have to compromise, you have to resolve conflicts."[71]

Rufus' discovery has profound theological significance: There is effort involved in forming godly character; and there is inherent reward. When we submit to God's design, we may experience rewards in our physical health, in our relationships, and in our emotional state of being.

In perhaps one of the most exhaustive studies of the leading outdoor education organizations in the United States, Stephen Kellert recorded the sentiments of many participants involved in a variety of outdoor experiences. His research affirms that wilderness adventures are inherently predisposed to character development and personal reward for young people. One participant shared: "The strength of the friendships and bonds that my group created were life changing. This strength was inextricably linked to the difficulty and nature of the work we were doing, and to the fact that we were living outdoors."[72] And another participant noted:

> Getting us out into the real world, showing us what exists outside of TV, neon lights, suburbs, cement, and noise. Creating a genuine sense of community where each person is important for the survival of the whole—cooperation to exist, finding value in self and others, loving what is finally revealed—hacking labor, laughter in the valleys and baths in glacier waters.[73]

Pack Light for Maximum Effectiveness

God wants us to have a right attitude toward possessions. Through wilderness experiences, God taught his people to pack light for maximum effectiveness in building his Kingdom. There are many examples of this in the lives of Abraham, Jacob, David, Joshua, etc. We also see Jesus instilling this principle in the disciples as he commissioned them on their first evangelistic journey: "Do not acquire gold, or silver, or copper for your money belts, or a bag for your journey, or even two coats, or sandals, or a staff; for the worker is worthy of his support" (Matthew 10:9-10). A highlight for me in leading wilderness adventures has been to observe people discovering this principle of "packing light." In my experience whether backpacking, backcountry skiing, biking, or paddling it is remarkable how much people enjoy the experience with so few material belongings. In the wilderness, we are more naturally able to comprehend a counter-cultural reality that *we need very few material possessions to enjoy a full life.* In this context we learn firsthand the age-old proverb: "You can't strip a naked man." Or in the words of Solomon, "Everyone comes naked from their mother's womb, and as everyone comes, so they depart. They take nothing from their toil that they can carry in their hands" (Ecc. 5:15). In the words of Jesus, "One's life does not consist in the abundance of one's possessions" (Luke 12:15).

These refining character development experiences can often be the beginning of a deeper understanding of what Dietrich Bonhoeffer called the "work" of discipleship. In his description of the twelve he writes:

> They are not to go about like beggars and call attention to themselves, nor are they to burden other people like parasites. They are to go forth in the battle-dress of poverty, taking as little with them as a traveler who knows he will get board and lodging with friends at the end of the day. This shall be an expression of their faith, not in men, but in their heavenly Father who sent them and will care for them. It is this that will make their gospel credible.[74]

This is a description of the kind of leaders we need for missions today. Wilderness ministry programs where leadership training to live a Great Commission lifestyle takes place will prove to develop and multiply leaders with the David, and Daniel-like courage and skill to engage the challenging mission fields of our day.

Authentic vs. Appointed Authority

Just because someone has a "position" does not give him or her much authority. In the wilderness setting this is magnified a thousand times. In times of need and crisis, leaders rise up. People choose to follow them because they have *authentic*, earned authority, not *appointed* authority. Young leaders especially need to learn about the need for humility, skill, and wisdom so they can earn the right to lead others. I think of one trip in particular where the guide was clearly incompetent, but he had been appointed to the "position" of guide for that trip. Yet in the same group there were other highly competent guides who, in a very short span of time, became the quiet leaders of the group. They humbled themselves so they wouldn't usurp the authority of the guide who was *appointed* to lead, but people looked instead to them for guidance because they were the *authentic* leaders. These more competent guides in many instances bailed out the trip because they were truly skilled and deeply cared about the group. So the people on the trip looked to them in decision-making scenarios because they had earned the right to lead.

They had *authentic* authority rather than *appointed* authority. Outdoor leadership in the way of Christ does not rely so much on age or pedigree, or even credentials. Rather it depends on character, an ability to teach God's Word, adequate technical skills, and a passion to lead others. People quickly assign authority to those who are true spiritual leaders. Positions are only useful for a brief moment in the leadership timeline, so don't lean on your *title* or lack thereof. Just figure out how to be a servant leader and you'll eventually find yourself leading people.

Training on the Move

As a good shepherd, Jesus paid attention to the environment in which he tended his flock. Jesus taught in a variety of urban and wilderness settings. He taught indoors, outdoors, in homes, along the road, on the sea, in the desert, on top of mountains, and next to rivers. One thing is for certain, though: Jesus trained on the move. He did not stay in one place very long. He went from village to village, through fields and valleys, journeying with his disciples through various landscapes to provide experiences and a laboratory from which to teach them about the Kingdom of God.

Much like we try to use multimedia today to capture people's interest, as Jesus trained on the go, the landscape around him spun like a film reel of visual illustrations. The landscape was like a potter's wheel for hands-on instruction. The outdoor setting provided him a dynamic duo of graphic and tangible object lessons he could craft into parables that confronted his followers with realities of the spiritual realm.

C.H. Dodd in *The Parables of the Kingdom* helps us see how Jesus did this by looking at the context of each of his parables. As he traveled along he made observations from nature, which became the prime source from which he made illustrations on the Kingdom of God. The parables in the Gospels are remarkably true to everyday life. Each story is a perfect picture of something that can be observed in the world of our existence.[75] In creation, we see at work the very principles of the Kingdom:

> Since nature and super-nature are one order, you can take any part of that order and find in it illumination for other parts. Thus the falling of rain is a religious thing, for it is God who makes the rain to fall on the just and the unjust; the death of a sparrow can be contemplated without despairing of the goodness of nature, because the bird is not forgotten by your Father; and the love of God is present in the natural affection of a father for his scape-grace son. This sense of divineness of the natural order is the major premises of all the parables.[76]

When Jesus taught people about the Kingdom, his aim was not to provide moral generalities for the religiously inclined. When Jesus taught, he created an atmosphere that aroused the senses and heightened learning in his audience. He did this very often by tapping into the visible and tangible setting around them as they walked along. Understanding *where* Jesus taught will make us a more effective outdoor leader, because we too can *use the natural environment* in the same way he did. For example, Jesus illustrates the power of faith by analogies from nature. F.F. Bruce writes: "If faith is present at all, even if it is no bigger than a mustard seed, it can accomplish wonders: think what a large plant springs from something as tiny as a mustard seed."[77]

In *The Parables of Jesus,* Joachim Jeremias provides a detailed description of the context of Jesus' teaching from a Palestinian perspective. He writes: "The parables of Jesus...[were] *uttered in an actual situation* of the life of Jesus, at a particular and often unforeseen point...they were preponderantly concerned with a situation of conflict. They correct, reprove, attack...Every one of them calls for immediate response."[78]

Jesus continually drew teaching material from what Archibald Hunter called the "open book of Nature."[79] It seems like every bend in those desert roads on which he strolled with the disciples was like a new Wikipedia page that gave opportunity for teaching. For example, in *Interpreting the Parables,* Hunter illustrates how Jesus used metaphors from weather to paint a vision of the Kingdom:

> The cloud in the west foretokening rain, the south wind with its promise of heat; or the budding fig tree which is the harbinger of summer; or all the images of men going forth to till and reap the fields: the ploughman, with his eyes fixed straight ahead; the seed growing secretly, first the blade, then the ear, then the full grain in the ear; and then the fields white with a plentiful harvest, with the labourers putting in the sickle because the time for reaping has come.[80]

Another vivid example of how Jesus teaches on the move transpires along the road to Emmaus. The two disciples who encountered Jesus along their journey were in need of understanding and encouragement. Sharon Cheston writes:

> Jesus met two discouraged disciples immediately following the crucifixion. Not knowing that it was Jesus who was walking with them, the disciples indicated their confusion and discouragement over what they had just witnessed. Jesus listened, gently pointed out how the prophecy had been fulfilled, went to their house, and broke bread with them. Then he revealed himself to them. They were so encouraged that they immediately ran the several miles back to Jerusalem.[81]

It is important to note that Jesus did not prevent these men from experiencing pain and discouragement. Rather he met them in the midst of their struggle as they walked the lonely path into the dark hours of the night.

Actively Listen

Spending hours or days with a group in the wilderness affords much time for asking questions and listening deeply to a person's soul. In a weeklong camp a youth leader will typically spend as much time with a young person as they would during a twelve-month period of typical youth ministry activities back at home. As a result, people usually open up more because of spending so much time on the log. What a person offers in conversation is largely related to the level of safety they feel in the relationship. *Active listening* is a way to take captive one's thoughts to create space for genuinely listening to the other person when they open up. By seeking to understand a person's history and what has most shaped them, we offer a transforming gift.

Discussions on the trail naturally arise out of shared experiences that happen each day. This provides opportunities for asking good questions. One of the most transforming aspects of any wilderness adventure is the opportunity each person has to share their *life story*: This is a time for each person (within the safety of confidentiality) to share the milestones and memories of their lives. They are able to share what has most shaped them to be who they are today. They are even able to talk openly (maybe for the first time) about the brokenness of their lives as a result of sin or others hurting them. This allows participants in the context of community to experience forgiveness and meaningful hope through grieving, confession, being understood, and embracing a new future in Jesus Christ. Sharing life stories provides an opportunity for the group to move toward one another, demonstrating genuine interest by asking meaningful follow-up questions. This is one of the most influential aspects of a multi-day trip.

Doors of Hospitality

The apostle John commended his friend Gaius for his willingness to show hospitality to itinerant preachers sent out to evangelize in the early church:

> Dear friend, you are faithful in what you are doing for the brothers, even though they are strangers to you. They have told the church about your love. You will do well to send them on their way in a manner worthy of God. It was for the sake of the Name that they went out, receiving no help from the pagans. We

ought therefore to show hospitality to such men so that we may work together for the truth. (3 John 5-8)

The apostle Peter's model for effective evangelism also involved a commitment to the ministry of hospitality: "Offer hospitality to one another without grumbling" (1 Peter 4:9). One of the most common ways of demonstrating hospitality is through sharing meals. On wilderness adventures meals are a community experience, usually sitting in a circle so that everyone can see one another face to face. Often after everyone is served, we will ask a question to get to know something new about each person.

Hospitality is a ministry of creating safe and welcoming environments where folks feel at home. This is an essential skill for outdoor leaders to master. We have found in our ministry that many young people may go a week or more without hearing their name called in an affectionate way. Even this simple aspect of the journey where the leaders call everyone by name in a loving way day after day can cause a lasting impact. As cities become more violent and impersonal, young people feel anxious and vulnerable. On wilderness trips, even though kids may initially be scared by the unfamiliarity of the outdoors, ironically, they're often deeply affected by the sense of *safety* they feel in being a part of such a caring group even though it is in such a *wild* environment. As the group works, eats, and rests together, a sense of safety and belonging develops over the course of a few short days. For example, one activity most people associate with a sense of belonging is the sharing of stories. Storytelling around the campfire at night or during a shared meal can be an intimate and enjoyable way to connect more deeply with others. Unfortunately, at times well-meaning adults diminish the importance of "fun" in creating an environment of hospitality. Yet creating an environment of fun and humor on the journey can be like rain to a parched field. Humor allows a person to share deeply of themselves and to feel more connected to the group.

Many young people are hurting from broken family relationships or from lack of respect and tender love from the adults who mean the most to them. Jesus was concerned about the whole person, and an effective outdoor leader will be constantly aware of people's needs along the journey so that he or she can provide *practical help* (which is hospitality at its best).

Art of Guiding

When starting out, guiding can be a little overwhelming because you are responsible for people in an environment that can potentially turn dangerous. But similar to being a part of any guild or learning a craft or art, it takes time and practice to develop these skills. Watching a master at work is the best way to learn an art. In relational evangelism and experiential teaching, the skillful guide will be able to amplify Kingdom truths as situations arise. Like any apprenticeship model, after you've been leading people a while your apprentices will begin to grasp your priorities and some will even begin to live by them. It's more about who you are than what you do. You can't take a cookie-cutter approach to discipleship because you have to tailor your relationships and goals based upon whom you are apprenticing. Jesus also engaged different personalities along the journey; some were more tender requiring gentleness, and others required more severity because they were strong-willed.

One aspect of the art of guiding is the *attitude in which we serve.* Jesus demonstrated a hopeful and encouraging attitude especially as he ministered to tired or discouraged people. Applying first aid to someone is a wonderful opportunity to identify compassionately with him or her through a personal touch. Addressing their physical pain assures the patient something is being done to alleviate the ache, whether it is physical or emotional.

One irony I've observed in the art of guiding is the more seasoned, experienced outdoor guides tend to rely more and more on the ministry of prayer in leading people on wilderness adventures rather than their own ability or strength to facilitate the activities. That's because they have learned that seeking the mind of God on behalf of others, and interceding for them in the spiritual realm, is our greatest contribution to the transformation of people. This reminds me of the scene when Jesus spoke to the crowd that was about to stone the woman caught in adultery: "When they kept on questioning him, he straightened up and said to them, 'Let any one of you who is without sin be the first to throw a stone at her...At this, those who heard began to go away one at a time, the older ones first'" (John 8:7,9). The oldest people left first because they had a thick memory of experiences under their belts that made them humble. Likewise, when an outdoor leader realizes people need the intervention of the Holy Spirit, prayer becomes a paramount discipline in the art of guiding. This is learned through experience much like the skill of a weathered artist.

Closure

Bringing an adventure to a close is necessary in *validating the experience as "real"* for each of the participants. Inadequate closure will cause people to wonder or doubt whether what happened to them on the trail was just a mountaintop experience. One way we provide adequate closure is by simply allowing the group to encourage one another by acknowledging the transformation they witnessed in each other during the journey. We find as well that commending others for their gifts and contributions strengthens our own witness as we freely build up others and value them as they are created in the image of God.

The Great Commission was a concrete closure-event for the disciples, and Jesus' ascension was the culmination of that closure-event, marking the decisive point that the disciples were now being sent out to act on the commission they had been given. Interestingly, the "doubting" episode (where some worshiped and others doubted) Matthew mentioned preceding Jesus' commissioning words to the disciples, indicates *the tendency we all have to doubt the validity of the new orientation which occurs following a life-changing experience.* It's kind of like the feeling we have after a really impactful retreat where we are excited about what happened, but then we soon begin to wonder if what we experienced will actually have any bearing on our life. Satan loves to snatch away seeds of growth. His scheme is always to discredit the Word of God, which is one of his primary modes of attack. We see this clearly modeled in the temptations of Christ where all of Satan's lures sought to discredit the Word of God. *Satan desires to derail vital closure-events. Paradoxically he will either throw a wet blanket on new flames of faith or he will try to fan into a blaze any smoldering doubt that might still be resonating in our heart.* For this reason we need to carefully provide closure and debriefing opportunities for people to validate their experience so they can make a game plan for implementing any direction they received from God.

The parable of the Two Builders provides another rationale for our concept of *closure*; asserting the critical nature of *immediate application and follow-up plans.* The parable occurs at the conclusion of Matthew's Sermon on the Mount and at the end of Luke's Sermon on the Plain (see Luke 6:20-49)—thus exemplifying the pressing urgency of an obedient and practical response to Jesus' preaching. This is relevant because at the end of a wilderness trip or retreat we must impress upon people the urgency of responding to what Jesus has spoken to them. What Jesus speaks to us doesn't change, so it is urgent that we respond immediately. Even in the parable of the wise and foolish builders Jesus clearly states that the wise builder is the one who listens to the Word and acts on it daily (see Matthew 7:24-27). As we help people process what has occurred in their lives and what they've heard Jesus say to them, we need to help them consider how to continue abiding daily back at home so their lives are built on rock rather than sand. Most likely very little has changed in their home context when they return from a wilderness experience, so it is all the more urgent for us to help people make a plan for mission-commitment and spiritual growth as they go back to a situation that may even be hostile toward what they have learned.

Regarding this closure-principle, we have found Psalm 1 to be very practical. Here David teaches us to be careful about: 1) The *foundation* on which we build our life, and 2) Our *relationships* and *priorities*. In other words, whom do we allow to influence us? It is vital for people to consider if they are building their life (structure, patterns) on a human foundation to fit in, to impress others, or to get ahead, etc. We must warn them that building their life on a foundation of self-oriented priorities will crumble at some point because of the weak base it is built upon. Equally, we are to be careful about our relationships because they are one of the key foundations of our lives. If our relationships are poor then our foundation is poor. Our relationship with Jesus Christ needs to be the central relationship in our life—out of which all other relationships will find their meaning and vitality.

Adequate closure is perhaps the greatest challenge for an outdoor leader. Preparing someone to go home to the city after experiencing a "peak experience" is especially difficult. We often find lessons learned in the pristine wilderness may be lost without an obvious parallel in a busy, violent, impersonal city environment. Arnold Berleant has explored this quandary and discovered the value of *viewing the city as a type of wilderness*. As we reflect on the organic nature of the city, we are able to uncover many facets of the city environment that are analogous to a wilderness experience. This may be helpful for relating one's wilderness experience to life back at home. Berleant writes:

> One can find a parallel between the momentary respite from immersion in the density of a city or wilderness either by the panoramic view from the observation deck of a skyscraper or a broad boulevard, or by the sweeping panorama one might obtain from a mountaintop, bluff, or tall tree. The aroma emanating from a bakery or restaurant might remind one of the odors of different vegetation or ground surfaces, such as pine needles or wet soil. The odor of decaying leaves or the effluvium of a marsh or swamp in the hot sun may resemble the smell of garbage containers on the sidewalk awaiting pickup or the exhaust of motor vehicles. Moving among buildings and along streets has some of the perceptual quality of moving among stands of trees and through openings in the vegetation. The background hum of traffic is reminiscent of the wind rushing through the trees when a front was coming through. Pushing one's way through a crowd

resembles the experience of pressing through dense growth. Constant concern over making a misstep influences our passage through both city and wilderness, while the background apprehension of danger from motor vehicles and muggers parallels the constant threat, real or imagined, from the deadly creatures thought to inhabit a wilderness.[82]

However you decide to do it, in shepherding people, you need to consider what your participants have learned and then give them guidance on how to apply those lessons in their home-context.

Follow-Up

Following up with people after they go home is also essential in helping them mature and practically apply the decisions they have made in their home environment. Leaders who make contact with young people and build relationships with them in the city need to make every effort to be the ones who *bring* those young people on a wilderness journey. Telling someone they should go do something without being willing to go along with them is relationally counterproductive. The best model for follow up is when the youth leader brings the young person on the trip and then goes home with her to follow up long term after the trip.

We find this in Paul's own conversion experience. Coleman explains: "After Paul affirms Christ as Lord, the question of knowing his specific direction still remains. Here follow-up is essential."[83] So the Holy Spirit drew Paul out into the desert to re-orient his life through a time in the wilderness of Arabia. That time of follow up on his conversion experience was crucial for setting him on a new course of true discipleship. The goal of youth ministry is to make disciples and bring them *to maturity in Jesus Christ beyond their mountaintop experiences.* Young people especially are at a crucial stage in their maturity where they are making decisions about the frontiers of their lives. So they need leaders who will follow up with them until they have their feet underneath them enough to start discipling others.

So how do we recognize maturity in those whom we are apprenticing? Just as growth on a vine can vary in appearance, Roy

Zuck describes some recognizable fruit of maturity in Jesus' disciples. According to Zuck's review of Jesus' teaching, spiritual fruit becomes mature or ripe as the believer grows, by: 1) Loving the Lord, 2) Loving others, 3) Obeying God's Word, 4) Doing good deeds, 5) Putting spiritual priorities first, 6) Fellowshipping with God in prayer, 7) Exercising faith in the Lord, 8) Resisting temptation, and 9) Manifesting spiritual virtues. This is a very useful list to help you organize your discipleship plan based upon the specific needs and development stages of your disciples.

The writer of Hebrews also provides timeless wisdom pertaining to the need for follow up. These principles apply to all stages of maturity:

> And let us consider how we may spur one another on toward love and good deeds. Let us not give up meeting together, as some are in the habit of doing, but let us encourage one another.... (Hebrews 10:23-25)

Follow-up is possibly the most important aspect of the journey in order to help people solidify decisions or commitments they made in the wilderness. I find that, in many ways, faith is a group journey, especially among adolescents who are especially friend-centered. Again Coleman asserts: "Faith inspires faith. One person believing creates a positive climate that will influence others. Unbelief also tends to be contagious. Where there is massive doubt, as in Nazareth, miraculous works of God are rare."[84]

SECTION II: THEORY

CHAPTER 6
RESULTS

Aim Small, Miss Small

In *The Patriot*, Benjamin Martin taught his sons to "aim small, miss small." The idea is that if you aim at the bullseye on a target, you are more likely to hit it. If you aim at the whole target you might hit somewhere on the object but you won't hit the bullseye. In leadership, we need to guard against trying to do too much and stay focused on the task at hand. If we keep a small, sharp aim at a particular outcome then we are more likely to hit the mark and see the results we are hoping for. If we deal only in generalities then we will probably either miss or barely hit the target. Outdoor leadership has a target...the target is our audience. We need to know them, study them, love them, and seek spiritual guidance from Jesus in how to lead them. As we keep a keen eye on our audience and choose outcomes and objectives that create an environment of spiritual formation for our group then we will be more satisfied with the results. Outdoor leadership is much more than just going outside to hang out with people.

As an outdoor leader, you will be more organized and effective if you know what you are aiming to see happen. This chapter is about desired outcomes. They will vary from group to group, but there are common spiritual fruits that seem to ripen through outdoor adventures. Grasping some of these common outcomes will help you establish good goals and plans for your trip. I have been asked many times, "Why is adventure camping in the outdoors so effective?" Many of us who have been taking people out into the wilderness and leading people on adventures know it is effective from our experiences, but could we explain why it works in a thirty-second elevator conversation? We need a practical way to weave the Five Smooth Stones of Wilderness Theology into our adventures, but we also need a way to cast the vision of wilderness ministry to our church or organization. This chapter pulls back a curtain on the mystery of why adventure evangelism is so effective. It is set up as a tool for memorizing the basic framework of a theology of wilderness. I want to get better at leading others in the outdoors *and* in the city. Don't we all? Having a thirty-second spiel on the tip of your tongue for what outdoor ministry is all about will help you cast compelling vision to people who may need a little coaxing toward adventure.

This chapter is about outcomes and objectives for outdoor adventures. We will offer a simple acrostic for memorizing five of the most common spiritual outcomes we see happening in the biblical wilderness journeys. A useful acronym I use to easily remember the basics of wilderness theology is *"ABCDE"*. We will look at each letter of this acronym and then later in the chapter, we will list ten common *objectives* or goals of a typical outdoor adventure.

Before we look at some of our objectives, we need to look at the umbrella themes or outcomes that come right out of the pages of Scripture. The reason I am presenting the following model is for ease of memory. My hope is that as a Christian outdoor leader, you will know by memory the Five Smooth Stones of Wilderness Theology: TEMPO, TERRAIN and TIMING, TRIALS, TRUST, and TRAINING, which we've been talking about in preceding chapters. I also hope that you can learn to recognize the *ABCDE's* of common outdoor adventure outcomes. The most effective outdoor leaders are able to facilitate experiences toward measurable outcomes such as these.

Having a theological framework helps us to focus on the essentials. I realize that any generalization (like this model I'm about to present) is an approximation of reality. I can already hear many of my outdoor leader friends saying, "Don't put me in a box!" I assure you, the opposite is actually what I intend. I'm merely aiming to help us think this through. If this type of ministry is to grow we need many more people who can articulate why wilderness experiences are so effective for evangelism, discipleship, leadership development, and spiritual formation. I hope this will help shed light on your own experiences and enhance your future endeavors as a Christian outdoor leader.

ABCDE's of Outdoor Leadership Outcomes

The field of wilderness medicine has paved the path for more simple thinking about effective wilderness leadership. For example, if you take a Wilderness First Aid course, you will learn that very little equipment is needed to treat a patient in the wilderness. All you need is a little confidence, some basic skills, and a *bunch* of creativity to use the bits and pieces available to you in your surroundings. In first aid training, the *ABCDE*'s stand for "Airway, Breathing, Circulation, Disability, and Environment." These are the essentials for making an initial assessment of a patient to diagnose if there is a threat to his or her life. In the same way that Wilderness Medicine training organizations try to make their training as simple and memorable as possible, the following model is meant to introduce "Christian outdoor leadership" in an easy-to-remember paradigm.

When planning a trip, it is a good idea for you to have the desired results in mind so you can prayerfully guide others toward those outcomes. The *ABCDE* outcomes I've identified are five mega-themes under which you can categorize the types of transformation that happened for people as a result of their wilderness experience in the Bible. And we have every reason to pray and hope for similar outcomes on our trips as well.

The five most common outcomes we see emerging from people's wilderness experiences in Scripture are as follows:

1. **A**WARENESS of God's existence through observing his creation
2. **B**ELIEF in Jesus Christ
3. **C**OMMUNITY: Experiencing biblical fellowship
4. **D**ISCIPLINE: Finding freedom and joy through spiritual disciplines
5. **E**XAMEN: A habit of Christ-centered contemplation

Wilderness experiences heighten our AWARENESS of the existence of God. Colossians 1:15-20 says that Jesus is the One who made all of creation, so it should be of no surprise that his handiwork has a limitless number of illustrations to elicit awe for God. The wilderness changes our perspective. It expands our comfort zones and shows us our need for God's grace.

Adventures also invite us to take risks. BELIEF requires taking a risk. Trusting other people may come with some perceived risk, but the actual risk of putting your trust in Jesus Christ is nil. It's just that our pride gets in the way of humbling ourselves before him. God used the wilderness to expose Israel's disbelief and Jesus used storms and struggles to reveal the disciples' lack of trust.

Experiencing biblical COMMUNITY changes our wrong views of God, others, and ourselves. If we embrace individualism and neglect community then our ideas of success and failure are going to be warped. Biblical community turns the world upside down in all the right ways. For example, we find out that washing other's feet brings joy because Jesus came to serve not to be served—and that includes us; he came to serve us! The wilderness teaches us that the foundation of community is grace upon grace.

The opposite of DISCIPLINE is chaos and confusion. Ordering your life to enjoy the presence and peace of Christ is counter-cultural. It means saying no to many things that everyone else is saying yes to. Yet it also means experiencing freedom that most others will never enjoy. Spiritual disciplines teach us that limitations are good because of our sin and pride. Be comforted if God disciplines you. It's a sign of his love.

St. Ignatius coined the term EXAMEN to refer to a lifestyle of Christ-centered contemplation. *Examen* is a habit of taking time each day to reflect and pray in order to hear God's voice of guidance. Time in the wilderness helps us remember God's faithfulness. The silence and solitude of the outdoors exposes the emptiness we feel when we hide from God and it ushers in the healing balm of brokenness, honesty, and confession.

As an outdoor leader, you will be more effective if you know what you are hoping to see happen in your group. *ABCDE* is an acronym for five of the most common spiritual outcomes that result from outdoor adventures (Note: you can download this model at the book's website, www.outdoorleaders.com/resources). If you choose one or two of the *ABCDE* outcomes as an umbrella theme for your trip, you'll notice more intentionality in everything you do. Then, if you choose one of the ten primary learning objectives suggested in the next section, your teaching content will have a sharper aim at your audience and result in a lasting impact. "Aim small, miss small!"

The grid on the next page is an abbreviated attempt to illustrate the way these *Five Smooth Stones of Wilderness Theology* intersect with the five common *ABCDE* outcomes I have proposed. Each box in the grid lists a theological principle discussed in the book and how it is connected with these desired outcomes. And for reference, in the grid on the next page, some of the pertinent chapters are listed for each theological principle for further study. Again, the main application for you as a leader is to think through how you can lead others toward these *ABCDE* desired outcomes, recognizing that there is a theological basis for what you are doing in that God has used the *tempo*/rhythm of retreats, the *terrain and timing* of wilderness experiences; and he has orchestrated *testing, trials*, and *trust-building* experiences to *train* and *transform* his followers throughout the ages.

Five Smooth Stones of Wilderness Theology	TEMPO Jesus had a rhythm of hard work and regular retreat "The Eleven went to Galilee..."	TERRAIN & TIMING Jesus made His ideas STICK: Setting + Timing + Intentional Content=ties the Knot The Disciples went "to the mountain"
AWARENESS of God's existence and character	Wilderness provides vistas for new perspectives Ch. 7	Mountains inspire awe of God Ch. 2
BELIEF in Jesus Christ	The wilderness prepares us for spiritual conflict & helps us discern Kingdom strategy. Ch. 1 & 7	Fearful situations can evoke belief Ch. 3
COMMUNITY Experiencing Biblical fellowship	Experiencing Biblical community changes our view of God, ourselves, and others. Ch. 7	Jesus redefines success & failure through desert solitude Ch. 2
DISCIPLINE Finding freedom and joy through spiritual disciplines	Limitations are good and have a spiritual purpose Ch. 1	Hunger, thirst, & physical trials in the wilderness forged character development Ch. 2
EXAMEN A habit of Christ-centered contemplation	Wilderness experiences help us remember God's faithfulness Ch. 1	Silence & solitude exposes the emptiness that results from hiding from God. Ch. 3 & 7

OUTCOMES OF CHRISTIAN OUTDOOR LEADERSHIP

152

INSTRUMENTS OF TRANSFORMATION

TRIALS	TRUST	TRAINING
Physical, emotional, intellectual, and spiritual challenges forge our character into the likeness of Christ **"they worshipped... but some doubted..."**	Jesus' Disciples are marked by trust in Him. There is <u>no</u> *actual* risk in trusting God. All *perceived* risk is false. **"All authority... has been given to Me..."**	Leadership is more about who you are than what you do. Healthy leaders reproduce healthy ministry. **"therefore go make disciples."**
Adventure expands our comfort zones Ch. 3	The Desert elicits trust. We realize it is by *grace* we are chosen and saved. Ch. 3	Through intense decision-making scenarios God used the wilderness to draw out leaders
God questions us to examine our integrity Ch. 3	Peter's reinstatement: God is faithful even when we are faithless Ch. 4	Because of its lack of distraction, the wilderness was a common scene for commissioning leaders Ch. 5
Working together in adventure teaches us the foundation of Biblical community is grace Ch. 3 & 4	Jesus' relationship w/ the Father epitomizes how trust is the foundation for relationships. Ch. 4 & 7	Jesus intentionally involved His Disciples & we are called to do the same for others. Ch. 13
Through intentional resistance God exposes whether we fear Him or man Ch. 3	God interrupts those whom He chooses to reshape their identity Ch. 4	Pack light for maximum effectiveness in advancing the Gospel Ch. 5
Wilderness teaches us the rhythm of the Psalms: orientation, disorientation, new orientation, Ch. 9	The desert challenges our pride: take the pressure off yourself, this is God's work! Ch. 7	The wilderness teaches us the difference between positional and legitimate authority. Ch. 5

W.I.L.D.E.R.N.E.S.S. Learning Objectives

As you consider leading others on wilderness journeys you need to consider your potential audience. Depending on the church you want to serve or the organization you are representing there are at least ten primary *learning objectives* you may want to consider for your camps. Again these are ten common and somewhat timeless objectives that I think are worth aiming at as teaching themes or content for wilderness adventures. The difference between the five *ABCDE* outcomes above and our ten objectives which follow the acronym W.I.L.D.E.R.N.E.S.S. is slight but worth noting.

I believe the *ABCDE* outcomes are largely what God accomplishes in us as a part of his work of sanctification. In other words, God is sovereign, and whether or not we intentionally try to work toward those *ABCDE* outcomes on our trip it seems that God brings about fruit in these areas through wilderness experiences even despite us just because of the intrinsic power of encountering God in solitary places. But that doesn't mean that we *shouldn't* try to organize our trips to focus the learning toward a desired outcome. I think being more intentional toward a desired outcome will make you a better leader and by God's grace you will see more fruit. So it's worth working on these skills rather than just winging it and heading out to the hills without a plan. Jesus is our model and he seemed to have a rationale for what he taught. So should we.

Objectives, on the other hand, are different than outcomes. They are steps we can attempt toward those outcomes. For example, in a soccer game the outcome or "end" you hope for is to *win* the game. Each goal you score is an *objective* toward that end. If you don't score any goals then you won't achieve your desired outcome either. Reaching the desired outcome is somehow intimately and mysteriously linked to our effort.

So following this rationale, our ten W.I.L.D.E.R.N.E.S.S. objectives are more focused steps to help us move toward our *ABCDE* desired outcomes. I encourage you to start small as you grow in your leadership ability because if you try to do too much you'll water down the impact. So, you should filter your objectives through a narrow funnel and just focus on a few.

Below is a list of ten common funnels to direct your efforts. It is beyond the scope of this book to provide fully developed plans for each learning objective, but this overview will give you a start in developing your own curriculum or trail talks. Hopefully you will be able to measure in some small way if you've hit the mark on your trip. Again, this does not depend on you alone—this is God's work. All we are doing is seeking to be good stewards of the limited amount of responsibility we've been given under *God's absolute sovereignty* over our group. So, without further ado, here are some suggested themes or learning objectives for your outings:

W – Worldview

David Noebel, in *Understanding the Times,* writes: "Your worldview is like the trees roots, it is essential to your life and stability...Roots are essential for the tree's stability. We can't see one another's worldview, but we can see the exposed part of it—your actions."[85] Now there's a great trail talk! The next time you are leading a group on a hike, stop at a stream where there is a big tree with roots fed by the water and ask them to come up with a handful of ways that a tree's roots are like a person's worldview. See what they come up with and then help them solidify this image in their minds.

What is a worldview? There are a number of ways to look at one's worldview, but Paul's letter to Titus provides us with a model for looking at the four main questions imbedded in one's worldview:

1) Where did I come from?

2) What is the meaning of life?

3) How do I determine right from wrong?

4) What happens to me after I die? (see Titus 2:11-14)

Utilizing Scripture and your knowledge of contemporary culture, you might decide to focus the content of your adventure on helping people honestly appraise their worldview and identify where it does not align with Christ's worldview. You could set up quiet times to address each aspect of Jesus' worldview, or you could have groups work on two or three different worldviews throughout the trip and present what they learned to the rest of the group. We would be remiss in this day and age to discuss the content of Jesus' teaching without giving some attention to his basic worldview. With growing interest in a wide variety of religious and cultural worldviews today, it is increasingly important to find ways to help people filter what they are learning from worldly sources through Jesus' coherent and unparalleled worldview.

I – Intercession

(Preparation for Spiritual Conflict)

Jesus retreated to the wilderness often for blessing and preparation for spiritual conflict or "warfare." Luke the Evangelist shows how the *wilderness was a place of preparation for conflict with Satan* (see Luke 4:1-13). The Gospel of Mark also shows Jesus retreating to the wilderness before handling the spiritual burden of healing the multitudes by the sea (see Mark 3:7-12). And after the apostles returned to him, having engaged in evangelism and spiritual conflict in the towns and village of Galilee, they were in much need of rest— so they retreated (see Mark 6:30-31). Mark also shows how Jesus went away to receive spiritual guidance and perspective from his Father through prayer. From Mark's account, we learn that although doors for ministry were wide open in a certain region, through a time of retreat where he listened to his Father in prayer, Jesus chose to go to other towns and villages. We need time away to pray and listen so that our strategy is formed in the *spiritual realm* rather than in the realm in which we can only *see*.

L – Leadership Development

The sky is the limit in terms of how you could design a week of content for this subject. Topics can include servant leadership, understanding spiritual gifts, and how leaders are commissioned to equip and increase the potential of others. We could study what shepherding should look like in the church and the kinds of things leaders should look for in the lives of people under their care. We could use the week to demonstrate a biblical understanding of how to form and carry out a vision or we could emphasize how we might motivate and empower others to get involved and participate in what God is doing around them. Chapter 5 offers more ideas on how to maximize learning toward this objective.

D - Discipleship

You may want to spend a few days of your trip gaining a deeper understanding of worship, or how to more effectively make disciples. You may want to focus on the fruit of the Spirit, or how we are called to show mercy and pursue justice for vulnerable people in our world. Whichever angle we take, focusing on discipleship as a learning objective will help funnel our content and discussions around how we are engaging our world for the glory of God.

E - Evangelism

As followers of Jesus we want to bring the rain of the gospel to dry and thirsty souls. There are a myriad of ways to share the gospel effectively with people in the context of a wilderness journey. Three goals worth considering are: 1) Learn to be the initiator in bringing the rain of the good news to thirsty souls (see Hosea 6:3); 2) Learn to pray for the soil of people's hearts to be ready for the very rain of the gospel coming their way through you as the messenger (see John 4:13-14); and 3) Submit to Christ and humbly decide to step out of your comfort zone to be a faithful leader who is a *rain cloud* that actually brings rain rather than a cloud that doesn't (see Jude 12). A soul that needs the rain of the gospel is left hanging when what apparently looks like a rain cloud passes over and doesn't leave a drop for its parched soil. How often do we do this by *not* bringing Christ into our conversations with people who don't know him yet?

Here are a few questions that might help you effectively share the gospel through your week in the wilderness:

1. What would I want if I were (*put a person's name here*)? The answer to this question is what we can strive and pray for. Assume more often than not that we are the one to provide that need rather than think it is someone else's role.

2. Don't assume or expect that (*name of lost person*) will care about you at first. We don't need to talk about ourselves much at first, but rather focus on asking questions that probe for understanding.

3. Be **CHEER**ful:

    CURIOUS: Always seek to learn something new in conversations.

    HUMOR: Don't stay serious. Share funny stories and laugh at yourself.

    ENTHUSIASM: Let them experience your own enthusiasm about life.

    EMPATHY: Put yourself in their shoes. Seek to understand them.

    RELATE: Find common ground to talk about. Seek to learn from them. Be selfless and other-centered

4. Recognize "wants" versus "needs": Ask yourself, "What does (*name of person*) want that Jesus has to offer? What does (*name of person*) need, but doesn't know it yet?"

5. Restate objections into a goal: People always have concerns and issues that must be satisfied. For instance: the cost of following Jesus, the reliability of the Bible, the relevance of Jesus to their life, misconceptions of who God is as "Father," etc. After identifying their objections to the gospel, restate their objections into a goal. For example:

    Objection (they might say): "I would lose so much freedom if I become a follower of Christ."

    Restate Goal (ask yourself): "How can I help my friend see that he or she can still enjoy freedom if they choose to follow Jesus?"

6. Write a gospel path through your Bible:

Below is a sample template to scribble into your Bible. It provides a simple pathway to explain the gospel through the Bible. First go to 1 John 5:13. Highlight that verse and then write next to that verse the next verse in the gospel sequence, i.e., Proverbs 14:12 and so on (see the table below for a suggested sequence to articulate the gospel clearly). So if you have a chance to walk someone through the whole gospel, you can just remember 1 John 5:13 and go there in your Bible, then you can follow the verses in your margins to lead you to the next verse and so on. It's a simple way to have the gospel *mapped out* in your Bible for ease and simplicity.

A Gospel Path Through Your Bible

SCRIPTURE	Main Points
1 John 5:13	God is not playing hide-and-seek with us...We are able to seek and know him.
Proverbs 14:12	Man's ways are not God's ways.
Romans 6:23	The path of grace.
Romans 3:10,23; Isaiah 53:6	All have sinned and have fallen short of the glory of God.
Titus 3:5; Ephesians 2:8-9	We can't save ourselves from our predicament.
James 2:10; Galatians 3:10	Just one sin makes us cursed. This highlights the gravity of sin.
Isaiah 14:12-15	Satan's one evil thought cast him out of the presence of God.
Luke 18:9	Trusting in ourselves will not save us from sin.
1 John 4:8; Genesis 1:31	God hates sin because sin destroys his creation, which he loves!
Romans 5:8	God loves us even though we are sinful and rebellious against him.

John 3:16	God has a plan to save humankind from eternal separation from him.
Isaiah 53:6; 1 Peter 2:24; John 15:13	Jesus paid for our sins and laid down his life for us.
John 19:30	Jesus paid for our sins in full. Jesus paid the penalty for those who believe in him.
John 14:2	God has prepared a place in heaven for those who believe in his Son, Jesus.
Ephesians 2:8; Hebrews 11:6	In order to be forgiven of our sins and given the free gift of eternal life, one must put their faith in Jesus Christ.
James 2:18-19; John 14:6	Faith is a choice. It is not just intellectual agreement. One must put their full weight on Jesus Christ and trust that he is the Way, the Truth, and the Life.
1 John 1:9	God will forgive those who confess their sins and put their trust in Jesus.
Romans 10:9	How do I go about choosing to follow Jesus?
John 3:16; 6:47	Assurance of one's salvation.

R - Relationships

In Chapter 7, we'll look at how our lives are connected to a network of relationships. What should healthy family relationships look like according to the Bible? What do healthy relationships look like with your friends, church, local community, or across cultures? The wilderness is a laboratory for discovering God's design for relationships. Make this a learning objective for your trip, and hopefully you will be able to measure in some way if your group goes home with a renewed perspective and commitment to God's design for relationships. I have seen small groups of high school kids be so affected by God's design for relationships that they initiated radical change to their whole church community and eventually their high school after they returned home. Some passages to focus on could be: *Acts 2:21-47; Romans 12:9-18; 1 John 3:13-18; and John 13:35.*

N – Nurture
(Adventure Therapy and Mental Health)

Wilderness or adventure therapy in the psychological sense is largely about identity formation and trust issues discussed in Chapter 4. In the process of orienting our lives to Jesus Christ, our True North, we find that he is the Great Physician and the Rock of our salvation. In leading others therapeutically on the trail, we may need to help them sever old ties to behaviors or thinking patterns that have greatly damaged their relationship with God or others. This is not a book on wilderness therapy, but as far as a learning goal, the wilderness is an ideal setting for giving people space to change wrong ways of thinking or to anchor their whole identity to Jesus. This may require healing old wounds, forgiving others, or having a chance to be heard and understood. We see Jesus modeling relational therapy in an adventurous setting with his disciples, individuals, small groups, and whole crowds who sought him out. Fostering better mental health is a noble and appropriate goal for wilderness ministry.

Many agree that the wilderness is an excellent environment for counseling young people with behavioral challenges through an experiential process. Patricia Doucette asks an important question at the outset of her study regarding the value of walking in the outdoors verses sitting in an office while counseling young people. She writes, "Do preadolescent and adolescent youths with behavioral challenges benefit from a multimodal intervention of walking outdoors while engaging in counseling?"[86] Her study reveals that walking outdoors during counseling is definitely beneficial to the process of behavioral transformation among at-risk youth.

Author and adolescent researcher, Rebecca Cowan discovered similar results in the lives of several participants she led in the wilderness. One camper described her experience in terms of how it increased her self-esteem:

> "Lord," wrote one camper in his journal, "You know that I am struggling with a bad self-image. Lots of times Satan puts thoughts in my head about not being worth anything. But I know that is wrong. You especially designed and made me—just like you made this beautiful vast wilderness around me."[87]

Another camper wrote about his solo experience where he slept alone for a night under the stars: "Being alone on the solo made me realize how much I really do need people and how much I take them for granted...I enjoy being with people and sharing my life with them and having them share their lives with me."[88]

E – "Expect great things, attempt great things!"

In studying the heroes of missions we find that many of them got their vision from reading stories and biographies of other adventuresome missionaries who had gone out before them. William Carey, a hero of modern world missions, is famous for saying, "Expect great things, attempt great things!" This learning objective focuses on how to infect others with the missionary spirit. The Bible makes it clear *God has used the wilderness as a special place for choosing and commissioning people into his mission field (see Gen. 12:1-5, Matthew 28:16-20).* This can be a powerful learning goal to pursue with a group of people who desire to discern God's call on their life or to determine strategies for how to use all that God has given them (including time, talents, and treasure) to advance his Kingdom locally and globally.

Many Scripture passages provide a foundation for this theme, but a few worth mentioning could begin with Luke 19:1-10. What does it mean for a person to be lost? What keeps us from pursuing those who aren't in Christ? Or we may focus on 2 Corinthians 5:14-21 and highlight how both the *message* and the *ministry* of reconciliation have been entrusted to us as believers. You could focus a whole week on coming to grips with what the *message* of reconciliation encompasses and what living out the *ministry* of *reconciliation* could look like back in our community. Or you could highlight a particular missionary using short excerpts from their autobiography or journals to spark dialogue about why there is still a need for cross-cultural missions today.

S - Spiritual Formation

It goes without saying that one of the primary values of the wilderness is the solitude with God it provides toward developing a conversational relationship with him. There are four main elements to this ongoing conversation with him in prayer: 1) *We speak to him; 2) We believe that he listens to us; 3) He speaks back to us; and 4) We exercise discipline to listen and obey him.*[89] People often need to reboot from the spiritual paralysis that comes from habitual disobedience or disbelief. Make this a learning objective for your trip and you can help people enjoy a week of more intimate experiences with God. This might help them see the value of developing a pattern of regular retreat, which increases the likelihood that they will take initiative in their spiritual formation process back at home. Some possible passages to explore could be: *Luke 10:38-42; Mark 1:35; Luke 5:16; Matthew 14:23; Matthew 6:7-13; 1 John 1:8-9; Hebrews 4:14-16; Matthew 11:28; and Philippians 4:6-7.*

S - Scenarios

This learning objective focuses on critical thinking, decision-making, and discerning the will of God. How to make sound decisions for survival or for charting a vocational path varies from person to person. But in most cases, developing an ability to process environmental conditions, group needs, and biblical wisdom to make a sensible decision involves handling four types of knowledge:

1) Knowing *what* to do, 2) Knowing *how* to do it, 3) Knowing *when* to do something, *and 4)* Knowing *why* to do it. If there was ever a need for this generation, it is to help people throw off the shackles of decision-paralysis so they can do something with their lives in the full freedom of Christ. Especially in the developed world, our younger generation has had many things handed to them, and, as a result, hasn't learned how to weigh decisions and assertively decide a good moral direction to glorify God. The wilderness offers a veritable cornucopia of decision-making scenarios.

Programming this learning goal into your week simply requires you to anticipate a handful of scenarios that will come up based upon the route you are taking. Then prepare how you are going to present those situations to your group so they can participate in the decision-making. Learning how to make decisions in adventure or survival situations actually teaches them a skill that will be useful in every aspect of decision-making back at home. Your job is to connect the dots and help your group see how the lessons learned from decision-making in the wilderness directly applies to their life back home.

CHAPTER 7
REELS

Anticipatory Sets (Movie Trailers to Capture Your Audience)

When I was twelve years old, the pastor of my church, Doug, invited my dad, me and another friend, Mike, to go on a backpacking trip to the base of Chair Mountain near Marble, Colorado. I could not have been more excited. Days seemed like months as I waited for our big expedition. That warm summer day finally arrived and as we clunked along the four-wheel drive road to the trailhead, I imagined facing mountain lions, dodging rock slides, and spelunking into caves to protect us from the wild splashes of lightning common at that time of the summer. I was ready for adventure!

Near sunset at the end of our first day, after clamoring thousands of feet to the doorway of Buckskin Basin, I saw a beauty I had never before imagined. At the base of cathedral cliffs that seemed to reach to heaven, an opal-blue lake sat like a jewel, quietly reflecting the canvas of the red sky above. Like an orange ball coming to rest on the distant ridge, the sun set. I sat in the quiet, and with every fresh breath of air that filled my little lungs, it was obvious to me that this wild and pristine basin had been created as a place for *me* to sit and gaze into the glory of God. "Wow," I wondered, "Did God have me in mind when he created this alpine wonderland?" It seemed possible that maybe he did. In many ways, this special place, in the seat of Chair Mountain, marked the beginning of my journey with the Lord. Buckskin Basin marks the spot on the map where the Lord imparted a vision in me to do everything I could to help other young people around the world encounter Jesus Christ in the captivating theater of his creation.

The next morning I awoke to the serenity of Buckskin Basin and soon got the lesson of a lifetime. I learned how to fish for native cutthroat trout that day. My dad pulled out a strand of fishing line and tied it to a hook for me. After finishing his cigarette, we tied the butt of that Camel to the fishing line to use as a bobber and affixed a chunk of cheddar cheese to the hook. With the end of the line wrapped around my hand I catapulted that tangled twine out into the lake with every hope that I would catch something. The cheese barely had a chance to sink below the surface when a wild trout swallowed my bait! We caught our limit that morning with nothing more than that funky but effective little rig my dad set up for me. This was unforgettable.

One thing you have to know about fishing is how to *reel* them in. If you pull too hard they'll get away, but if you give too much slack they'll spit out the hook. There is a fine balance. The same is true about your audience. (After working in youth and college ministries for more than twenty years, I realize now more than ever that our real challenge today is to capture the attention of young people through meaningful relationships. Maybe that's why Jesus used the fishing analogy with Peter. Fish don't just go out of their way to jump into a net or chomp down on a hook...you have to persuade them.)

One handy trick I've found to help keep folks *on the line* and involved in the learning process during a wilderness experience is to give them a glance of what's ahead so they are convinced it's worth all the hard work to get to our destination. Another type of *reel* we commonly see used these days to draw people in is a movie *reel*. Movie trailers help people decide if the film interests them enough to sit through it. They also give us a preview to the theme so we can follow the story line from the opening scene. The task for you as an outdoor leader is to come up with a movie trailer for your trip. I call these "Anticipatory Sets," because they help people anticipate what's coming up to keep them committed to the journey.

As an outdoor leader, you need to know the story you want to present and you need to know your audience. By knowing the outdoor environment, your desired outcomes, your objectives, and your audience, you should be able to thoughtfully write down a short vignette to prep your audience for the content you hope to present to the group throughout the adventure. Making a movie trailer forces the producer to narrow down the message to sixty seconds or so. An *anticipatory set* forces us to do the same. Being forced to narrow your message down to its most simple and vivid terms, you will most certainly do a better job of shaping and planning your week toward a worthwhile outcome.

Part of what makes teaching as you go more fun and more effective in the wilderness is when you have a crystal clear vision of the primary and secondary objectives you are aiming for. This frees you up to focus on discerning the needs of the group rather than following some manual. In a nutshell, you want to find a variety of ways to give your group a sneak peek into what they are going to *do* and what they might have an opportunity to *learn without giving away all of the surprises. Then design your plan to facilitate that learning process.* Anticipatory sets are a great place to start your trip.

In this chapter I'll offer four sample *anticipatory sets* that give an overview of the learning objective I'll be aiming at accomplishing in a week with a group. They are not necessarily in any kind of order, they are just samples for you to look at before you try to write out your own. Some are longer than others and they are not meant to be used verbatim. Rather I use these as a tool to help me think through how I can tell a story to prepare folks for what we're going to do and hopefully what we might learn on the forthcoming adventure.

There is a Purpose to Discomfort

An Anticipatory Set for a *Discipleship* Learning Objective

We live in a day and age where immediate gratification is considered a virtue not a vice. Unfortunately (or fortunately depending on your point of view), we don't always get what we want, so this often leaves people scratching their heads wondering if God really loves them because he has allowed difficulty in their lives. When we finally reach a point where we are being stretched, we either blame God or learn to thank him for loving us so much that he allows hardship in our lives to keep us from running amuck with pride. Our theme this week is to process a hugely present theme of Scripture that flies in the face of immediate gratification. *We are going to learn this week that God is actually in the business of expanding our comfort zones to keep us humble and dependent on him. Yes, God actually removes familiarity at times to foster humility and guard us from the dangers of pride.*

One of the first examples of this occurs at the Tower of Babel (see Genesis 11:1-9). The people of ancient civilization had become confident, self-sufficient, and overly comfortable. Seeing this as a danger (a vice not a virtue), God pressed them outside of their comfort zone by confusing their language. He scattered them throughout the wilderness with many languages to keep them dependent on him. If you've ever traveled to another culture where you don't understand the language, you can relate with how uncomfortable this is and how much it causes you to be dependent on God and on other people.

God is not against comfort but he actually sees value in *discomfort* to keep us humble. Humility is more important to him than our personal comforts. So when we are stretched beyond our comforts on the trail this week, hiking, climbing, serving, getting wet, whatever happens... look at it as a God-ordained opportunity to experience more freedom and richer blessing in life because we will be freed from the slavery of always having to selfishly satisfy our own desires. God wants us to know that through Christ we can say "no" and be okay with *not* having what we want. In doing so we will actually be freer than others around us who are *enslaved by materialism or an addiction to recognition.*

Later in Scripture we see this principle come to light through Abraham's calling to mission (see Genesis 12:1-13:18). One obvious feature of his calling was the intentionality God expressed in removing familiarity and comfort from Abraham and his family for the purpose of blessing all people through him (see Genesis 12:17-18). Familiarity is a blessing and a curse in every culture. We can rest when we are familiar with our environment (i.e., culture, family, music, food, surroundings, art, etc.), but familiarity can also lead to complacency. Wilderness journeys were used by God to remove familiarity (i.e., comfort zones), to get us moving on the challenging but purposeful adventure of reconciling those who were estranged from God back into relationship with him!

One can relate to the concept of expanding comfort zones if he or she has experienced being new to a group or an alien in a culture. This is a humbling experience and usually causes a change of heart toward those who are different from us—because we know how it feels to be a foreigner. Abraham was an alien everywhere he traveled through the wilderness, bumping into people who spoke different languages, having to borrow land to graze his flocks, etc. Nothing about his life was comfortable, except his position of dependence and favor with God.

When we experience a small dose of this by spending time in another culture or doing something way beyond our comfort zones, we can relate better with what Abraham experienced. After my first mission trip overseas years ago, upon returning to the United States I had a new sense of compassion and understanding toward foreigners living in my native culture. God stretched Abraham's comfort zone by having him sojourn as an alien in a foreign wilderness. This developed in him a heart of compassion and understanding for the lost. *God's mission is to seek and save the lost through his chosen people and he saw it was necessary to first humble them by making them aliens so they would be a mission-committed people, with compassion for those outside their family—the other nations.* They had to wear the shoes of a foreigner first to gain a heart and vision for reaching out to the nations estranged from God.

Familiarity is a danger for the church even today. The moment we become comfortable and over-familiar with our own culture, we tend to disregard those who are foreign to our "family." This principle has direct implications for believers in every church: *Mission-commitment in the church is dependent on God's people being pushed into unfamiliarity in order to develop compassion for the lost.* Remaining comfortable hardens the heart of the church for the lost... we must live and feel as aliens or strangers in the world to remain a *missional* church.

Until Jesus returns, God is going to continue to push his people out of their comfort zones to keep them humble and mission-committed. The forty-year wilderness sojourn of Israel is a good paradigm for us to understand what Jesus meant when he spoke about how the church's citizenship is in heaven. We are aliens in this world, it's not our home. Wilderness experiences provide limitless opportunities for stretching comfort zones: sleeping on the ground, having few baths, eating different food, having no media to cause distractions, experiencing real physical demands, visiting the toilet in the woods, etc. Jesus' goal is to purify for himself a people who are transformed; a people who are a possession for him, who will eagerly lay their lives down to desire only one thing: God's good, pleasing, and perfect will (see Titus 2:14, Romans 12:1-2). And the unavoidable reality is that this singleness of heart God desires is usually developed and shaped through trials and challenges.

Continuance Indicates Covenant Relationship

An Anticipatory Set for the *Relationships and Community* Learning Objective:

In the first half of the letter to the Hebrews, we learn a principle about trials and testing: *Pressing* on in our relationship with Jesus is the true test of reality—*our continuance in faith is an assurance of our belonging to Christ.* God disciplines those he loves, and those with true faith in Christ will continue to follow him to the very end. Faith is measured over a lifetime, so seasons of struggle or even disbelief may come our way, but at the end of the day, those who belong to Christ will continue and press on. The writer of Hebrews speaks at great length about the rebellion of the Israelites in the wilderness at *Meribah*. We learn the reason the Hebrew people were not allowed to enter into the Promised Land was because of their *persistent unbelief*. And the message of the writer of Hebrews to his audience was that this principle remains true throughout the ages. Beginning well with Christ is not the test of reality, that's easy. Rather the continuance of our belief and submission to his authority even in the hard times is the sign of our belonging to him.

In Hebrews 5, we see how the expanding of Israel's comfort zones in the wilderness broke their laziness and disbelief. We see this lesson in our own lives as well; when we're stretched or challenged, we become more dependent on Christ. He forces us to sever old ties that hold us back. The writer warns against falling away in our faith: "For though by this time you ought to be teachers, you have need again for someone to teach you the elementary principles of the oracles of God, and you have come to need milk and not solid food" (Hebrews 5:12). The author's Hebrew audience was sluggish; they had settled down and were comfortable. Going further in their faith would mean they would have to sever old ties with legalism, and comfortable family traditions that provided false hope. Turning 180 degrees away from all you've ever known is not easy, but it's exactly what this letter to Jewish Christians exhorts its readers to do. F.F. Bruce comments: "The intellect is not over-ready to entertain an idea that the heart finds unpalatable."[90] We need young leaders today to respond to this message, to sever their old ties and forge new paths in missions to the lost—free of the snares and shackles of familiarity and comfort.

Bruce explains the contrast between mild and solid (spiritual) food was a common subject in the early church. Paul writes to the church at Corinth: "And I, brethren, could not speak to you as to spiritual men, but as to men of flesh, as to infants in Christ" (1 Corinthians 3:1). And Peter writes: "Like newborn babies, long for the pure milk of the word, so that by it you may grow in respect to salvation" (1 Peter 2:2). Peter was writing to a church of primarily *new* converts. Yet here in the letter to the Hebrews, the audience is those who are *mature, yet sluggish* in their faith. These "mature" Christians had built up a standard of righteousness by which they were passing discriminating judgment on others, yet their hearts remained resistant to change and non-committal toward missions.

Maybe you have a group of people who have grown up in the church and they've developed an edge of superiority or separateness from others. They can be judgmental of others but won't deal with the sin and complacency in their own hearts. As mature or blessed as they may feel, having grown up in the church, a group like this is to be pitied and pushed hard to stop relying on spiritual milk. It's time to grow up and feed on spiritual meat—to focus on becoming Christ-like rather than staying true to traditions or patterns of life that hinder us from relating with those who are broken and enslaved to their sin.

This same heart condition was cause for the Lord to initiate the transformation Israel experienced at the end of Moses' life when they had to go through forty years of reformation in the desert. And this same heart attitude was the occasion for the book of Hebrews. We would be wise to recognize this warning is also fully relevant for many Christians who've grown up in churches today. A wilderness adventure may be just what the doctor ordered to push a group of "religious" people toward a faith-life that is anything but comfortable. Starting out well with Christ is only the starting point; it is how we continue growing in Christ-likeness that is the mark of authenticity in our relationship with him.

Severing Old Ties and Shedding Spiritual Blinders

An Anticipatory Set for the *Nurture/Adventure Therapy* Learning Objective

Due to the fall of Adam and Eve we do not naturally sever old ties, but rather hold on to what we know, e.g., the comforts and familiarity of our sinful nature. This is why Paul wrote similarly in his letter to the Colossians these instructions to sever their old ties:

> Therefore if you have been raised up with Christ, keep seeking the things above, where Christ is, seated at the right hand of God. Set your mind on the things above, not on the things that are on earth. For you have died and your life is hidden with Christ in God. When Christ, who is our life, is revealed, then you also will be revealed with him in glory. Therefore consider the members of your earthly body as dead to immorality, impurity, passion, evil desire, and greed, which amounts to idolatry. For it is because of these things that the wrath of God will come upon the sons of disobedience, and in them you also once walked, when you were living in them. But now you also, put them all aside: anger, wrath, malice, slander, and abusive speech from your mouth. Do not lie to one another, since you laid aside the old self with its evil practices, and have put on the new self who is being renewed to a true knowledge according to the image of the One who created him— a renewal in which there is no distinction between Greek and Jew, circumcised and uncircumcised, barbarian, Scythian, slave and freeman, but Christ is all, and in all. (Colossians 3:1-11)

Again, he gave similar instruction to the church in Rome:

> For those who are according to the flesh set their minds on the things of the flesh, but those who are according to the Spirit, the things of the Spirit. For the mind set on the flesh is death, but the mind set on the Spirit is life and peace, because the mind set on the flesh is hostile toward God; for it does not subject itself to the law of God, for it is not even able to do so, and those who are in the flesh cannot please God. However, you are not in the flesh but in the Spirit, if indeed the Spirit of God dwells in you. But if anyone does not have the Spirit of Christ, he does not belong to him. If Christ is in you, though the body is dead because of sin, yet the spirit is alive because of righteousness. But if the Spirit of him who raised Jesus from the dead dwells in you, he who raised Christ Jesus from the dead will also give life to your mortal bodies through his Spirit who dwells in you. (Romans 8:5-11)

Through the expansion of our comfort zones in the wilderness, old ties and spiritual blinders are removed, opening our eyes to the reality of the spiritual realm. This is possibly one of the most important fruits of transformation to come through wilderness experiences. We live in a society that disregards the spiritual realm as imaginary or unreal. Yet God's Word clearly teaches that only through Scripture and prayer are we able to discern what God is *thinking*, and thus hear from him what he would like us to *do*. Since we, in our busy society, often lack the discipline to quietly listen to God in prayer, wilderness experiences are needed even more so people can experience God speaking to them in solitude. The apostle Paul explains this principle that *spiritual blinders are removed through prayer* in the first letter to the Corinthian church, where he explains this mysterious reality in a simple earthly analogy. He writes:

> But just as it is written, "Things which eye has not seen and ear has not heard, And which have not entered the heart of man, All that God has prepared for those who love him." For to us God revealed them through the Spirit; for the Spirit searches all things, even the depths of God. For who among men knows the thoughts of a man except the spirit of the man which is in him? Even so the thoughts of God no one knows except the Spirit of God. Now we have received, not the spirit of the world, but the Spirit who is from God, so that we may know the things freely given to us by God, which things we also speak, not in words taught by human wisdom, but in those taught by the Spirit, combining spiritual thoughts with spiritual words. But a natural man does not accept the things of the Spirit of God, for they are foolishness to him; and he cannot understand them, because they are spiritually appraised. But he who is spiritual appraises all things, yet he himself is appraised by no one. For who has known the mind of the Lord, that he will instruct him? But we have the mind of Christ. (1 Corinthians 2:9-16)

In other words, a person has no way of knowing the thoughts of another unless the other person reveals his thoughts to him. One of the greatest causes of psychological angst in both Christians and non-Christians is we make ourselves believe we know what others are thinking. We trust our perceptions when, in fact, our perceptions are often (or maybe most often) wrong. Paul here provides a tonic for freedom to those of us who struggle with anxiety. We cannot know others' thoughts in the same way others can't know ours.

Here is a very interesting flip side of this reality: In the same way we can't know the thoughts of other people, we similarly cannot know the thoughts of God unless his Spirit reveals his thoughts to us. What we need more than anything else is to hear the voice of the loving Heavenly Father speaking to us, so his voice drowns out other condemning voices (our own or others'). We need true healing from those destructive voices, but this is only possible if we can hear God's voice. Yet Paul clearly says here that if you do not have a relationship with Jesus Christ, if you have not repented of your sin and humbly submitted your life to Christ, then you will not be able to hear the voice of the Heavenly Father speaking to you in the way that those who are in Christ are able to enjoy. That is only possible through Christ. He is the gate, the door, the Way. It is crucial for non-Christians to wrestle with this.

And for Christians, we need to be reminded that unless we are in a posture of listening and communing with God through prayer and his Word, we will not know his thoughts either. The thoughts of God are only accessible through his Spirit and as he desires to reveal them to us. Paul's analogy is both common sense (we see this operating in the world of relationships), and a spiritual reality. *Only through prayer and meditation on God's Word are our spiritual blinders removed!* This is why prayer and Bible study is vital for growing in Christ. There are many spiritual *blinders that hinder us from "continuing in our faith and belief."* Mankind is tempted to believe lies and if we remain sluggish and "prayer-less" we will be entangled by many hindrances. E.M. Bounds gives us instructions on how to guard against this "prayerlessness":

> Prayerless praying, which has the form and motion of prayer but is without the true heart of prayer, never moves God to an answer. It is of such praying that James said, "Ye have not, because ye ask not. Ye ask, and receive not, because ye ask amiss."[91]

The wilderness is a special place where God has removed spiritual blinders through leading his people into discomfort and suffering in order to open their eyes and ears to his glory and goodness. The result is unhindered belief and trust, which transforms us, fanning into flame the fire of the gospel that shines in the darkness of our world-influenced minds. The gospel washes over the lies we have believed and cleanses our thinking to align with the mind of Christ. Rather than letting our minds run down every rabbit trail or wind of false doctrine thrown to us on the radio, in books, or on TV, we are called, through faith and prayer, to submit our minds to be "controlled by the Spirit" (Romans 8:11). Paul promises if we allow the Spirit to control our minds, we will experience "life and peace." Life and peace are marks of a transformed mind. That is the goal of any kind of psychological therapy. And the Great Physician is able to bring that healing to our minds.

Who Sets the Terms of Discipleship?

An Anticipatory Set for the *Discipleship* Learning Objective

From a theological perspective, the stubborn essence of one's personal comfort zone is that he is dangerously close to trying to set the terms of his discipleship. Yet Jesus is the one who sets the terms of our relationship with him, not us. Michael Knowles explores this idea in the Parable of the Unworthy Servant (see Luke 17:7-10). Quoting John Calvin, he writes: "The object of this parable is to show that all the zeal manifested by us in discharging our duty does not put God under any obligation to us by any sort of merit; for, as we are his property, so he on his part can owe us nothing."[92] In this parable, the follower is denied setting the terms of discipleship... his relationship is on the master's terms and the master is by nature good. Knowles continues, "And the second half [of the parable] denies the possibility that service for God is intrinsically meritorious... Discipleship is not self-determined, and that one is not compensated according to one's merits, but on some other principle."[93]

We learn by expanding our comfort zones and removing familiarity—a crucial principle which is foundational to enjoying the abundant life Christ desires for us: *Being a disciple does not give us a special status—this side of Heaven there are no guaranteed "fringe benefits" or bonuses for service.* Now that is counter-cultural! And it is most certainly opposed to the prosperity gospel. At times this principle may even be an unwelcome truth for Christians. But God's aim is not always our comfort. Sometimes we need rebuke and exhortation if we've drifted off course.

Part of the art of guiding outdoor adventure experiences involves taking advantage of opportunities to challenge comfort zones by modeling the principle in this parable. We can often set the terms of an activity during a trip rather than allowing the participants to set the terms of the experience (i.e., defining boundaries, facilitating adventure, communicating aspects of the journey which are not optional for safety, health, etc.). Eating backpacking food and drinking treated water are two common examples of things that cause some discomfort for the average person. What is your list of things that you've seen causing discomfort on a wilderness adventure? The list is undoubtedly long.

Speaking to the group I might say, "On this outing you will have a guide who has some skills you may not have learned yet. This may be humbling to you, but embrace this as a great opportunity to think about how Christ is our 'Master'—we rely on him daily to teach us and lead us through things we have little or no experience dealing with. You may not have the skill to survive and thrive in the outdoors on your own, but if you humbly listen and learn from your guides and practice what they teach you, you will likely be able to survive and thrive on your own the next time you go out into the wilderness. This is what discipleship is all about. Your guides are not going to lord this over you, we are here to help you learn and become more comfortable navigating in the outdoors."

God's will is for all of us to humbly learn from those leaders who have spiritual authority in our lives. In fact, that is one of the reasons why God designed the local church to have leaders: "Obey your leaders and submit to their authority. They keep watch over you as men who must give an account. Obey them so that their work will be a joy, not a burden, for that would be of no advantage to you" (Hebrews 13:17). Discipleship is on Jesus Christ's terms, and we will thrive, grow, and make a more significant impact in our world the more we humbly submit to learning from those who know more than we do. Ultimately, our Guide is Jesus Christ, but in his love for us he also provides leaders here and now who can invest in us as apprentices. I might say something like this to a group at the beginning of a trip: "Even though your guides are far from perfect, at the end of the trip, I'd like you to journal a bit about how their role as a guide this week has shaped your understanding of how Jesus Christ is your Guide through all of life."

CHAPTER 8
RELATIONSHIPS

Master/Disciple Relationship

The wilderness is like a comprehensive social networking school. Like a cohort of students that studies together for a period of time, Jesus' relationships with His disciples went far beyond the classroom. They did all of life together. Our lives are oriented around relationships, but how healthy are those relationships? Today we can hide behind an Iphone or put the best face on our identity through Facebook, MySpace, or Twitter. I'm afraid our society might start enjoying texting more than talking at some point. Wilderness adventures provide a very healthy place to learn God's design for relationships. I think most would agree it's time we revisited this topic before technology rather than earned trust becomes the basis for relationships.

Who Jesus Christ taught is not a mystery to us. We see that he regularly taught individuals and groups of all sizes, yet he invested most of his time with Peter, James, John, and his other nine disciples. He invested time with a group of seventy-two, and an even larger group of one hundred and twenty whom he sent out to preach. He also spent a considerable amount of time with the masses. Jesus shared meals with "sinners," which seemed to be an activity he greatly enjoyed. (e.g., sharing a meal with Matthew and his tax-gatherer friends as well as reclining with Zacchaeus at his home). And he spent time in dialogue with Pharisees and religious teachers. He prioritized engaging the people of Israel but also pursued a few selected Gentiles and others like the women at the well in Samaria.

We can presume from what we know of the twelve that many of Jesus' disciples probably would not have initially chosen to be best buddies. For example, Simon the Zealot would have likely been an extreme nationalist and *proponent for the independence* of Israel from the Roman government—even as this meant taking up arms. Levi the tax collector would most likely have taken a position of *accommodation* to the Roman Empire in order to survive and thrive—capitalizing on the financial benefits of Hellenization. Thus, their opposing political views would probably have affected their respect for one another.

Yet respect is a critical component to enjoying meaningful relationships. So Jesus, through His teaching and various adventures, worked hard to forge respect and trust among even the prickliest of acquaintances in his community of disciples. Teams must be unified, and leaders sometimes have to do the hard yards to provide an anvil of experiences to break down pride and self-sufficiency, so everyone in the group learns to give and receive. Short-term wilderness journeys can be a fertile environment for bringing a variety of people together into a fulfilling community of relationships. For example, Simon Beames, in his article "Critical Elements of an Expedition Experience," interviewed several participants during an adventure experience in Ghana who affirmed this reality:

> Rufus felt that "living in a tight community where there's no escape" was an important aspect of the experience. He explained ...that unlike the UK, where "if you don't like someone you can just walk away or not phone them again or stay out of their way," the circumstances of the physical setting demanded that people get along with each other. Rufus expanded on this point by saying "you have to get along with people, you have to compromise, you have to resolve conflicts"...Gordo's observation about how the physical setting affects social interactions..."It's not just about speaking to people you get on with best. It's about learning to speak with people that you want to avoid!"...In her matter-of-fact manner, Tracy summed up this point by stating that "the fact that we're miles from anywhere and thrown together in this situation is important."[94]

These young people make a poignant observation about the nature of learning in community. Similar to Rufus and Gordo's experience, the disciples usually understood the significance of what Jesus taught *in retrospect.* Jesus did not expect his disciples to *immediately* grasp the significance of what he taught them. He was confident that transformation was happening regardless of any outward signs of growth. Peter Scaer agrees: "Often in pedagogy, the student learns to perform tasks, and only later to understand their significance."[95]

In discipleship we learn to imitate Jesus Christ (often through certain tasks) and then only later, after submitting our will in obedience to Christ, do we understand the significance of our actions. Today people, especially in western societies where entitlement has become an idol, will often say, "Show me the benefit first, then I'll do the task if it seems to be worth my effort." If we are honest, we must admit that Christian teaching to some extent today is focused on persuading believers toward discipleship by attempting to illuminate the *significance or purpose* for obedience rather than our obligation to obedience. This only feeds an entitlement view of discipleship, i.e., "Show me it's worth my time and then I'll commit to it." Does that in any way sound like the vibe of Jesus' invitation? Not even close.

In contrast, Jesus stakes a claim to the entire life of his disciples. And *as we take steps to obey him, then we begin to grasp the significance of what we are doing.* We walk by faith, not by sight. This principle must not be ignored regardless of how entertainment-oriented, enlightened, or postmodern our culture has become. Churches today are struggling with syncretistic tendencies to make following Jesus "relevant," "significant," or "worthwhile"—this is an inadequate and inappropriate response to Jesus Christ and will only grow shallow-rooted followers who lack perseverance when pressed (see Mark 4:4-6).

Jesus invited a variety of friends into community. He embarked with them on a quest to, in the words of George Müller, *"get glory for God."*[96] There is no greater pursuit than this, individually or corporately. And it was to the Father's glory that a diverse group of men and women would bear much fruit by modeling God's timeless design for holy relationships (see John 10:10; 15:8).

Jesus' Method was Relationships

One of the first things an outdoor leader needs to do is get to know his or her group. The deeper we go in knowing those we're leading, the richer the experience will be. Jesus modeled this priority of personal relationships. Think back to a group you've experienced an adventure or mission trip with, and try to imagine all of the characters that were in the group. I'm sure it was full of a variety of personalities and giftedness. Keep that group in the back of your mind as we look now at the main group Jesus led on multiple wilderness adventures.

To begin his mission, *Jesus started with a small group*. Like a wise architect who knew how to build a lasting foundation, or a seasoned warrior who knew the art of war, Jesus sought to gain a *strong base of operation* first in the Holy Land.[97] Jesus spent most of his three years of ministry with the twelve. Clearly, the heart of his strategy was to build a mission community that would carry his message to the ends of the earth. In other words, *people were His method, not programs*: "His concern was not with programs to reach the multitudes, but with men whom the multitudes would follow."[98] His disciples were a group of ordinary people whom he called into an extraordinary relationship. The disciples' varied personalities offer many insights into how Jesus transformed his friends. His mission community would be *unified, but certainly not uniform*!

William Barclay, in *The Master's Men*, provides insight into the personalities of the twelve. Jesus was the Master of bringing individuals and groups to maturity. Peter, the man who became known as a "Rock," was a Galilean fisherman who was part of Jesus' inner circle of disciples along with James and John. Galileans were traditionally a courageous stock of men.[99] We see from the outset that Jesus chose men who were prepared to follow him... those whom the Holy Spirit had quickened to forsake all for him: "Jesus did not have the time or the desire to scatter himself on those who wanted to make their own terms of discipleship."[100]

Peter had several unique experiences with Jesus, witnessing the raising of Jairus' daughter (see Mark 5:37; Luke 8:51), the Transfiguration (see Matt. 17:1; Mark 9:2; Luke 9:28), and Jesus' agony in the Garden of Gethsemane (see Matt. 26:40; Mark 14:37). Jesus also sent Peter ahead with John to prepare the last Passover in Jerusalem.[101] He is known for his declaration that Jesus was the Messiah, and his great discovery that no one else had the words of life.[102] He was the recipient of Jesus' *great promise* (that Jesus would build his church upon him), as well as his *great rebuke*, "Get thee behind me, Satan."[103] Ironically, Peter is known both for his *denial of Jesus*, and *Christ's loyalty toward him* as he imparted to him his calling at the Sea of Tiberias. And Peter is remembered for grasping that the *Missio Dei* (mission of God) included Gentiles as he received Cornelius into fellowship of the church.[104]

We also have much historical data about the apostle John. In Barclay's words, "He was the Son of Thunder who became the Apostle of Love."[105] The synoptic gospels (Matthew, Mark, and Luke) primarily describe John in an unattractive way—highlighting the "thunderous" aspect of his personality, whereas the Gospel of John highlights a transformed John—the Apostle of Love:

> At first sight John appears as a man of ever-reaching ambition, a man with an explosive temper, a man of an intolerant heart ...John is the supreme example of how Jesus Christ can take a man as he is and use his natural gifts and powers and temperament for greatness. Power itself is always neutral. Power becomes good or bad according to the mind and heart of the person by whom it is controlled and used. In John there was always power and the power was united with loveliness when it was controlled by Jesus Christ.[106]

Andrew, the second disciple chosen by Jesus, was uniquely devoted to introducing others to him. Every strong leader needs a follower like Andrew: "Andrew was the kind of man who never received the first place; yet he was also the kind of man on whom every leader depends, and who is the backbone of the Christian church and the salt of the earth."[107] He displayed several wonderful qualities in his relationship with Jesus. First, he was *selfless*. Andrew knew his brother Peter was a natural leader so he quickly introduced him to Jesus: "For Andrew missionary work began at home."[108] Second, he was *optimistic* and *enthusiastic*, eagerly bringing people to Christ; for example the boy with loaves and fishes.[109] Third, he was a man ahead of his time in that he saw the universality of Jesus' invitation; that the grace of God which brings salvation to all men had appeared in the person of Jesus Christ: "He understood Jesus so well that he knew that there was no one whom Jesus did not wish to see, and that there was no time when Jesus was too busy to give himself to the seeking and the inquiring searcher for the truth."[110]

Thomas was the disciple who became certain by doubting.[111] He is known by several unique qualities: 1) He was a man of courage, supporting Jesus' desire to see Lazarus: "Let us also go, that we may die with him" (John 11:16); 2) He was often bewildered (see John 14:1-6); 3) Initially, he could not wholeheartedly believe in Jesus Christ (see John 20:25); and 4) He became a man of devotion and faith (see John 20:26-28). Two principles emerge from observing Thomas' relationship with Jesus: 1) Jesus blames no man for wanting to be sure of him,[112] and 2) Certainty is most likely to come to a person in the fellowship of believers—thus making the need for being a part of the believing community clear.[113] As we read of Thomas' conversion, although he doubted that Jesus had risen from the dead, he remained close enough to the community of disciples to be around when Jesus appeared in the upper room, where Thomas saw him, touched him, and believed. Thomas provides a wonderful example to many people who participate in wilderness journeys: Although they may be searching and have many doubts, the environment of Christian community itself is often a climate that promotes new faith. When consistently connected to community, those with doubts are often illumined to the truth of the gospel. Thomas' experience can give us hope, and remind us to make every effort to keep skeptical or doubting personalities involved in the group discussions.

Matthew was the disciple who, previous to his submission to Jesus, was probably despised by most of his community because of his profession as a tax collector.[114] Yet we learn from Matthew's example that Jesus called self-promoting sinners to follow him. He was concerned for all kinds of people. A.B. Bruce highlights the importance of Mathew's call:

> The call of Matthew signally illustrates a very prominent feature in the public action of Jesus, viz., his utter disregard of the maxims of worldly wisdom. A publican disciple, much more a publican apostle, could not fail to be a stumbling block to Jewish prejudice, and therefore to be, for the time at least, a source of weakness rather than of strength... Aware that both he and his disciples would be despised and rejected of men for a season, he went calmly on his way, choosing for his companions and agents "whom he would," undisturbed by the gainsaying of his generation—like one who knew that his work concerned all nations and all time.[115]

The New Testament does not tell us much about the rest of the disciples. Judas Iscariot was the man who became the one who betrayed Jesus. Philip was the first man called to follow Jesus and Simon the Zealot was the man who began with anger, but ended full of love. James, the brother of John was the first of the twelve to become a martyr.[116] From Scripture and church history we know very little about Nathanael, James the son of Alphaeus, and Thaddaeus. So take heart when you lead a wilderness adventure with a group and for some reason you weren't able to connect equally with every participant. This is normal. You'll know some students more deeply... this is just the nature of relationships. Our capacity for depth is not limitless like Jesus' was, and even he seemed to prioritize his time with Peter, James, and John.

When invited to follow, the disciples did not enter their community as in the typical rabbi-student relationship, but followed Jesus in a personal way. Jesus' call was stern and uncompromising, even more so than some Old Testament examples.[117] In 1 Kings 19:20, Elisha was called to follow God as Elijah's apprentice, but when he asked if he could go back and say goodbye to his mother and father, he was allowed to take leave. In contrast, Jesus forbade His disciples from putting their hand to the plow and looking back:[118]

> He said to another man, "Follow me." But the man replied, "Lord, first let me go and bury my father." Jesus said to him, "Let the dead bury their own dead, but you go and proclaim the kingdom of God." Still another said, "I will follow you, Lord; but first let me go back and say goodbye to my family." Jesus replied, "No one who puts his hand to the plow and looks back is fit for service in the kingdom of God." (Luke 9:59-62)

A loyal and courageous mission community was the goal of Jesus' fellowship, so he invested heavily in the lives of those he trained. "The more concentrated the size of the group being taught, the greater opportunity for learning. In a profound sense, he is showing us how the Great Commission can become the controlling purpose of every family circle, every small group gathering, every close friendship in this life."[119]

The twelve were also Jesus' *traveling companions*. They were with him almost all the time, "witnessing all his work, and ministering to his daily needs."[120] The disciples were under-shepherds who would carry on his work. Jesus was limited in his humanness, therefore he could not spend time with everyone; instead he chose to develop spiritual leaders whom others would follow.[121]

In preparing the disciples, Jesus heightened their awareness of Satan's strategy to defeat them. A.B. Bruce provides insight into Satan's twisted creed:

> The whole aim of Satanic policy is to get self-interest recognized as the chief end of man. Satan's temptations aim at nothing worse than this. Satan is called the Prince of this world, because self-interest rules the world; he is called the accuser of the brethren, because he does not believe that even the sons of God have any higher motive...There is absolutely no such thing as a surrender of the lower life for the higher; all men are selfish at heart, and have their price: some may hold out longer than others, but in the last extremity every man will prefer his own things to the things of God. All that a man hath will he give for his life, his moral integrity and his piety not excepted. Such is Satan's creed.[122]

Since Jesus was taking his disciples on a journey (spiritually, physically, emotionally, and intellectually) and the dangers were imminent because of their foe, the Devil, he instructed them to *pack light.* Like any good soldier or shepherd, they had to learn to live on little and keep their lifestyle simple so they could focus their efforts on the *mission* rather than on the cares of the world. In other words, Jesus' message to his disciples was:

> Go at once, and go as you are, and trouble not yourselves about food or raiment, or any bodily want; trust in God for these. His instructions proceeded on the principle of division of labor assigning to the servants the kingdom military duty, and to God the commissariat department...God would provide for them through the instrumentality of his people.[123]

Any group on a journey will experience the dynamics of group formation. Living in community can bring out the best and worst in one another. As groups form, natural leaders arise, and those who have the appropriate gifts fill various roles needed for the group to function. Jesus' band of disciples provides a living parable of group dynamics in that he brought unity among a group with vast differences in personality, thus providing vision for the Kingdom of God: "This union of opposites was not accidental, but was designed by Jesus as prophecy of the future...So in the church of the future there should be neither Greek nor Jew, circumcision nor uncircumcision, bond or free, but only Christ."[124]

The Relational Apprenticeship Model of the Early Church

Robert Coleman, in his book *Master Plan of Evangelism,* traced the underlying strategy of Jesus' personal ministry, highlighting a model of working with the three, the twelve, the seventy-two, and the masses. In *The Master Plan of Discipleship,* he shows how (after the ascension of Jesus Christ) the *apostolic church* carried out its mandate for mission. This model of discipleship is largely observed in the book of Acts. Coleman writes, "The Book of Acts makes it clear that bringing the gospel to every creature is God's program, and it can be accomplished."[125] Early in church history there is a precedent for small group ministry. Learning in small groups leads to transformation. This happens not only because people are able to know one another and feel safe in the small community, but also because it is easier for the shepherd or leader of the group to facilitate learning through real life experiences. Coleman notes:

> One has to ask, in all honesty, why did not the Christians erect special buildings for their corporate meetings, especially after leaving the synagogues?...It seems probable that, "The Christians simply saw no compelling reason to erect buildings for worship." They gathered at home, where they lived their faith every day. In this relaxed atmosphere they learned together even as they shared one another's burdens.[126]

Sometimes parents recognize a unique gift in their child, so when it's time to choose a university or trade school to send them to, they will try to find somewhere they can get specialized training. Whether it's a private music or art institute, or a specialized engineering school, it's most parents' dream to provide the best education they can to help them develop their talents to their utmost potential. What about a school for learning how to develop healthy relationships? So much of life is about interactions with others whether it is family, marriage, friendships, or even work relationships. People today need godly models of healthy relationships. This is a responsibility that falls on leaders.

If you are a leader then you have people following you. People depend on your leadership at some level. This goes for parents, teachers, bosses, and even peer leaders. Leaders need to be able to name their desired outcomes both in their own life and in the lives of those whom he or she is apprenticing. This is what it means to have a vision for someone else. And then once you have a vision for someone else, your work becomes figuring out all of the ways you can help your apprentice increase their potential in all areas of their life: in wisdom, in stature, in favor with God and man (see Luke 2:52; Ephesians 4:11-13). Leaders help others learn how to aim the frontiers of their lives toward glorifying God through relationships. In an outdoor leadership context, your objectives will vary from group to group, but one significant area of growth we see through outdoor adventure is in the realm of relationships. The wilderness is truly a school for learning how to grow healthy relationships.

Establishing Relationship With God and Against Satan

Identity crises can cause a debilitating limp through one's whole life. It breeds insecurity, which ruins relationships like one bad apple among a bushel of good ones. So it is not surprising that identity formation was at the top of Jesus' list of desired outcomes in taking his disciples on adventurous wilderness journeys. Through his own baptism and immediate choosing thereafter of his first disciples by the Sea of Galilee, we see Jesus emphasizing a concern that the disciples establish firm and fulfilling relationships *with* God and *with* others. He also wanted them to develop a hardened posture in their relationship *against* Satan. This is a different sort of relationship; he is our foe not our friend. Our most foundational relationship is with God. Once reconciled to him, our relationship with the Trinity becomes one of *rest*. The Holy Spirit supernaturally helps us order all of our relationships with others based on self-denial and love. In contrast, our relationship toward Satan is one of unceasing conflict. And the wilderness prepares us for this battle. The Gospel of Mark illustrates how Jesus used the wilderness as a terrain to prepare for temptation and conflict: "At once the Spirit sent Jesus into the desert, and he was in the desert for forty days being tempted by the devil" (Mark 1:12-13).

We see a bit of Elijah's relational boarding school experience during his many sojourns in the wilderness. One of his lessons occurred in a cave with God (see 1 Kings 19:1-21). Leading up to this unforgettable seminar, Elijah had an amazing power encounter between the prophets of Baal. Elijah called upon God, and "the fire of the LORD fell and burned up the sacrifice, the wood, the stones and the soil, and also licked up the water in the trench" (1 Kings 18:38). Then Elijah had every prophet of Baal slaughtered. Upon hearing of this news, Ahab, the King of Israel, told his wife Jezebel what Elijah had done. In her rage she sent Elijah this message: "May the gods deal with me, be it ever so severely, if by this time tomorrow I do not make your life like that of one of them" (1 Kings 19:2). Naturally, Elijah turned tail and ran for his life. Strengthened by a meal from a messenger of grace, the Angel of the Lord, "He traveled forty days and forty nights until he reached Horeb, the mountain of God. There he went into a cave and spent the night" (1 Kings 19:8). And the LORD met him that day in such a way that changed his course forever. It's important to remember that preceding this tutorial with God, Elijah had fasted forty days and nights. He was tired and hungry. We see through this round table experience God was preparing him in the wilderness for further prophetic ministry. That is what school is for, right? To prepare us for what's next.

God could have given him a holiday on a Mediterranean beach to provide him rest and prepare him for the road ahead. But that isn't the way God usually prepares us for conflict. Instead this retreat was preceded by hunger and fatigue and culminated in a frightful encounter with the Living God. This "Relationship School" class held in the wilderness blessed Elijah immensely. Now with his trust established even deeper in God, he could reject the human fears that plagued him from Jezebel's power trip. Now he was prepared for new work ahead and could stand up to the conflict against Jezebel with confidence that the battle was the Lord's and he would be okay as long as he remained steadfastly faithful to God rather than wavering in his human fears. *The wilderness exposes the origin of our fears.*

After this peak experience on the mountain, with certificate of completion in hand, Elijah was sent back down into the valley with a new mission to anoint Hazael king over Aram, Jehu king over Israel, and Elisha his successor. And immediately after descending the mountain, the spiritual realm heaved with conflict in the days after anointing Hazael and Jehu. God had shaken Elijah up a little bit to ensure he could handle the mantle of responsibility he was giving him.

Elijah's cave account has very similar parallels to Jesus' temptation in the desert in preparation for his ministry. The climax of Elijah's encounter was meeting God in a "gentle whisper." Similarly, with words spoken from heaven, Jesus was blessed in the desert like Elijah at his baptism. And identical to Elijah, Jesus' blessing and baptism happened right before the unfolding of a long season of intense spiritual conflict in his ministry. In order to remain steadfast in our relationship of conflict against Satan we must constantly abide in Christ for the spiritual sustenance we need. Trials will come, but he is faithful to prepare us and get us through them.

The Gospel of Mark shows Jesus first retreating to prepare for ministry and it's corollary spiritual conflict. Before he healed the multitudes by the sea, he went up on the mountain to pray and choose his disciples (see Mark 3:7-12). Another example is when the apostles returned to him in need of rest after their first evangelistic mission (see Mark 6:30-31). And in preparation for the passion week leading up to the cross, Luke records Jesus continuing his rhythm of retreat in preparation for spiritual conflict: "Each day Jesus was teaching at the temple, and each evening he went out to spend the night on the hill called the Mount of Olives" (Luke 21:37). He retreated to the garden each evening in preparation for the intensity of spiritual conflict that was building up to a climactic point at the cross.

From Genesis 4 onward, we see God unfolding his mission plan to restore relationships to their proper design: 1) Man is meant to relate to God under his authority and blessing; 2) He is meant to relate to Satan in conflict as God relates to him in conflict; and 3) Man is meant to relate to fellow mankind in community and interdependence. Both Elijah's and Jesus' wilderness experiences were ordained by God to further establish these men under his authority and blessing so that they would be able and willing to engage in the upcoming conflicts with Satan for God's glory and purpose. In the context of outdoor adventure, you might get in the habit of asking those who you are leading about the spiritual battles they face back at home. As an outdoor leader, we have the privilege of purposefully facilitating adventures to help our participants have a life-changing encounter with God to prepare them for spiritual conflict in their life back in the valley where they live.

Jesus does not seem to tarry in establishing his disciples' relationship with himself and their relationship in conflict with Satan. Very soon after calling his first disciples, Jesus sent the seventy-two on a mission to preach the good news to every town and village he intended to visit. Before sending them, he *prepares this band of followers to encounter conflict* because they are now identified by his name in the spiritual realm. Thus, conflict was inevitable:

> After this the Lord appointed seventy-two others and sent them two by two ahead of him to every town and place where he was about to go. He told them, "The harvest is plentiful, but the workers are few. Ask the Lord of the harvest, therefore, to send out workers into his harvest field. Go! I am sending you out like lambs among wolves. Do not take a purse or bag or sandals; and do not greet anyone on the road. (Luke 10:1-4)

When the seventy-two returned, they rejoiced because many demons had submitted to Jesus Christ's name as they preached. Jesus spoke apocalyptically about the effect of their preaching within the spiritual realm saying: "I was watching Satan fall from heaven like lightning. Behold, I have given you authority to tread on serpents and scorpions, and over all the power of the enemy, and nothing will injure you" (Matthew 10:18-19).

It is an awesome experience to see lightning fall within just a few hundred feet in the wilderness. I've witnessed this on more than one occasion. The image of Satan falling like lightning is an earth-shattering analogy—literally. Lightning crashes to the earth, it does not descend like a feather. The nature of our conflict with Satan is one of decisive battle; it is nothing less than full-scale war. Jesus knew this. The call on his disciples' lives was not a game, not an add-on to their daily lives; it was a wholesale call on their lives. Jesus, being the Good Shepherd, prepares, protects, and fights for his flock. And through wilderness experiences he empowered his disciples to shepherd others in the same way.

Jesus also warned the seventy-two about the dangers of complacency. We see Jesus continually testing and training his disciples to
protect them from laziness. He constantly redirects their attention to
himself rather than their own sufficiency or power: "Nevertheless do
not rejoice in this, that the spirits are subject to you, but rejoice that
your names are recorded in heaven" (Luke 10:20).

The wilderness is a unique place where relationships can be
deepened. In fact, man and woman's relationship with God and each
other was first established in the garden (see Gen. 1-3). Then in
Genesis 4 we see the fall of Adam and Eve resulting in *conflict in all
their relationships*. Adam and Eve now found themselves in conflict
with God, with Satan, and with each other. What a mess. This is the
ultimate picture of loneliness, as a result of rebellion. Then God
sends them into the wilderness to humble them and restore dependence on him, as well as to establish interdependence between one
another. The wilderness is full of harsh realities, and if you've ever
been out in the wilderness with a group, you know that a properly
functioning community that submits to God's design for relationships is the best way to survive and thrive there. Alone, a person
doesn't stand much chance for very long. This reality, so easily
understood in the wilderness, is a perfect analogy for how the church
is so vital as salt and light to the world.

Wilderness Changes our View of God, Self, and Others

In addition to establishing the disciples' relationship with himself,
with others, and against Satan, God often changes his followers' view
of himself, themselves, and others through retreat into the wilderness. Three texts are particularly instructive in regard to this
principle. First, in the Gospel of Luke we are given a clear record of
those who first heard the news of the newborn king, Jesus Christ.
The shepherds who were tending their sheep out in the surrounding
desert were the first worshippers invited to come adore the infant
Jesus. In this account, we see Luke engaging his audience to help
them understand the shepherd's significantly changed view of God

after visiting the rustic scene. This ruler, Jesus, who was the expected Messiah was not the warrior king whom much of Israel was awaiting, rather he was a humble King born in a manger. Luke also uses this account to communicate how God was also changing the shepherds' view of themselves. Go figure: they were the first to hear the good news. The upside down Kingdom was at hand! The humble and marginalized were invited to see the Son of God first. What a message of good news to the poor on the fringes of society, like these shepherds were.

The second passage illustrating how Jesus changed wrong views of God, self, and others in the wilderness is Luke 5:1-11. Jesus takes Peter and his workmen out on the sea because, in God's timing, Peter's time was up. Today was the day he would call Peter to follow him unconditionally. In this account, Peter *understands himself* in a new light; that he was sinful, *and* yet he was chosen. After the miraculous catch of fish, he cried out to Jesus, "Go away from me, Lord; I am a sinful man!" (Luke 5:8). According to Jesus, *embracing this paradox of being sinful and yet chosen is how one enters the Kingdom of heaven.* After reaching the shore, Peter left his boat on the beach and followed his Master.

The third passage relevant to this principle is Jesus' encounter with the woman at the well on the outskirts of town by a lonely cistern (see John 4). Jesus changes her *view of God* in that *God shows no partiality.* Even though she was a sinner and a Samaritan woman, he asked her for a drink of water. He changed her view of God in revealing her hidden sins, yet at the same time inviting her to enjoy the living water through repentance and belief. He radically *altered her view of God and of herself* in revealing the reason *God hates sin is because sin destroys those whom he loves.* God did not hate her because of her sin; he loved her (see John 4:13-18).

Having her wrong views changed, with great enthusiasm and gratitude, she took the free gift of grace Jesus offered her. Then many of her fellow townspeople believed from the testimony she proclaimed in the streets following this life-changing event by that solitary well. Through this powerful testimony we also see the disciples recognize *they had a wrong view of the Samaritans.* Now they too had been changed: "Just then his disciples returned and were surprised to find him talking with a woman. But no one asked, 'What do you want?' or 'Why are you talking with her?'" (John 4:27).

There are so many opportunities to challenge people's views of God in the wilderness. After having one's eyes and ears open from being surrounded by God's creation for a few days, people often recognize more easily how they have a tendency toward self-absorption. This trait commonly manifests itself in our character in several ways: looking down on others who are different, viewing ourselves with false superiority toward others, feeling insecurity toward ourselves, or living on the basis of entitlement (i.e., believing we deserve a certain standard of life or material comfort rather than maturing into an attitude of gratefulness for the gifts God has freely given). All of these false views of self and God keep us from experiencing true life through dying to self. The wilderness is a great leveler, bringing us back to reality and giving us an invitation to repent.

CHAPTER 9
RETREATS

In fourth-century Egypt, many devout Christians were struggling to survive in a society that seemed to have an unbridled disregard for God. Like a house burning violently from within, the only choice many devout Christians felt they had was to run for their lives before being consumed by the culture. They ran to the desert of all places. They weren't running away to find a nice patch of grass for a picnic. No, instead they ran deep into the desert to reclaim their culture through spiritual warfare and renewal. Many of these Egyptian anchorites left the fertile and inhabited regions of the Nile valley or delta to plunge into a desolate wilderness. The terms anchorite (male) and anchoress (female), came from the Greek word ἀναχωρέω (anachōreō), which signifies "to withdraw," or "to depart into the rural countryside." These men (and a few women as well) withdrew from society to be able to lead an intensely prayer-oriented ascetic (spiritually disciplined) life.[127] To the anchorite, society was to be considered a wholesale shipwreck, and the only proper response in that scenario is to swim for your life: "These were men who believed that to let oneself drift along, passively accepting the tenets and values of what they knew as society, was purely and simply a disaster."[128]

Their retreat to a reclusive lifestyle in the desert is an uncomfortably foreign concept for many of us today. Because of our modern perspective, we may have some natural "prejudices" against these desert hermits. Here are a few common turnoffs to their decision to escape to the desert to seek spiritual renewal:

1. Weren't they being selfish for leaving the people of their cities who were lost without the gospel to go out into the desert to seek spiritual purification? Shouldn't they have

stuck it out and lived among the culture as salt and light rather than choose to only rely on prayer to do the work of turning their society around?

2. The Desert Fathers wrote extensively about a belief in the reality and personality of demons. They believed every temptation was an act of a special demon (demons of anger, despair, etc.). Were these just spiritual fanatics who went crazy in their caves?

3. They were too severe in their asceticism. The details of their war against the flesh through seemingly unbearable spiritual disciplines are almost unpalatable. Yet we read of them joyfully seeking out suffering and "crucifying their bodies." Were they overdoing it or were they truly sharing in the sufferings of Jesus Christ?

4. They aimed at a literal imitation of Christ. For example, they regularly carried out forty-day fasts like Jesus did in the wilderness. And just as he lived as a virgin, so did they. They literally became homeless and poor because Jesus had no place to rest his head during his years of ministry on earth. And since he ended his life on the cross, they sought to join in his sufferings by always finding new ways to deny themselves and die to their flesh. It seems a little extreme doesn't it?[129]

What do we do with the Desert Fathers and Mothers? We often want to explain away their spiritual experiences thinking that maybe their long fasts made them delusional or that their deeply solitary lifestyle made them a bit mad. Some of this may be true, but it could also be that they saw reality much more clearly because of their wholesale renunciation of all things secular. Susan Bratton reflects on some of our biases with a few disturbing contemporary implications for us to consider:

In the west, a material culture has obtained so strong a hold on religious activity that entire denominations count success in numbers attracted, building programs consummated, and funds solicited. Caught in the pressures of becoming Christian achievers, individual believers cease to reflect on the real substance of their lives—or on the essence of their relationship with God. Biblical wilderness experience is associated with spiritual transition, acquisition of a deeper knowledge of God, strengthening for ministry, and liberation from cultural or personal bondage—all functions that are potentially threatening to material religiosity. Some contemporary reluctance to define Christian relationship to wilderness may, thus, arise from the deep fear that God might actually send the church back into the desert.[130]

Rather than discounting these passionate desert dwellers as a bunch of wild-haired hermits that we can't relate with, we might instead seek to learn something from them. But in order to learn from them I think we must come to terms with the reality that we may have never "hungered and thirsted after righteousness with such intensity as these early monks did."[131] We may view them as crazy for retreating to the wilderness but *maybe they did this because they valued being pure more than being useful.* I think if we consider the context in which they lived, the choices they made might make a little more sense. Although we may not agree with their escape from the secular to become wholly engrossed in the sacred, we can at least appreciate that these desert hermits were more interested in who they were *becoming* rather than being preoccupied with what they were *producing* (which is more of my bent if I'm honest).

Those of us who live in task-driven societies could benefit greatly from embracing their rejection of building one's identity on his or her *usefulness.* One of the reasons why I am so passionate about wilderness adventure ministries is they can serve to shake our souls away from building on this sandy foundation of self-promotion. We must find ways to routinely re-attach snugly to our Vine, Jesus Christ, so that we organically (from the inside out) become the sap our society needs. The sad alternative would be to continue fitting blandly into the spiritual vacuum of worldliness that brings an even worse *death* than the "death to self" we are called to. This was the lifestyle that the Desert Fathers and Mothers spat out. Enough was enough!

Their solitude with God exposed the most common ways Satan routinely deceives us away from God's best. The wilderness reshaped their eyes into microscopes for observing the soul. They began to see how *odd* it was that men and women would go to great *extremes* for such *small gains*, rather than giving themselves to the greater gain of possessing Christ. One hermit, Macedonius' story, illustrates this point:

> A certain captain of soldiers, who took a great delight in hunting, once came in search of wild animals to the desolate mountain where Macedonius dwelt. He was prepared for hunting, having brought with him men and dogs. As he went over the mountain he saw, far off a man. Being surprised that anyone should be in a place so desolate, he asked who it might be. One told him it was the hermit Macedonius. The captain, who was a pious man, leaped from his horse and ran to meet the hermit. When he came to him he asked. "What are you doing in such a barren place as this is?" The hermit in his turn asked, "And you? What have you come here to do?" The captain answered him, "I have come to hunt." Then said Macedonius, "I also am a huntsman. I am hunting for my God. I yearn to capture him. My desire is to enjoy him. I shall not cease from this my hunting."[132]

Touché! Macedonius observed the cost and effort that this man had taken to enjoy a recreational hunt, and gently asked him whether he would also be as passionate to put out the same effort to hunt for God as his life-goal. Being an avid hunter, I get the point of this parable. I spend weeks preparing for my annual big game hunt with my kids and brothers, and I'm quite passionate about it. The lesson of Macedonius' story gives me a healthy pause to consider how I too am much like the hunter in this narrative: Do I exert the same planning, passion, and effort into my *hunt* for knowing God more intimately? I want to know more about this kind of hunting. Thank you, Macedonius, for this wisdom gained from your solitude in the desert!

Drawn to the Desert?

Escape to the desert was critical to these Coptic believers, but it came with a cost. The desert east of the Nile was a rocky, mountainous terrain with altitudes in some spots of 6,560 feet. Beyond these deserts was called the "interior desert."

This inner desert was uninhabitable land because it was sterile and unsuited for supplying people with the bare essentials of livelihood, e.g., good soil and water for crops. Some of the most well known Desert Fathers like Anthony actually found a way to live in this extremely harsh climate, which usually involved walking four or more miles for water. What was it that drew them to this inner desert? They weren't getting paid to entertain others' curiosity in how to survive in the wilderness. They did this because they wanted to, and there were no tangible rewards for doing so. As we consider some of their reasons, it is helpful to ask ourselves an important personal question: What would cause me to make intense sacrifices to start journeying further toward the interior of my soul where Jesus resides and beckons me? As an outdoor enthusiast, do I love adventure for what I can get out of it, or do I love it because it humbles me and bends me toward getting glory for God? If we were to become desperate for inward spiritual health and peace as these desert dwellers did, we, too, might do some radical things to see that transformation happen.

There are all kinds of reasons to explain their withdrawal to the desert, but we'll look at a few of the more common ones mentioned by these uniquely qualified spiritual guides. Here is a list of the most common reasons for their flight into the desert.

1. Renunciation of all entanglements
2. To unify one's heart and life by getting rid of everything that distracts and divides, such as earthly goods and human concerns
3. To remove oneself completely from the world's grasp
4. To fully belong to God

Taking literally Jesus' call to deny oneself, they sought to renounce all attachments to the world so they could only draw life from the nectar of the Trinity. For example, one time a philosopher asked Saint Anthony what it was like to renounce even his books. He replied, "My book, O Philosopher, is the nature of created things, and whenever I want to read the word of God, it is usually right in front of me."[133] Although some criticized their seeming extremist views, even Saint Athanasius, the great bishop of Alexandria who was the revered and ardent defender of Christ's divinity against the Arians, turned out to be a fervent apologist of the monastic life. He sided with their extremism as an appropriate response to the absence of Christ-worship in their culture.

Taking only what was required to sustain the body, yet never enough to fully satisfy it, these wilderness adventurers lived a life of prayer and work to become spiritual athletes running their race for God. They would recite words of Scripture throughout their day because most of them knew by heart a good part of the Bible. One of the lessons we can learn from what they gained through their wilderness experiences is:

> Christian holiness doesn't depend on spectacular exploits but on humble gestures carried out each day with love by the sons who seek only to please their Father, by doing everything he asks them to do with a ready heart...This was the main point of the desert hermit's daily life.[134]

Mining Spiritual Gems from the Desert Fathers

Circa 420 A.D., Bishop Palladius wrote down some simple instructions for monastic living. Palladius was a desert monk himself and spent many years interviewing and learning from some of the most famous Desert Fathers.[135] Below are sixteen guiding principles he gleaned from their wisdom. I imagine if we too begin to prioritize solitude with God in the inspiring setting of his creation, we might begin to make our own list to live by. Then we could pass it on to those whom we are apprenticing as a guide to know Christ more fully. What words of wisdom would be on your list if you could make one? Here is Palladius' list:

1. To do good to the fool and to bury the dead; both are alike.[136]

2. It is beneficial that a man should put on armor over the breast, and the word of our Redeemer Christ over grief; armor and shield will hide the breast, but only faith and action can hide the soul.

3. As it is possible to see the skill of the painter on a small tablet, so a small gift shows the greatness of the disposition of the soul.

4. Have no confidence in the belief that that which is placed outside your soul is your possession.

5. Clothes and outfits drape statues, but habits and manners drape men.

6. An evil word is the beginning of evil deeds.

7. Speak according to what is right, where it is right, and concerning what is right. Don't speak about things that are not right.

8. It is better to shake a stone vainly than to utter a vain word, and it is better to be under subjection to the Barbarians than to evil passions.

9. The excellence of a horse is made apparent in battle, and the disposition of a friend is put to the test in tribulation.

10. It is impossible to divide the sea, and it is also impossible to still the waves, although for them it is always easy to still themselves.

11. The wise and God-fearing man is he who hates that which is not right.

12. The gentle and gracious man is he who treads pride under foot; but he who is set upon that which is contrary of this is one who is governed by arrogance.

13. Constant prayer is the strength, the armor, and the wall of the soul.

14. Wine makes the body warm, and the word of God warms the soul.

15. Know that one act that you think must be hidden, will quickly bring you to oblivion.

16. The believing mind is a temple of God, which it is beneficial for a man to adorn daily and burn incense therein, inasmuch as it is God Who dwells there.

Maybe next time you go alone or take a group out into the wilderness, try to write down a couple of your own words of wisdom that the Lord teaches you through solitude. I think you'll be surprised what wisdom he gives to you as you ask him for it and listen to what he offers. Then see how putting those into practice can offer hope to people in your life who are looking for an alternative to the dead-end roads they keep going down. With the world becoming more and more urban it is becoming increasingly more challenging to "remove" oneself from the hustle and bustle. But doesn't this make it even all the more important that we retreat regularly so we can offer lifeboats of good news to those in our society who are headed for a wholesale shipwreck?

What's Your Wilderness Quotient?

With a special concern for youth today, I believe in a philosophy of youth ministry that combines relational youth work on the turf of where kids hang out with regular opportunities for purposeful adventure camping. I want young people to learn Jesus' rhythm of working hard for God's glory and then retreating for rest, renewal, and perspective. The climate of our times may not call for a flight to the desert like the Desert Fathers did, but we also can't deny our need to routinely remove ourselves from the world in order to sharpen our spiritual saw. Having a high Wilderness Quotient (WQ) means you value adventures, camps, and wilderness retreats as a regular part of spiritual formation, evangelism, discipleship, and leadership development.

I want to have a high WQ like Jesus did in his model of ministry. One of my favorite wilderness settings to seek solace is along a lonely ocean beach. I've learned that waves generally come in sets of two to five breakers, but sometimes can come in sets of up to fifteen—which makes for a great surfing day! Before paddling out into the water, a seasoned surfer will perch on a mound of sand and watch the waves to get an idea of the intervals between sets. Then, after diving in the water, the surfer will have an idea when to prepare to ride. Although I'm a grommet when it comes to surfing, while living in New Zealand I began to see a lot of comparisons between youth ministry and surfing. Interestingly, movements in mission throughout history also seem to come in sets; from the highly active missionary journeys of

Paul, to the radical accomplishments of St. Patrick's mission to Ireland, to the modern missionary movement led by William Carey that spawned a host of mission agencies committed to engaging unreached people. What waves do we see coming in today? What is the surf doing?

One thing many missiologists see happening in the world is a *bulging youth population* among many nations. There are significant implications when large numbers of young people enter societies where they have limited leadership from older, wiser leaders available to lovingly mentor them. The church worldwide must grapple with this challenge of equipping adequate numbers of younger leaders who can set an example for their peers.

Another *set* coming in is the effect of a global youth culture on the world as a whole but, more importantly, on a micro-level in neighborhoods, villages, and cities. *Globalization* has many implications among youth. Young people around the world are able to watch similar TV programs, access the Internet and interact through social networking in their own language. It is of great concern that many youth, because of the effect of the global youth culture, are, in some cases, pulling away from their traditional tribal/family patterns. This is causing conflict between youth, parents, and grandparents. For example, in traditional non-western cultures where young people have been expected to help provide income for the family, youth are now getting higher paying jobs in faraway places, and grappling with how to reconcile their new lifestyle and the needs of their extended family. Should they still submit to a system where all the money they make is under the authority of their father or grandfather for distribution? This is just one of many examples of how youth culture and globalization are causing family tension and cultural seismic activity. So what is the church to do?

Unfortunately, all too often the church is very slow to address these seismic-wave changes in culture. Then tension arises, leading to overreaction and the pendulum swings too far in the other direction. This makes the voice of the church seem irrelevant to the dominant culture. Working particularly within youth culture, we have to resist this temptation to look the other way and hope things will just fix themselves and change for the better. Instead, we have to courageously grapple with God's Word and provide answers to the questions the dominant culture is really asking. Maybe you can take a moment and write down five to ten questions that you think young people are struggling with. Can you offer biblical answers to their questions? *If you can do that, I guarantee you can become an instrument for catalytic change in your neighborhood or city, or even your nation.* This is the kind of thinking and theological inquiry we need today to ride the youth culture waves coming toward us.

For youth missiologists, these problems and challenges also present exciting opportunities. The well-known youth evangelist, John Mott, had the same perspective on the challenges of his day (nearly one hundred years ago). He once wrote in his journal that there was "no more important work on earth than influencing students."[137]

Today, we need more young leaders who take time to see the waves coming so they can harness their power and ride them. Without visionary leadership in making young disciples, many young, well-meaning youth workers will likely be rolled by a clean-up set; pummeled rather than prepared. I view leadership just this way. Those who sit and watch and formulate a game plan before jumping in the water are going to have a much better day in the surf. You'll have more fun and a lot better ride when the force of the wave propels you forward, rather than laundering you if you're deluded enough to actually fight *against* the waves coming in. Such is youth mission. We try to harness the power of the dominant cultural shifts and bring redemption, reconciliation, and good news to *transform* it, rather than rejecting it all together. Thinking we can stop all of the waves of culture change is silly. *Nature teaches us it is not wise to try to stop waves—it's more realistic to learn to ride among them.*

Richard Niebuhr explored this phenomenon in his classic book *Christ and Culture.* His conclusion was that Christ came to transform culture. He was not *against* culture, he was not *of* culture, and he didn't even try to claim the higher ground *above* culture. No, he came to *transform culture*. Jesus said it this way:

> No one sews a patch of unshrunk cloth on an old garment. If he does, the new piece will pull away from the old, making the tear worse. And no one pours new wine into old wineskins. If he does, the wine will burst the skins, and both the wine and the wineskins will be ruined. No, he pours new wine into new wineskins. (Mark 2:21-22)

Any given day on the beach presents a surfer with varied intervals and sizes of waves. Similarly, local youth ministry can look different everywhere you go. So we have to work at respecting our unique context to communicate the gospel cross-culturally. We need to evaluate how much time we *personally* take to enjoy time with God in solitary places. There he can shape us into leaders who know how to engage the culture while we lay our lives down as stepping stones for others to walk on. If your WQ is low and you *aren't* taking time to sit and watch the waves regularly (so to speak), then you may want to develop that habit first before you continue your surf career in youth ministry, pastoral work, marketplace ministry, missions, or outdoor leadership. I hope some of these reflections will help you improve your WQ for the sake of your own health, the health of your ministry, and, most of all, for the glory of God.

The One True Thing

Great teachers are able to simplify what they teach so even the simplest of minds can understand the meaning and implications of their teaching. The psalmist models this type of teaching with simplicity in Psalm 27, stating there is only "one thing" that he desires...to dwell in close *relationship* with the Lord forever. Jesus in like manner boils down what it means to follow him in the Great Commission. The stark simplicity of his marching orders stands out as the ultimate model of great teaching. Simply stated, followers of Jesus Christ belong to him, and are called to make disciples (students) for the rest of their lives.

One challenge to maintaining a healthy WQ in your life is finding time to get out of your city for brief interludes in the outdoors. Many cities have great trails and parks, which is great, but there is still something unique about getting away from the manmade environment and into the pristine creation seldom touched by man. This is a growing challenge because our world is becoming more urbanized by the day. But leaders do not give up in the face of obstacles, do we? No, we step over them or navigate through them. So I propose that if you are serious about growing your Wilderness Quotient, you need to prioritize some regular retreat time *outside the city* for your own spiritual formation and those you are leading. You need it as much as those you are leading.

This section has taken a theoretical approach to Christian outdoor leadership. *A theory is a set of principles upon which the practice of an activity is based.* It gives justification for a course of action. Most would agree that there could not be a one-size-fits-all exam to pass in order to be a "certified" outdoor leader. Yet for this reason we must continually *strengthen the theories and principles* upon which we practice outdoor adventure ministries. The preceding chapters have provided a *biblical, theological* and *theoretical* rationale to justify a course of action for practicing this kind of ministry in organizations, churches, and universities, etc. Now we'll put our theology, theory and philosophy to work in the next section as we propose a vision for the *practice* of Christian outdoor leadership.

Section III: Practice

Chapter 10
Inspire

How Jesus Motivated Learning

Not only did Jesus captivate the imagination of his audience, he also motivated them to change. He did this by creating a thirst for learning by challenging them to actually "hear" what he was saying. If we were to teach like him, we would have a reputation for asking a lot of questions, we would be known for telling stories, and we could be counted on for using visual props to drive a point home. Jesus also endeared himself to people by calling them by their name (see Luke 10:41, 19:5, 22:31; John 1:42), and he often took people off guard by making uncommon requests like asking the Samaritan woman to give him a drink (see John 4:7).

A few years ago, I was leading a group in the West Elk wilderness of Colorado during a very dry summer. We couldn't find water for hours because many of the intermittent streams had dried up. The group began to grumble of unbearable thirst. Finally, late in the afternoon, as we came within earshot of a long-awaited stream, we stopped under a shade tree and read this Psalm: "My soul thirsts for God, for the Living God. When can I go and meet with God?" (Psalm 42:2). Before dropping our packs to wet our parched tongues with cool water, I said to the group: "Imagine what it would be like if we thirsted for God the same way that we thirst right now for a drink from the stream we hear just around the bend?"

This is my feeble example of how Jesus motivated his followers. By drawing attention to our physical thirst that day, we were able to appreciate a little more the relevance of passages that speak about our soul's thirst for Christ. Jesus is the Living Water. He knew the hearts of his audience, and *spoke when they were most thirsty.* To teach as Jesus taught challenges us to bring Kingdom principles to light in the context of *when our audience is motivated to "drink."* Do you know your sheep that well? Have you tried to step into their shoes and relate with their thirsts? We observe quite often that Jesus purposed to motivate his listeners first, before offering an invitation to himself. He is the Bread of Life and the Living Water that can quench all people's hunger and thirst—but he seemed patient to wait until people were sufficiently at the end of their rope before intervening with a lifeline.

One way Jesus stirred interest in others was by identifying their needs. Research has shown when people wonder about the answer to a question or the solution to a problem they face, their attention is aroused. Howard Hendricks asserts one of the best ways to motivate is to "help the learner become aware of his need."[138] Another way Jesus motivated his disciples was through stories. "The most effective stories are those that follow the storytelling principle: the greater the unpredictability within a familiar situation, the greater the audience interest generated."[139] Jesus was the master of drawing people in with surprise and unpredictability.

Experiential Learning Discoveries

A wide body of literature is available to study the ways experiential learning inspires the student. Although this is beyond the scope of this book, it is worth noting a few pertinent case studies that relate more directly to faith-based experiential learning. For example, an interesting pattern developed in Keijo Erickson's study of a group of students enrolled in a religious education course in Sweden. His objective was to determine the kinds of experiences he could develop to teach and challenge his students in the areas of most concern. When the group of students was asked to write about what was most important to them in life, the following categories emerged (in order of popularity):

1. Family
2. Education
3. Social concerns
4. Leisure time
5. Sympathy and understanding
6. The environment
7. Health and keeping fit
8. Religion
9. Death
10. The joy of growing up and the satisfaction of making progress
11. Peace
12. Security in one's social environment[140]

Providing further synthesis, the three main categories of greatest concern for this group of adolescents were:

1. Individuals and their relationships
2. Society
3. The concept of God and religion[141]

There are several ways you can help people in your group recognize their needs and show them how Jesus fulfills them. First, prioritize talking with your group about their *fears and expectations* before they set out on a trip. Then make a list of what they share and use this list of "fears and expectations" to develop teaching material through the week. This list is also a good prayer list for you to leave back with a group of people to pray for your trip specifically while you are out. Secondly, you can work on developing outdoor quiet time questions that suit both girls and boys. For example, girls often want to explore issues of *relationships and security* and boys need to be asked questions that probe their *opinions*.[142] Thirdly, boys especially need to be encouraged to journal so they can process what they are thinking or decisions they need to make. And fourthly, incorporate meal discussions into the daily routine of the wilderness journey. Meals are an opportune time to give your group a chance to share what they wrote in their journals. In addition to helping them solidify what they are thinking and feeling, this will also help you establish relevant teaching content aimed at their biggest concerns.

Essentials of an Authentic Wilderness Experience

In 1996, wilderness and outdoor education specialists gathered at the Aldo Leopold Wilderness Research Institute in Bradford Woods, Indiana, to explore the daring question of what composes an authentic wilderness experience. After the papers and lectures were presented, a smaller group wrote a report to describe several elements that most outdoor education specialists agreed were the essential components of an authentic wilderness experience. Although this gathering was seeking a secular rationale for outdoor education, their findings coincide with our theological *raison d'être* for the transformational character of wilderness experiences.

The first characteristic identified was the way wilderness experiences develop *humility* in participants. They wrote, "Wilderness is a great leveler, reminding us, perhaps, of our rightful place within the natural world, and engendering an intellectual humility."[143] The second is the aspect of *primitiveness*, which is a quality of experience most city dwellers rarely experience. As an example, the authors quoted Thoreau to illustrate the meaning of primitiveness: "I went to the woods because I wanted to live deliberately, to front only the essential facts of life...I wanted to live deep and suck out all the marrow of life, to live so sturdily and Spartan-like as to put to route all that was not life."[144] Although this is a very humanistic description, I agree that living in the primitive sense does confront the wilderness traveler with the essentials of life. A Young Life staff member, who served as a wilderness guide for high school young people in Colorado, communicated well the effect wilderness has on one's understanding of God and the bare essentials of life:

> Being on the trail created raw space for God to work in me and the girls that I guided like nothing else has. I was face to face with myself and face to face with the wildness and adventure of Jesus. The climb doesn't just teach you, it changes you and

makes you into more; it forces you to move. I was honored to watch transformation not only in myself, but also within the lives of dozens of teenagers.[145]

Third, we encounter an element of *timelessness* in the wilderness, which confronts the idol of busyness that poisons the roots of community and fellowship. This is especially a problem in western society where personal progress and ambition is often valued more than relationships:

> Wilderness provides an opportunity to leave behind the frantic pace of modern life, and to experience a far less controlled and perhaps unmeasured pace. Some may find a natural affinity with the ancient rhythms of life, the cycles of the seasons, and the day/night patterns of light, temperature, and activity...Olsen, for example, was convinced that given sufficient time, all visitors to wilderness can experience timelessness and that as they "accept the time clock of wilderness, their lives become entirely different. It is one of the great compensations of primitive experience, and when one finally reaches the point where days are governed by daylight and dark, rather than schedules, where one eats if hungry and sleeps when tired, and becomes completely immersed in the ancient rhythms, then one begins to live."[146]

Another leader provides a vivid description of how one's view of community is profoundly changed through small group adventures in the wilderness:

> One of my favorite things about the trail is the community it brings. Defenses come down. Barriers are breached. Authentic relationship is possible. Once you get a taste of that, reality changes. Your expectations are higher. Desire comes alive. In this post-modern culture, often marked by isolation and loneliness, the community formed on a backpacking trip meets the core hunger of both teens and adults today.[147]

A similar quality to timelessness that the symposium identified as a critical aspect of an authentic wilderness experience is *solitude*. The psalmist declares that because God cares for his creation, he desires for his people to experience solitude so that their lives are fueled by his pleasure toward them. We hear the words of our Creator-God in the psalm: "Be still and know that I am God" (Psalm 46:10). Being still can really push us into a new level of communication with God. For example, one camper named Holly, reflecting on her week on the trail, said, "I really felt out of my comfort zone when we had a four-hour quiet time."[148]And Riley summed it up this way after his first solo experience during a weeklong trip in the backcountry of Colorado: "Solo time = good."[149]

For young people, wilderness experiences are often characterized by the most uninterrupted amount of time they may have ever experienced in solitude reading God's Word. They discover that many others (young and old) have been searching for God for millennia, and the Bible contains an account of their quest. Thus, a personal encounter with God through solitude and reading the Scriptures is an indispensable element of outdoor ministry.

Lastly, it was agreed at this meeting at Bradford Woods, a final quality of any authentic wilderness experience will forge a more *caring attitude* among those who tread its paths: "The wilderness visit can induce profound changes in people's relationship to nature, and in their value system."[150] In Christian outdoor leadership we call this *biblical community and biblical stewardship*. Christians are called to excel in caring for creation as well as caring for people. As we explore ways people today can engage the challenges of poverty, violence, differing religions, and the clashing of cultures and civilizations, a prerequisite for significant influence as a leader will require an attitude of care and love for those who are walking in darkness—those who are different from us, or maybe even violent toward us. The wilderness can forge that attitude. Andy summed it up this way after his weeklong wilderness adventure: "Something I learned about community from this experience is that even though you're supposed to pull your own weight, you still have to let people take SOME of the burden off of you."[151]

Luckner and Nadler present an adventure-based learning process model in their book, *Processing the Experience*, which provides a good synopsis as to why adventure-based learning is so effective. Essentially, here is the sequence of what happens in experiential learning:

1.   First, individuals experience some form of disequilibrium or out-of-comfort zone experience by being placed in a novel (unfamiliar setting) like the outdoors.

2. Then within a cooperative and supportive environment,
3. They are presented with a myriad of problem-solving situations in the course of the adventure. This could be as simple as how to stay warm and dry in a rain storm, or as complex as how to get from the bottom of a rock face to the top using newly learned rock climbing skills.
4. This leads to feelings of accomplishment which is unpacked through a...
5. Debriefing process, which promotes...
6. Generalizing and transfer of what has been learned to other future endeavors.[152]

Principles in Practice

Many organizations have discovered the effectiveness of experiential learning models. Outward Bound is an outdoor education school that excels in facilitating this type of learning environment. Emily Cousins in her book, *Roots; From Outward Bound to Expeditionary Learning,* synthesizes several expeditionary design principles:

> Given fundamental levels of health, safety, and love, all people can and want to learn. We believe Expeditionary Learning harnesses the natural passion to learn and is a powerful method for developing the curiosity, skills, knowledge, and courage needed to imagine a better world and work toward realizing it. Learning happens best with emotion, challenge, and the requisite support. People discover their abilities, values, "grand passions," and responsibilities in situations that offer adventure and the unexpected. They must have tasks that require perseverance, fitness, craftsmanship, imagination, self-discipline, and significant achievement. A primary job of the educator is to help students overcome their fear and discover they have more in them than they think ...Learning is fostered best in small groups where there is trust, sustained caring, and mutual respect among all the members of the learning community...All students must be assured a fair measure of success in learning in order to nurture the confidence and capacity to take risks and rise to increasingly difficult challenges. But it is also important to experience failure, to overcome negative inclinations, to prevail against adversity, and to learn to turn disabilities into opportunities.[153]

The National Outdoor Leadership School (NOLS) also specializes in wilderness education. In *The New Wilderness Handbook*, Paul

Petzoldt (the founder of NOLS) outlines several principles of experiential teaching in the outdoors:

> The very act of backpacking is a learning experience. Rhythmic breathing, use of leg muscles, methods of going up and downhill, and other trail techniques are explained, demonstrated, and practiced during the walk. Expedition behavior is learned as stronger members share the loads of weaker persons and the pace is determined by the slowest hiker.[154]

Opportunities arise in situations that, if recognized by the leader, can be used to illustrate and teach life-changing principles:

> Someone develops a blister. While the leader treats the sore, he explains why it happened, why it should be attended to immediately, and how the situation can be avoided in the future...A pack breaks. A tent is damaged by improper placement. A finger is cut. Someone falls, has a narrow escape, or performs well. All are opportunities for teaching while students' attention and motivation are stimulated. "Opportunity teaching" is not intended to point a finger at or embarrass any individual. The leader must indicate his appreciation of that person and the specific situation as an opportunity for teaching.[155]

Another outdoor leadership textbook provides further insight in terms of the significance of capitalizing on timing (opportunities) in teaching:

> One of the most powerful outdoor teaching strategies involves motivating the participant to learn by creating the "need to know." Outdoor leaders can facilitate situations that motivate participants to seek knowledge and skills. The leader does this by placing the participants in a situation where they seek knowledge and skills in order to accomplish the task.[156]

Opportunity teaching opens doors for spiritual lessons as well. The common occurrence of a blister on the trail provides an opportunity for teaching a vital spiritual principle at the moment when it can be best illustrated in real life. In 1 Corinthians 10:13, Paul writes, "No temptation has overtaken you except what is common to mankind. And God is faithful; he will not let you be tempted beyond what you can bear. But when you are tempted, he will also provide a way out so that you can endure it."

Before blisters are formed, "hot spots" develop on one's feet; serving as "warning signs" that something is wrong and needs immediate attention. If a person stops immediately and puts on Moleskin or Duct Tape, they can prevent the "hot spot" from turning into a crippling blister. This is similar to the situation Paul describes in the Corinthian church. All of us will experience temptation in our lives. Temptations are like "hot spots"—a sign of potential danger. When we are tempted, the proper response is to stop and deal with it immediately so that it does not become a crippling wound. A wise wilderness traveler will stop when he feels the warning signs of a potential blister in the same way that a wise person will stop and heed the warning signs of temptation, to avoid a painful consequence. Using the object lesson of a *blister* to teach about the nature of *temptation* models the way Jesus used physical analogies to explain deep spiritual realities.

There is another spiritual principle to draw from the simple blister analogy. In 1 Corinthians 12, the apostle Paul describes the beauty of the Body of Christ (i.e., the church). When someone feels a "hot spot" forming on his foot during a hike, he may be reluctant to speak up and ask for help because he does not want to be a burden to the rest of the group. In 1 Corinthians 12:12-31, Paul explains how the community of God (The Body of Christ) is analogous to the human body. In verses 26-27, he writes: "If one part suffers, every part suffers with it, if one part is honored, every part rejoices with it. Now you are the body of Christ, and each one of you is part of it." Thus the experiential lesson learned is that even though only one person suffers, the whole group must acknowledge the "hurt" and stop to take care of the individual part (i.e., the blister). If the group doesn't stop, then ironically the group (Body) will suffer even more in the long run as the crippled hiker becomes a greater burden to the group.

I remember one trip where a young person neglected to reveal his "hot spot" because he did not want to annoy the group by stopping for treatment. A painful blister formed on his foot. And as a consequence we had to shorten our route and the group had to disperse the load from his pack because he was in such pain. Thus, the whole group suffered more because of his unwillingness to stop to treat his "hot spot." We truly are a part of a larger body, and our wounds, if un-treated, do affect the rest of the Body.

Petzoldt refers to the "Grasshopper Method" to explain the reality that when leading a group in the outdoors, one is able to address various subjects like the blister analogy as circumstances demand. Teaching in real life situations is not systematic:

> The most effective method of teaching outdoorsmanship is in the field, where introduction of a subject, its demonstration, and practical application are presented in close time sequence. We cannot cover any one subject all at once, since initially we must teach the things most necessary for that first day of walking, camping, cooking, and conservation. The next day we might cover the same subjects again and add new techniques. In this "grasshopper method" of teaching, we hop from one subject to another as circumstances demand.[157]

Since Jesus came to change lives, it makes sense that he would have repeated himself often—teaching as circumstances (often initiated by him) arose to provide opportunities for learning and reinforcement.

Surprisingly, there are only a few books and articles that focus on this aspect of outdoor adventure ministry. Brett DeYoung's thesis highlights much of the pertinent research:

> Wilderness learning is an educational process that was rediscovered by Dr. Kurt Hahn, a German Christian educator, who implemented these principles into his schools and eventually started Outward Bound in Wales, in 1942. This process was a discovery of the educational principles used by God to prepare men and women for leadership. It is a process involving the acceptance of responsibilities: of focusing on reachable challenges, of spending time in contemplation and reflection, of experiencing deprivation, of examining values, of developing compassion for others, and of testing one's faith and character.[158]

His study provides a history for how wilderness ministry has been an effective tool for developing leaders in the past few decades.

Norman Rose also conducted a particularly relevant study on moral development among adolescents who have been involved in experiential learning environments. He concludes that one of the greatest needs in working with adolescents is training them to *think clearly*, and experiential learning environments accomplish this:

Adolescence would be an excellent time to introduce novel types of learning settings. Apprenticeships and mentorships would require the young person to think clearly, to acquire real (not imagined) expertise in an endeavor of interest, and to learn to avoid trivial emotional distractions. Outdoor experiential learning would also provide experiences for testing one's ability to process thought clearly, on one's own and within a group context.[159]

Responding to Skeptics

As I've talked with people all over the world about how to combine outdoor adventure with their ongoing youth ministries, some have expressed a bit of skepticism. In this section, I offer responses to the two of the most common questions people have had regarding the viability of outdoor adventure ministry in churches and faith-based organizations.

Criticism #1: Aren't outdoor adventure experiences only available to the affluent?

My vision for the future of outdoor ministry is that every young person would have an opportunity to encounter Jesus Christ and grow in his or her faith through a guided outdoor adventure. Yet such a radical statement welcomes quite a bit of criticism and skepticism. Some have claimed wilderness experiences are only available to the affluent—that poor inner-city young people could never enjoy an opportunity to experience a wilderness adventure. This criticism rightly challenges the potential limitation and usefulness of our hopes and dreams to give people the gift of a wilderness experience in the beauty of God's creation. Is this only possible for the culturally privileged? I would argue this apparent conflict is at the heart of the missionary problem we are seeking to address.

As an advocate for relational youth evangelism, my objective is to generate strategies and conceptual models to identify, train and sustain young leaders from among every socioeconomic stratum of each city. Even though there seem to be insurmountable obstacles to this dream, I believe pursuing it with unwavering passion will bring glory to God. I guess one could call that a *theology of hard-headedness*. I would welcome that title as a badge of honor. I believe there is a long list of witnesses throughout the ages who have modeled this hard-headedness to pursue what seemed to be impossible in missions. That has always been the mantra of missions.

Possibly the most complex cultural concern we must consider in our vision to provide an opportunity for every person to encounter Jesus Christ through guided outdoor experiences, is the issue of poverty. Here we have what appears to be a conflict as our theology of journey is built on the principle of *Missio Dei* (the mission of God to proclaim the good news to *every* people group). To my concern and utter dismay, due to the expense of equipment and transportation, wilderness or outdoor programs in existence today mostly serve young people whose parents have enough extra money to afford an adventurous experience. Parents of young people in poor societies cannot afford to provide special "experiences" for their child when they often cannot even feed their families. In India, Nepal, or Indonesia, for example, we have found it difficult at times to convince parents to allow their child to go off for a few days of "adventure" when they're needed to work or develop further skills to help the family. Parents may not see the value in this experience for the health of their son or daughter's soul. Nor do they see the benefits of potential leadership development that may occur because the pressing needs they face might not allow for longer-range thinking. This is the privilege we have in developed communities—we can offer "extra" opportunities to our children to help further their education and development. Most people in the developing world have to think of their immediate needs, so a retreat for spiritual formation or leadership development seems like a luxury.

In terms of issues of transportation, many of the world's slums are deep in the heart of cities, where it takes considerable effort and cost to provide transportation for a young person to leave the city for a short period of time to enjoy a wilderness experience. Sadly, in the inequitable world we live in, enjoyment is not usually a priority among the poor as they are concerned more with survival.

These realities throw a serious proverbial wrench in our assertion that every young person deserves an opportunity to encounter Jesus Christ in the beauty and serenity of his creation. *Yet, with every missionary dream there are always seemingly insurmountable obstacles.* Most would agree that cities are certainly in need of transformation. Thus, our dream to give young people an opportunity to experience Jesus Christ through guided wilderness adventures cannot be hindered by any obstacle, including poverty. We must find a way.

The problem of how to offer adventure experiences in the context of poverty requires us to embrace several principles in the developing world: 1) God stands with the poor and so must we in developing a mission model to reach people through outdoor adventure ministries; 2) The Gospel is translatable in every culture, and so our strategy to present the gospel and make disciples must be translatable in poor societies as well; thus we must pursue reproducible ways to provide the highest quality experience at the lowest possible cost; and 3) Equipment and transportation are our two greatest obstacles so we must adopt a strategy that utilizes some already-available technology rather than solely introducing foreign technology. We must adopt a culturally sensitive strategy for equipment use, which I refer to as "local tech."

This means that the equipment we use during an adventure experience to keep people warm and dry might be made from materials that are local and commonly used by farmers, shepherds, or others who do work in the nearby outdoor environment. Embracing "local tech" methods of ministry as much as possible, rather than using expensive high-tech equipment which is foreign to the people we desire to serve, may be one way to make this style of discipleship more possible and palatable to the poor. To address the issue of transportation, we have to consider ways we can provide experiences for those in urban areas by using public transportation to keep costs very low.

Criticism #2: Is wilderness and adventure just for certain personality types?

The short answer is, "No." We can say this definitively from a theological perspective just by looking at whom Jesus took along on His wilderness journeys. Some have proposed outdoor ministries appeal more to certain personality types, rather than being appropriate for all people, which is my conviction. Getting his disciples into the outdoors was a critical component of Jesus' discipleship. Some people honestly wonder whether outdoor adventure is important for every person or just a few who have a natural affinity for it. I have greatly appreciated these points of concern as it has caused me to question whether this really is a broad strategy for discipleship today. If I thought they were right, this book would end right here. But it doesn't.

Susan Bratton in her book, *Christianity, Wilderness, and Wildlife: the Original Desert Solitaire* also recognizes this potential bias:

> One of the more subtle reasons for contemporary difficulties in dealing with wilderness traditions is the assumption that the wilderness sojourn was restricted to the professional prophets, such as Moses and Elijah. This concept causes two problems. First, it makes wilderness experience appear exclusive and limited to those with a very specialized calling or a very unusual relationship with God. Second, since the Old Testament prophets seem to have disappeared, it makes wilderness appear to be an archaic site for spiritual activity.[160]

This critique is a potential showstopper for a truly relevant theology of wilderness journey that relates to all people. In searching for an objective response, I came across a helpful study conducted by Cashel, Montgomery, and Lane. It measures this potential critique through empirical research by raising some important questions. As helpful as it is, it also has huge limitations. Using the filter of Myers-Briggs categories, they found that of the outdoor participants they studied who had attended an Outward Bound-type experience,

"There were overwhelmingly high SSRs in the type categories of INTP, INFP, INTJ, INFJ."[161] Thus this report claims that certain personality types may be inclined to *choose* to participate in outdoor adventure programs more than others. "Wait a minute", you might say, "Doesn't this support the naysayers argument, that outdoor ministry mainly appeals to certain personality types?" Almost, but it actually supports my theological view even more. Let me explain: it is very important to balance their research with a theological response.

First of all, let us consider the types of people Jesus chose to be his band of companions. The twelve disciples were a motley crew (as we saw in chapter 8). Jesus' group included fishermen, tax collectors, military types, and even a dishonest accountant, Judas. Clearly, we can observe from the biblical data all of the disciples would not have been "outdoor types." Yet Jesus led *all* of his young disciples on wilderness experiences *regardless of their personality*. Whereas Peter, James, and John may have had more composure being tossed around in a fishing boat because fishing was their trade and maybe they had a personality type for this type of voyage, I am guessing Matthew may have been a little less serene in that moment because he spent most of his time manning a tax booth. In order to respond to this important question we have to consider that Cashel, Montgomery, and Lane's research is based heavily on *personality theory*, rather than a theological framework, which is our concern.

The main difference in the above-mentioned study and our theological perspective on the relevance of outdoor wilderness experiences for *all* people is this research only looks at what motivates a person to *choose to go* on an outdoor adventure experience. In other words, they are looking at the personality types that might naturally search out opportunities to go experience an adventure. On this point I would agree with them, there may be certain personality types that have a natural affinity for adventure. So if you were an organization that is trying to reach those types of people, then it would be great to know what personality types you should target.

By contrast though, the Bible emphasizes a distinctly different theological point of view. *Jesus took the initiative and chose his followers;* they did not choose him. We do not find in the biblical text that it was up to the disciples to choose when (or when not) to join Jesus on his adventurous outdoor journeys. What motivated them was being chosen and who chose them, not what they had a personal hankering to do because of their personality type. *Jesus wasn't organizing fun adventures and marketing the crowds to see who would sign up for a trip. No, he chose his disciples, and then took them out on adventures to grow them to be like him.*

Yes, we might need to exercise wisdom and adjust the outing to be an appropriate challenge depending on whom we are with, but Jesus modeled that being a disciple means to follow him, and part of that was to retreat with him often into the wilderness for solitude. This isn't just for certain personality types. Retreating to spend time with God in the outdoors is a noble goal for *anyone,* even if it doesn't *fit* his or her natural affinities.

CHAPTER 11
IMPART

Teachable Moments?

One of the most obvious patterns of Jesus' teaching in the outdoors was that he often capitalized on teachable moments. You know you are in the middle of a teachable moment when the natural creation around you all of a sudden becomes a bubbling laboratory for illustrating a truth from the Bible. Some teachable moments occur in the midst of stress. Others pop up in the most tranquil of circumstances as you sit by a gurgling brook or in the middle of a meadow that is gleefully bursting forth with color and aroma. Any time you and your group is presented with a hands-on object lesson from the journey itself, then you're on the cusp of a teachable moment. The more you spend time in the outdoors with groups, the more naturally you will be able to recognize these opportunities. The more intentional you are at increasing your Wilderness Quotient (see Chapter 9), the more your volume of stories will grow and expand into a treasure trove of Kingdom wisdom you can pass on to others. This chapter is focused on helping you anticipate potential teachable moments so you can effectively impart the wisdom these situations offer.

Opportunity teaching is the art of a well-timed story. In ancient Israel, this was a respected and sought-after skill. Swift writes:

> Possibly, as throughout all the towns of modern Palestine, there were found professional story-tellers who, whenever men gathered together for recreation, recite with gesture and action their bundle of tales. The stories appealed strongly to the imagination of people, for they told of courtship, marriage, intrigue, and of the achievements of their ancestors, or else answered the questions which were uppermost in their minds

[i.e., questions regarding the origin of man and the world in which he lives, differences in races and languages, etc.].[162]

One of the tricks of the trade is to first think through the topics of interest to your audience. Erickson's study, mentioned earlier, highlighted three categories that pique young people's interest: 1) Individuals and their relationships, 2) Societal issues, and 3) The concept of God and religion. Teachable moments will inevitably arise in the context of wilderness trips, so like Erickson I recommend you prepare a short list of topics that you think are currently most relevant to your group. Opportunities are endless so there will never be one book that can give an exhaustive list of teachable moments. What is more important is that you learn how to recognize a teachable moment when you are standing in the middle of one, and then have the skill to shape the experience into a learning environment.

The Five "T's": How to Facilitate a Teachable Moment

There are four steps to opportunity teaching: *TIMING, THINKING THEOLOGICALLY*, offering *TOOLS* for reflection, *TRYING IT*, and TRANSFER the learning to future endeavors in normal everyday life. The first step is *TIMING*. Always be attentive to what is going on in your group and what the landscape is offering you as a backdrop for learning. As you prayerfully reflect on the state of mind of your group, you will be able to identify topics that relate to them. Then look around and pray for the Lord to show you an object lesson to illustrate what you want them to learn.

The second step is to *THINK THEOLOGICALLY* about the topic. *Theology is simply asking questions and seeking answers to those questions in the Bible.* What questions do you have? What questions does your group have about God or about life? What do they want to know more about or understand more fully? Once you have a good list of people's questions, start finding Scripture that relates to their questions. As you hike along or paddle at sea, try to have in your mind a tool belt of good questions to ask. Be prepared to address people's questions from the Scriptures. Then, when you experience a teachable moment and the timing is right, you can stop and reflect on a pithy question that interests the group and poignantly connects to a creation analogy. Now you are ready to connect this timely object lesson to their experience by anchoring everything you are teaching to God's Word.

Third, you want to provide your group some TOOLS for reflection. You might have everyone grab one of the objects (maybe it is a piece of grass, a rock, a flower, an ant, etc.). Or you might just point it out to them so they can look at, touch, or taste what you are talking about. From here, you have lots of options. You might just ask a simple well-crafted question, and leave it at that. Sometimes a good question without you giving any answers is the best way for the group to chew on and discover the truth for themselves. Or maybe you could have them draw a picture or write a poem or prayer that relates to the object you are connecting to the Bible. Or you may ask them to dig further and answer your question with another deeper question that provokes an honest response. Jesus often answered questions with more questions.

Sometimes it may not be an object you are pointing out as a teachable moment, but it might be more nuanced like an attitude in the group, or an interpersonal issue you see going on. Either way, you want to be able to offer a tool for reflection to make the lesson memorable. If you can engage some of the five senses (see, hear, feel, taste, smell), then you've probably successfully given them a tool for reflection.

Fourth, you want the group to TRY IT themselves. After you model a few teachable moments for your group, one of the very best ways to bring about transformation in the minds and hearts of your group is to invite them to come up with their own teachable moments. You might say, "Hey, now that you've seen how we take advantage of teachable moments, I'd like you to try to think of one yourself while we are paddling to the next beach (or hiking to the next water break)...Maybe spend some time talking to God in prayer and ask him to reveal something he wants to teach you through his creation. Then come up with a passage of Scripture that anchors your analogy and share it with the group. I can't wait to hear what you all come up with!" You'll be absolutely floored by the stuff folks come up with. It's truly profound to see people digging into their relationship with God, searching his creation for treasures of truth to pull out and share with the group. Fifth, you want to help the group TRANSFER the learning to future endeavors. Simply ask them to share what difference this lesson from nature will make in their life at home.

Alpha and Omega

The Greek alphabet begins with alpha and ends with omega. The title Jesus takes in his last words to John was the Alpha and the Omega, the First and the Last (see Revelation 22:13)! Since Jesus is the One who made all of creation, it should be of no surprise that his handiwork has infinite illustrations to elicit awe and glory to God.

Now that you know how to facilitate a teachable moment by drawing upon the genius of creation, let's look at a sampling of great teaching moments from *alpha to omega* (A to Z) that may arise during your wilderness experience. We don't have room for an exhaustive list of possible teachable moments, but to get you started, I'll give some examples of how you could start putting together your own teachable moment notebook. The more time you spend in the outdoors with people, the greater you'll expand your dictionary of topics. If you flip back through the chapters of this book, you will find dozens of relevant theological topics or creation analogies that commonly occur as teachable moments.

Teachable Moments from A to M

Awareness

When John the Baptist was in prison, his hands were literally tied from doing more ministry, but he kept hearing stories of all Jesus was doing in the surrounding towns and villages. He paid keen attention to what Jesus was saying and doing, and came to the conclusion that Jesus was the long-awaited Messianic fulfillment of all of the Old Testament prophecies! Mark writes, "When John heard in prison what Christ was doing, he sent his disciples to ask him, 'Are you the one who was to come, or should we expect someone else?'" (Matt. 11:2). John the Baptist was a student of Jesus. He asked questions, observed his actions, and recognized God's pursuit of people through his cousin Jesus.

When we take people out into the wilderness, God uses his creation to awaken people's souls. If people are guided in such a way that they get time to be quiet and walk through Scripture and gaze into the face of Jesus Christ through the biblical text, they will become more aware of who he truly is. And like John the Baptist, we pray and hope people will connect the dots and see that his words matched his life. Jesus claimed to be the Way, the Truth, and the Life, and that there was no other religion or way back into a relationship with God. By pointing out the ways God's creation confirms his character, and by presenting the gospel in such a way that it truly becomes "Good News" to those on our trips...you have done all you can to facilitate the experience to heighten people's awareness that God exists and he rewards those who put their faith in him (see Hebrews 11:6). That's all we are called to do...the rest is out of our hands and simply a matter of prayer for the eyes of our campers' hearts to be open and illuminated to the glorious great news of Jesus!

> *Other references for writing quiet time questions or teachable moments that relate to this topic: Genesis 28:16; Exodus 34:29; Leviticus 4:14,23,28; Numbers 15:24; 1 Samuel 14:3; 1 Kings 8:38; 2 Chronicles 6:29; Nehemiah 4:15; Matthew 4:15, 12:15, 16:8, 24:50, 26:10; Mark 8:17; Luke 12:46; John 6:61; Acts 10:28; Galatians 4:21*

Beauty

How do we know that something is beautiful? This is a philosophical question that is impossible to test in a laboratory. But when we look at the wide-open spaces of a majestic mountain scene, or we meditate on the splendor of a sunset on the horizon of a rolling sea, we know we are looking at beauty. In a Christian worldview, we believe God created the heavens and the earth, and everything he created was good and pleasing to him. It was and is beautiful. The creation inspires awe, whereas the degradation of the earth causes repulsion. When I walk by polluted streams full of human waste and discarded trash in some developing countries, I am saddened by the ugliness of the scene, but even more grieved by the plight of the poor who cannot enjoy a safe and refreshing drink of water, which was God's intention for creation.

What God creates is beautiful, and what our sin causes is destruction of beauty. You might ask a group questions like: How do we see evidence of God's design in the beautiful landscape we are looking at today? In what ways do you see evidence of mankind's sin destroying that very beauty God intended for the human race? What does this say about God? What does this say about mankind? How does being a follower of Jesus Christ make you a restorer of beauty in God's world? How can we take a snapshot of the awe-inspiring beauty we see in this magnificent natural setting and go back to our cities with a renewed vision to restore God's intended beauty in our relationships, schools, churches, and city as a whole?

References: Esther 1:11, 2:3, 2:9, 2:12; Psalm 27:4, 45:11, 50:2; Proverbs 6:25, 31:30; Isaiah 3:24, 28:4, 33:17, 53:2, 61:3; Lamentations 2:15; Ezekiel 16:14, 16:25, 27:3, 27:11, 28:12, 28:17, 31:7; James 1:11; 1 Peter 3:3-4

Camping

Camping is a temporary activity. People eventually need to settle and establish a home. Israel spent many years camping in the desert. Still today, to remember their dependence on the Lord in the wilderness, Jews celebrate the Feast of Booths by camping for a week in the outdoors. In what ways does camping remind you of your need for God? How does camping make us more grateful for God's provision? What are some of the lessons we learn while camping that we probably take for granted in the comfort of our home?

References: Exodus 16:13; 2 Kings 7:5; Judges 7:11; 1 Samuel

4:6; Judges 7:15; 1 Samuel 28:4; 1 Kings 16:16; Numbers 11:26, 5:3; Deuteronomy 23:14; Exodus 33:7; Leviticus 9:11; Numbers 5:1, 11:30, 3:23, 3:29; Deuteronomy 23:12; Josiah 3:2, Leviticus 17:3; Numbers 11:9; Josiah 10:15,43; Judges 7:10, 20:19; 1 Samuel 17:53; Psalm 106:16

Devotion

Are you enthusiastic about your relationship with Jesus Christ? Spending time with God is less about piety (practicing religion), and more about experiencing and extending God's love to other people in our lives. Devotion to Christ is about being attached to him. What are some of the measurable results of this attachment? How does it make you feel that Jesus is completely loyal to you? What does it look like to be completely loyal to him?

The opposite of devotion is apathy. If I am indifferent or begin to show a lack of concern for a friend, what does that do to my relationship with them? How does it make you feel when someone you love shows indifference to you? God's design for us is to be devoted to him in the same way he is devoted to us. Has your relationship with God become routine? Are you bored? Maybe this time in the wilderness will strip away the things that are competing for your loyalty to Christ. Let's spend some time in solitude today and ask Jesus to speak to us about anything we might be attaching ourselves to that is causing us to drift away from him. Ask him to prune and cut away anything that is entangling you so that you can truly enjoy your relationship with him.

References: Job 15:4, 6:14; 2 Chronicles 35:26; 1 Corinthians 7:35; 1 Chronicles 29:19; 2 Chronicles 32:32; 2 Kings 20:3; Isaiah 38:3; 2 Corinthians 11:3; Ezekiel 33:31; Jeremiah 2:2; 1 Chronicles 29:3, 28:9

Earth

"Where were you when I laid the earth's foundation? Tell me, if you understand. Who marked off its dimensions? Surely you know! Who stretched a measuring line across it? On what were its footings set, or who laid its cornerstone" (Job 38:4-6). We need to spend time in awe of the earth and all of its dimensions. As we look more carefully at creation, we begin to more accurately acknowledge the greatness of the God who created it. Colossians 1:16 states that Jesus is the one who created all that we see on the earth and everything we don't see in the heavens! What does the design of the earth tell you about its Creator?

References: Job 38:4-6; Colossians 1:15-20

Forest

The theme of Psalm 96 is that the Lord reigns over all the earth. In fact, most scholars agree that God's reign is probably the main theme of the whole book of Psalms. Psalm 96:12 says, "Then all the trees of the forest will sing for joy." As we walk through the forest today, I want you to listen to the sounds of the trees swaying, creaking, and whistling in the wind. Why is it so appealing to our ears to hear the sound of leaves quaking or the hum of wind forcing its way through the harpsichord of pine needles on a spruce tree? Like the sounds of creation, we, too, can make music with our voices or instruments. God makes music in the rhythmic sounds of his creation. Today I want you to consider if right now your life is like a song of praise to God.

Are you in a place of self-absorption where all you can think of is your own problems or concerns? Maybe the way out of this is not necessarily getting all of your questions answered or getting your way all of the time. Maybe the way out of despair or discouragement is to stand up like these trees and allow God's breeze of love to make a new song as you surrender to his sovereign *reign* over your life. How can you surrender to his reign over you today so that your life becomes a beautiful song, like the beautiful sound of a quaking aspen tree that just responds naturally to the wind that blows around it?

References: Nehemiah 2:8; Psalm 80:13, 83:14, 96:12, 104:20; Song of Solomon 2:3; Isaiah 9:18, 32:15

Glory

George Müller was famous for saying that his goal was simply to, "Get glory for God." John the Baptist, in reference to the comparison of his ministry to the ministry of Jesus said, "He must become greater; I must become less" (John 3:30). Is this the path of our life? Are we on a path of exalting ourselves or seeking significance and recognition from the world? Or are we happier when we become unimportant—when knowing and worshipping Jesus becomes all-important?

People are tempted to glorify themselves and cut others down to build themselves up. But the sad fact is the path of self-glorification is actually the path of self-destruction. Today as you look out over this glorious scene of grandeur, isn't it easy to agree that we deserve no credit for the glory of God's creation? He did it all, and is worthy of all the glory for making it. In the same way, consider as you spend time in quiet solitude with God today, do you need to repent for being on a path of self-glorification? Are you taking credit when you should be giving God the credit for what he has done in your life? Has it left you empty, angry, and directionless? Confess this to God and offer yourself to a life of "Getting glory for God." This is the path of enduring peace that all of us are longing for.

> *References: 2 Corinthians 3:7, 3:10; Isaiah 60:1; Romans 8:18; 2 Corinthians 3:11; Ezekiel 3:23; Romans 9:23; Exodus 40:34; Matthew 25:31; Luke 9:26; Ezekiel 43:2; John 1:14; Ezekiel 10:4; 1 Corinthians 11:7; 2 Peter 1:17; 2 Corinthians 3:18; Proverbs 25:2; John 17:42; Isaiah 35:2; Psalm 24:10; Habakkuk 2:16; Haggai 2:9; Isaiah 66:19; 1 Thessalonians 2:20*

Hiking

If you want to be a marathon runner in life rather than a sprinter who burns out, you've got to take things one step at a time. Following God's will might feel like a grind at times but it's the easiest and safest path in the long run. When hiking gets hard, remember that if we discipline ourselves to walk in the Spirit, God will give us agility and stamina to navigate through those periods of our life where it feels like we are just plodding along. Take heart. He gives us "hind's feet on high places" just like the wild mountain goats and bighorn sheep (see Habakkuk 3:19). It's amazing how they don't fall in such steep craggy terrain. It's also amazing how the Lord keeps us from falling when we face trials of many kinds.

References: Colossians 1:19; Ephesians 5:17; Isaiah 40:27-31; Habakkuk 3:19; Psalm 121

Interpersonal Relationships

How we feel about ourselves can greatly affect how we treat others. Out in the wilderness this can become heightened because we don't have a shower or a mirror to doll ourselves up. Yet when everybody is in the same boat, it doesn't really matter. Everybody's outward appearance becomes much less important. Isn't it shallow how much our outward appearance matters back at home among our friends? God's Word teaches that he doesn't look at our outward appearance. Instead, he looks at our heart (see 1 Samuel 16:7). Take notice this week how much easier it is to get to know people and become good friends when outward appearances no longer matter. By focusing on how much the Lord loves us, we begin to realize and believe he doesn't really care much about our outward appearance.

When we're liberated from this paralyzing concern about our appearance, then we'll finally be free from the poison of comparison that plagues our culture. When we focus on the hearts of people, we will notice that our relationships will improve as well. Wouldn't you rather have deep relationships than shallow ones based upon outward appearances? The wilderness changes everything by opening our eyes to heart issues rather than just the outer shell of a person.

References:

1. Friendship: *Jeremiah 9:5; Luke 11:5; 2 Samuel 16:17; Proverbs 27:10; Matthew 26:50; Psalm 55:13, Proverbs 27:6; 3 John 1:1; 2 Samuel 15:37; Job 16:20; Proverbs 17:17; Isaiah 41:8; Jeremiah 3:4; Colossians 4:14; Judges 14:20; Job 6:27; Proverbs 19:4; Luke 5:20; Romans 16:9, 3 John 1:5; Psalm 88:18; Matthew 22:12; Luke 11:6; Proverbs 19:6*

2. Harmonious Relationships: *1 Peter 3:8; 2 Corinthians 6:15; Romans 12:16; Zechariah 6:13*
3. Helping Others: *2 Kings 6:27; Romans 16:2; Judges 5:23; Ecclesiastes 4:10; 1 Timothy 5:16; 1 Chronicles 12:18, 14:11; Isaiah 31:1; Psalm 5:2, 30:2, 38:22, 63:7; Judges 6:6; Psalm 44:26, 88:13, 121:2; Acts 4:20; Numbers 34:18; Job 6:21, 30:28; Psalm 60:11, 108:12, 115:9, 115:10, 124:8; Numbers 1:4; Job 6:13; Psalm 22:19*

Jesus

Jesus is fully human and fully God. This is a divine mystery, but it is essential to understand his humanity and his deity. God became a human being in the person of Jesus Christ. The Trinity (Father, Son, and Holy Spirit) agreed that Jesus would be sent to enter the world on our turf. He is able to identify with us in every way because he was fully human, yet he never sinned. Do you need a leader you can trust, one with authority and strength, yet who is compassionate and can totally relate with you? Jesus is that man.

If God came to earth, you would also expect him to do something no other mere human could do. In Mark 4:35-41, Jesus calmed the *storm* over the Sea of Galilee showing his authority over nature. Only God could be expected to do that, no one else. Jesus has the power to calm the storms of your life if you put your faith in him.

Common sense says if God came to earth, you would also expect him to be able to forgive people's sins since that is what has broken the relationship between him and us. Mark 2:1-12 is a story of an encounter that Jesus had with a paralyzed man. Yet before Jesus healed the man, he said, "Son, your sins are forgiven." The people must have been thinking to themselves, "How can a paralytic sin? What could a paralytic do wrong, he's paralyzed?" Here is the point: Jesus sees through us, to our inmost being. He forgave this man's sin first because that was a bigger problem than his paralysis. The bottom line is that only Jesus has authority over sin, disease, and whatever cripples us. Have you asked Jesus to forgive you of your sin and pride? Sometimes the stress of wilderness experiences can help us see what is really inside our hearts. The stress of strenuous experiences can squeeze us like a sponge to show us what's truly inside. On this adventure you may have felt angry, hopeless, or lonely. All of these feelings may be signs of an even bigger problem, which may be your separation from God if you haven't put your faith in Christ yet. Jesus is the only bridge from death to life (see John 5:24). Who do you say Jesus is?

References: Matthew 3:13, 4:1,12, 8:18, 9:1, 26:1, 27:11; Mark 1:9, 2:1, 6:30, 10:47,52, 11:12; Luke 4:38, 19:35, 22:63, 23:3; John 4:50, 11:17, 12:1, 17:1, 19:1, 19:38, 21:4,15; Acts 1:1

Kiss

The Song of Solomon begins with a poem from a bride to her husband: "Let him kiss me with the kisses of his mouth—for your love is more delightful than wine" (Song of Solomon 1:2). What a profound statement. The love of her bridegroom is so much better than anything the world could offer her. This is a picture of our relationship with Jesus Christ. The church is called the "Bride of Christ." That means that if you have put your trust in Jesus, you are like a bride to Jesus in that he loves you, protects you, and leads you.

Wine in this passage is symbolic of anything from which we have found satisfaction. Whether we delight in video games, buying stuff, or pandering to an addiction, there is no greater delight we could ever experience than the affection of Jesus Christ. In the Song of Solomon, the bride got it right. Anything else that had ever brought her pleasure in life now paled in comparison to the love of her husband. Is that how you feel about Jesus? Do you delight in anything else more than him? Would you rather spend your time drinking the "wine" of the world that only offers temporary enjoyment for an evening, or would you rather reach for the favor of Jesus Christ and the blessings of walking shoulder to shoulder with him for eternity?

Wilderness trips can help us recognize the things we have idolized (or put our delight in) back home. Now that we are out in the wilderness we don't have many of those distractions tugging at our heart. This is a unique time to stop drinking the "wine" of the world, and listen to the loving voice of the Heavenly Father who is wooing you to himself. Ask yourself if you agree with the bride in this verse...can you honestly say that closeness, faithfulness, and obedience to Jesus is more delightful than anything else you could get from the world? Is his favor the flavor you seek?

> References: Proverbs 24:26; 2 Corinthians 13:12; 1 Thessalonians 5:26; Job 31:27; Psalm 85:10; Luke 22:48; 1 Peter 5:14; Genesis 27:26, 31:28; Romans 16:16; 1 Corinthians 16:20; Matthew 26:48; Song of Solomon 1:2; Psalm 2:12; Luke 7:45; Mark 14:44; Luke 22:47; 2 Samuel 20:9, 15:5; Song of Solomon 8:1; 1 Kings 19:20; Hosea 13:2; Genesis 27:27, 29:11

Light

For this teachable moment, refer to the reflection on "light" from Psalm 119:105 in the section called, "Metaphors Pierce the Heart" in Chapter 13.

> References: 2 Corinthians 4:6; Revelation 22:5; Exodus 35:14; John 1:9; Ephesians 5:8; Genesis 1:4; Psalm 36:9; John 1:8, 5:35; Isaiah 9:2; Luke 11:36; John 3:19; 1 John 1:7; John 12:36; Matthew 4:16, 5:15; John 3:20; Genesis 1:16; John 8:12; Genesis 1:3; 1 John 1:5, 12:35; Isaiah 5:20, 13:10, 13:10, 50:11, 60:19

Mountain

God used mountains in the wilderness as a special geographic feature to teach about his authority and to cast vision for missions to the world. The opposite of mountains are valleys. We all experience valleys as well as mountaintop experiences. The valleys are just as important to the spiritual formation process as the peak experiences because they teach us to depend on God. David spoke of the Valley of the Shadow of Death in Psalm 23. Both mountains and valleys were literal wilderness landscape features through which the ancients traveled. These physical, outdoor features provide a wealth of perspective that can be translated directly into one's spiritual experiences. Christian outdoor leadership capitalizes on helping people connect the landscape of the outdoors with the landscape of their soul's experience with God. This is nothing new. Jesus did it all the time.

References: Exodus 19:12, 24:18, 34:3; Micah 4:1, 7:12; Numbers 20:28; Jeremiah 51:25; Deuteronomy 9:9; Zechariah 8:3; Ezekiel 20:40, 24:15, 25:40, 26:30; Job 24:8; Psalm 95:4; Exodus 19:14, 24:17, 27:8; Deuteronomy 1:6; Job 14:18, 39:1; Psalm 87:1; Song of Solomon 4:6; Ezekiel 11:23; Psalm 30:7; Isaiah 2:1; Hebrews 12:18

CHAPTER 12
INSTRUCT

Making Your Teaching S + T + IC = K

We have covered a lot of turf in the realm of teaching techniques. Yet the skills that are most helpful are those you can personalize and simplify so you can remember them in the heat of the moment. For this reason, I've come up with a schema or diagram to help capitalize on teachable moments. It's called the S + T + IC = K Model. As a teacher, I'm fascinated by how Jesus made his ideas STICK. The content of his teaching usually catches our attention, but what about the context? If you want to emulate the teaching techniques of Jesus, you have to pay attention to your surroundings. He didn't teach in a vacuum. The one-two punch of his teaching style was the way he combined $\underline{S}$etting + $\underline{T}$iming + $\underline{I}$ntentional $\underline{C}$ontent to tie a $\underline{K}$not around each learning event.

When rock climbing, if you tie the right knot, you can hang on it and trust it—it will hold you. I see Jesus doing this with his teaching...He hung his words in such a way that they stuck in people's minds like a bombproof knot that you could completely trust and put your full weight down upon. Jesus evoked a response from people. He closed the deal. So before you teach toward a desired outcome or objective, consider how you'll tie the elements of $\underline{S}$etting and $\underline{T}$iming together with $\underline{I}$ntentional $\underline{C}$ontent into a nice $\underline{K}$not to evoke a response. You can download the S + T + IC = K Model from the book's website (www.outdoorleaders.com/resources) to hang on your wall or stuff in your Bible to help you master this skill.

Teachable Moments from N-Z

Now that we've considered how Jesus made his instruction STICK, let's continue our journey through our teachable-moment-alphabet to glean some more potential ideas for how to facilitate learning on your trip! Remember, the best way to come up with your own journey talks is to first be attentive to the outcomes and objectives you are aiming at during the day. Then prayerfully tune in to what is going on in your group and the surrounding environment for light bulbs of learning to turn on somewhere along the way. Your five senses are also a natural conduit to get ideas for illustrations.

Names

We are identified by our name. It was given to us as a gift and our name has meaning and reputation. It is a great honor and privilege to give a name to someone else. Parents get the honor of naming their children, but ultimately whom we are is what gives meaning to our name, not vice versa. The idea of naming comes from God. Isaiah said, "Lift your eyes and look to the heavens: Who created all these? He who brings out the starry host one by one, and calls them each by name" (Isaiah 40:26). Imagine that. God has a personal name for each and every star! And he also has a name for us. He's had a personal name for you from before he created you in your mother's womb.

Jesus once said, "Indeed, the very hairs of your head are all numbered" (Luke 12:7). As you look at the night sky tonight, I want you to consider the reality that God had given each star a pet name. Then run your fingers through your hair and see if you can guess how many hairs you have on your head. What does it say about God that he knows your name and knows the number of hairs on your head? What does that say about you that he knows you that intimately? Spend some time talking to God about how well he knows you. Ask him to speak to you about how much he likes you. Think about how Jesus' death on the cross was the ultimate demonstration of God's love for you. How does that change your perspective of yourself, and your relationship with the Heavenly Father?

References: Mark 3:16-17, 5:9; Luke 1:31,59-53, 6:22, 8:30; John 1:6, 5:43, 17:11; Ephesians 3:15; Philippians 2:9-10, 15; 1 Peter 4:16; Revelation 2:17, 3:5,12; 20:15, 22:4

Obstacle

In the context of unbridled wickedness in his culture, Isaiah was given a vision from God. God accuses the wicked of depending on their idols to deliver them. Yet in all reality, even the wind can knock over an idol! God says with unmistakable clarity, "'He who takes refuge in me will inherit the land, and will possess my holy mountain.' And it will be said, 'Build up, build up, prepare the way, remove every obstacle out of the way of my people'" (Isaiah 57:13-14). While enjoying purifying solitude with God out in his creation it is good to think a little bit about what it is going to be like when you go back down into the valley of life back at home. There will inevitably be obstacles to block or prohibit us from being faithful to God when we plug back into the routine of our normal daily lives.

The idols of our culture easily become teddy bears of comfort to us and we need to recognize how much God hates idol worship. Yet if we turn away from them and seek to please God, he will remove obstacles out of our way and give us an inheritance that cannot perish, spoil, or fade. What obstacles have we faced so far on our wilderness trip? There have been peaks, rivers, and emotional challenges. We could have given up or backed down to those obstacles. But, instead, we leaned on God and took refuge in him, and he gave us the strength and perseverance to go through the obstacle rather than be stopped by it. What is stopping you from walking in the Spirit back at home? Are there personal sins or relationships that are hindering you? In quiet solitude try to identify the sin that entangles you and ask God for his help to completely remove those obstacles so you can freely pursue the adventure of the Great Commission where it counts, back in our city or community.

References: Romans 14:13; Isaiah 57:13-14; Jeremiah 6:21; Romans 16:17; Hebrews 12:1

Persevere

To persevere is to be persistent, to continue on and stick with something even when you feel like quitting. The opposite of perseverance is giving up. Life is full of very real moments where we are tempted to give in or give up. Although there may be an appropriate time to quit something, the biblical norm is to persist through trials and suffering. James wrote: "As you know, we consider blessed those who have persevered. You have heard of Job's perseverance and have seen what the Lord finally brought about. The Lord is full of compassion and mercy" (James 5:11). Job is an iconic model of perseverance in the Bible. He had every "human" reason to blame God for his sufferings, but he didn't. Although he and God had some very intense wrestling matches, the end result was a man who withstood trials that seemingly no human could endure. By sticking with it and pressing into God rather than running away from him, he received a reward far greater than any trinket the world could offer him as a prize. Our wilderness experiences may not hold a candle to Job's experiences, but they do push us to our limits. What have you learned about perseverance this week? Are there any trials or challenges that lay ahead back at home that you feel like running away from? In your solitude, consider if God has brought you into the wilderness to wrestle with him and press into him in some way. When we go home after our outing, God promises to give us the ability to run toward him, to overcome and win the race rather than run away from difficulty and come up more empty in the process.

References: Jude 1:17; Hebrews 10:36, 11:27; 1 Timothy 4:16; 1 Corinthians 13:7; James 1:12, 5:11; Revelation 2:3

Quiet

There are times when we need to be quiet, and there are other times when we should not remain silent. This is a holy tension. God in his jealousy for the fidelity of Israel spoke this through Isaiah: "For Zion's sake I will not keep silent, for Jerusalem's sake I will not remain quiet, till her righteousness shines out like the dawn, her salvation like a blazing torch" (Isaiah 62:1). There is a time to speak up and fill the airwaves with our voice for the sake of God's name being honored and praised. There is also a time to shout even if the levelheaded religious elite is staying quiet. One time two blind men made a real scene when they started crying out to Jesus for mercy: "The crowd rebuked them and told them to be quiet, but they shouted all the louder, 'Lord, Son of David, have mercy on us'" (Matthew 20:31). There is definitely a time to *not* be quiet.

Yet our lives should not only consist of making noise. Through the prophet Zephaniah, God speaks to his people saying, "The LORD your God is with you, he is mighty to save. He will take great delight in you, he will quiet you with his love, he will rejoice over you with singing" (Zeph. 3:17). At the end of the day, either our quietness or our speaking out should be signs of our resting in God's sovereignty over our situation. As you reflect on your relationship with Christ and your obedience to serve him however he calls you, are there any things he is calling you to stop being silent about? How can you step out in faith and speak up in a faith-filled and productive way?

On the opposite side of the spectrum, is God calling you to be quiet and rest in his sovereignty in some area of your life? Have you been taking something into your own hands that you need to quietly release to God? Whether you are called to speak out or be quiet, how can you know whether you are doing so obediently and in full confidence in God's sovereignty and authority over your life?

References: Genesis 25:27, 34:5; Judges 3:19, 18:19; 2 Samuel 13:20; 2 Kings 11:20; 1 Chronicles 4:40, 22:9; Nehemiah 5:8; Esther 7:4; Job 6:24; Psalm 23:2, 76:8, 83:1; Proverbs 17:1; Ecclesiastes 9:17; Isaiah 18:4, 42:14, 62:1; Amos 5:13; Zephaniah 3:17; Matthew 20:31; Mark 4:39, 6:31, 9:34, 10:48; Luke 4:35, 18:39, 19:40; Acts 12:17, 19:36, 22:2; 1 Corinthians 14:28; 1 Thessalonians 4:11; 1 Timothy 2:2; 1 Peter 3:4

Remain (or Abide)

This means to be inherently dwelling in something. We remain or abide (live) in our home as a branch abides or stays connected to its vine. While we are out in the wilderness this week, we will be taking up residence in makeshift tents that are vulnerable to the weather. More importantly, though, we have each other as companions. We will be dwelling in community this week, which is another form of "abiding." One of my highest hopes for this week is for each one of us to consider the invitation of Jesus Christ to come "abide" in a lifelong, eternal relationship with him.

We are going to consider many of his claims this week, and you will be presented with an opportunity to make Jesus Christ your home. As you climb in the tent to go to sleep tonight, consider giving him the keys to your heart so he will make his home permanently in your soul. When you yield your life to him through faith in his name, he covers you like a tent with his unconditional love. He is the perfect covering we all need, especially in the storms.

References:
1. Remain: *John 15:4, 15:7, 15:10; Ezekiel 44:2; Philippians 1:24; Exodus 25:15; Leviticus 11:37; Job 37:8; Psalm 102:27; 1 Corinthians 7:26; 2 Timothy 2:13; 1 Corinthians 7:20; Job 29:20; Galatians 2:5; Psalm 109:1; 1 John 2:24; Leviticus 25:51; 1 Corinthians 14:34; Revelation 14:12; Leviticus 25:52; John 1:32, 21:22: 1 Samuel 16:22*
2. Abide: *Leviticus 16:16, Job 24:13, Psalm 9:7, 15:1, 25:13, 37:27, 61:7, 91:1, 102:12, 113:9, 125:1; Isaiah 32:16; John 3:36, 6:56, 14:17, 15:4-15:10, 1 Corinthians 13:13; Galatians 3:10; James 1:25; 1 John 2:6, 2:10, 2:14, 2:24, 2:27-28, 3:6, 3:9, 3:14, 3:17*

Spiritual Disciplines

When rock climbing we wear a helmet at all times. One of the safety practices we teach is what to do if an object (a rock or water bottle, etc.) falls down the rock. Paradoxically, one's natural instinct when someone yells "rock" from above is to look up, step back, and then run away from the object. Yet the safest action to take is to immediately run toward the face of the rock and lean into it. The closer one is to the rock face, the safer he is, because the falling object will likely bounce over his head. This paradox has parallels to one's spiritual journey. As we are climbing the "rock of life," we will experience fear. Yet, even though our instinct is to turn and run, the safest posture to take is to face our fears and squeeze closely against the Rock, Jesus Christ.

When we encounter a difficult situation, we may be tempted to run away from the Body of Christ and forsake community. Yet, the spiritual weapons he gives us (listed in Ephesians 6) are meant to help us stand against the enemy rather than run away from him. This paradox relates similarly to the spiritual disciplines in that they are used to train our bodies and minds to act in ways that go against the inclination of our flesh. In Christ, we are enabled to say "'No' to ungodliness and worldly passions, and to live self-controlled, upright and godly lives in this present age" (Titus 2:12). Likewise we are called to have our minds "controlled by the Spirit" (Romans 8:6); which results in "life and peace" rather than being controlled by the flesh, which results in death. Like learning to press into the rock when something is falling from above, the spiritual disciplines of silence, solitude, prayer, study, service, confession, worship, etc., are ways to train ourselves to be controlled by the Spirit so we can lean *into* the spiritual battle rather than run away from it.

References: Deuteronomy 4:36, 11:2, 21:18; Job 5:17; Psalm 6:1, 38:1, 39:11, 94:12; Proverbs 1:2, 1:7, 3:11, 5:12, 5:23, 6:23, 10:17, 12:1, 13:18, 13:24,15:5, 15:10, 15:32, 19:18, 22:15, 23:13, 23:23, 29:17; Jeremiah 7:23, 30:11, 32:33, 46:28; Hosea 5:2; 2 Timothy 1:7; Hebrews 12:5-11; Revelation 3:19

Stress (or anxiousness)

There is a redeeming purpose within discomfort. To put it bluntly, familiarity leads to complacency. God pushed Abraham out of his comfort zone to make him more committed to mission (see Gen. 12:1-3). The same is true of the church today. God pushes us out of our comfort zones. He puts us in unfamiliar territory for a purpose: to bend our hearts more toward loving and pursuing those who are lost. In what ways have you been stressed or pushed out of your comfort zone the past few days on the trail or in the water? Can you see a purpose in feeling this way? Are there any areas of your life where you might be lazy or complacent back at home? Do you think it might be possible that God is pushing you out of your comfort zone to expand your horizons, so you will live more loyally toward his purposes when you go home?

References: Deuteronomy 28:65; Psalm 139:23; Proverbs 12:25; Ecclesiastes 2:22; Philippians 4:6

Trust

See rock climbing analogy discussed in the section, "Paradox Reconciles Seeming Opposites" in Chapter 13.

References: Psalm 20:7, John 14:1, Psalm 4:5, 31:14, 56:3; Deuteronomy 1:32; Psalm 78:22; 2 Corinthians 13:6; Psalm 37:5; Proverbs 22:19; Psalm 22:4, 31:6, 33:21, 37:3, 56:11, 115:9, 115:10, 118:8-9, 91:2, 115:11; Zephaniah 3:12; Psalm 119:42, 146:3; Proverbs 21:22; Nahum 1:7; 1 Corinthians 4:2, Luke 16:11

Un-Merited Grace

Possibly one of the most important truths one must grapple with in order to put their faith in Christ is that God saves people by extending them grace. He is merciful. Jesus willingly died on behalf of those who belong to him. This is grace: We do not get what we deserve and we get the gift without cost and by no merit of our own. Grace is the greatest, freest gift available to mankind. Evangelism is about helping people turn around to receive it!

If you've ever been lost, you understand this completely. Once when I was about twelve, I got lost while hunting with my dad. I went off on what appeared to be a straightforward mission to track a set of deer tracks that would certainly lead me to an astonishingly large buck to hang on my wall (or so I imagined). After about an hour I realized that I had been walking in circles and I could not find my father. I yelled, screamed, cried, and eventually started shooting my gun into a hillside to see if anyone could hear me. Eventually my father and the pastor of our church tracked me down because of the racket I was making. The sense of relief I felt was more than I could handle...I was holding back tears of gratitude the rest of that day, even though I never saw that buck deer again. All that mattered to me was that I was found—my potential accomplishment of getting that buck was irrelevant.

One day when Jesus was teaching a group of self-confident Pharisees about grace, he told a wilderness story to drive his point through the wax in their hearts:

> Suppose one of you has a hundred sheep and loses one of them. Does he not leave the ninety-nine in the open country and go after the lost sheep until he finds it? And when he finds it, he joyfully puts it on his shoulders and goes home. Then he calls his friends and neighbors together and says, "Rejoice with me; I have found my lost sheep. I tell you that in the same way there will be more rejoicing in heaven over one sinner who repents than over ninety-nine righteous persons who do not need to repent." (Luke 15:4-7)

There were probably some people listening who had grown up helping their fathers tend sheep. They would have understood the point immediately. A lost sheep is completely helpless. And when it is finally found, this is only by the work and grace of the shepherd who came searching for it. On wilderness trips, kids get "lost" in many ways (but hopefully never physically lost). What I mean is this: Many who haven't grown up spending time in the outdoors are lost from the moment they reach the trailhead to go on your trip. Everything is new. "What do I wear?" "What do I eat?" "How are we going to get across that river?" At every turn we have opportunities to love and extend grace to people who are out of their comfort zones and feeling lost.

After a few days of this, we can connect the dots for people and help them see how the various ways we feel "lost" or scared can help us understand our true state of being without Christ. Without him we are like a lost sheep: alone, afraid, and walking in circles. The good news is that he has come looking for us and, if we are willing, we can walk out of the Valley of Shadow of Death once and for all, and cross over from death to life into his loving arms for eternity. This un-merited grace is almost irresistible when fully grasped.

References: Psalm 45:2; Proverbs 1:9, 3:22, 3:34, 4:9; Isaiah 26:10; Jonah 2:8; Zechariah 12:10; Luke 2:40; John 1:14-17; Acts 4:33, 6:8, 11:23, 13:43, 14:3, 14:26, 15:11, 15:40, 18:27, 20:24, 20:32; Romans 1:5-7, 3:24, 4:16, 5:2, 5:15-21, 6:1, 6:14-15, 11:5-6, 12:3-6, 15:15, 16:20; 1 Corinthians 1:3-4, 3:10, 15:10, 16:23; 2 Corinthians 1:2, 1:12, 4:15, 6:1, 8:1, 8:6-9, 9:8, 9:14, 12:9, 13:14; Galatians 1:3-6, 1:15, 2:9, 2:21, 3:18, 5:4, 6:18; Ephesians 1:2, 1:6-7, 2:5-8, 3:2, 3:7-8, 4:7, 6:24; Philippians 1:2, 1:7; Colossians 1:2, 1:6, 4:6, 4:18; 1 Thessalonians 1:1; 5:28; 2 Thessalonians 1:2, 1:12, 2:16, 3:18; 1 Timothy 1:2, 1:12-14, 6:21; 2 Timothy 1:2, 1:9, 2:1, 4:22; Titus 1:4, 2:11, 3:7, 3:15; Philemon 1:3, 1:25; Hebrews 2:9, 4:16, 10:29, 12:15, 13:9, 13:25; James 4:6; 1 Peter 1:2, 1:10-13, 4:10, 5:5, 5:10-12; 2 Peter 1:2, 3:18; 2 John 1:3; Jude 1:4; Revelation 1:5, 22:21

View

Views give us new perspectives. When you look at the moon through a telescope, you get to see its wrinkles and craters. Yet when you gaze at it with the naked eye you can only see a milky-white ball sur-rounded by a sheet of black sky. The telescope gives a new and better perspective of this stellar natural satellite, which orbits the earth and reflects the light of the sun upon us. Jesus frequently opened up a new perspective or view for his followers through physical and emotional challenge in the wilderness. Wilderness experiences are like a telescope lens to help us see life in a completely new light.

For example, one day Jesus came to Simon Peter after he had been fishing all night to no avail. Having relied on his skill and his ingenuity to bring in a catch of fish for his family, he was totally exhausted and felt like a failure. Then Jesus gets in his boat and asks him to push out one more time. Peter reluctantly concurs and, to his amazement, catches one of the largest schools of fish he had ever seen! Jesus pushed him beyond his physical and emotional breaking point. His learning was heightened because he was not relying on his own skill and ingenuity anymore. And the result we read about in Luke 5 is that Peter was transformed into a *fisher of men* from that day onward. His perspective shifted 180 degrees. The fatigue, the failure, and the wilderness of the sea were the instruments Jesus used to change the trajectory of Peter's whole life!

In what ways do you rely on your own skill and ingenuity to get things done? Have there been any times the past few days on this trip when you felt like you got to a point where you pushed "auto pilot" because your strength ran out? Do you see this as a way that God might be changing your *perspective* on something? How might your self-confidence or "street smarts" be causing you to miss out on a great catch of fish God might have for you? Are you using your gifts and talents to drop the nets where Jesus is telling you to go, or are you just doing life in your own strength? How will you know the difference between going out in your "boat" alone and having Jesus in your boat? Jesus gave us ingenuity not just for personal gain, but for his glory. And if we resist him on this, he'll probably allow us to hit a wall of fatigue to change our view like he did with Peter.

References: Numbers 23:9, 33:3; Deuteronomy 32:49; Nehemiah 9:38; Psalm 48:13, 68:24; Proverbs 1:17, 5:21, 17:24; Isaiah 33:17; Mark 2:12; Romans 12:1; 1 Corinthians 9:8; 2 Corinthians 5:10; Galatians 5:10; Philippians 3:15; 2 Timothy 4:1; Revelation 13:13

Witnessing

At the end of a long day of hiking it was brought to my attention that the person who was carrying the meal for our dinner had accidentally left it on the ground behind the van back at the trailhead five days ago. Going back to get it was obviously not an option. Thankfully our campsite was near a small mountain stream. One of my little survival tricks of the trade is to keep a wad of fishing line and a dry fly in my bag. Here was my opportunity. I went down to the stream and caught a handful of brook trout in about thirty minutes. A little olive oil poured over a salad made of wild Blue Bell flowers along with the fish made for a welcome meal to our famished group.

Fishing provided a myriad of teachable moments for Jesus. While you are journeying along with your group, take time to stop by a pond or stream and tell a few fishing stories—people love 'em! Then after telling some tall tales, give the group some time to go off alone for some time with Christ to consider *whom they are fishing for back at home.* Jesus changed Peter's identity from a fisher of fish to a "fisher of men." What does your spiritual bait look like to the world? Do your friends think of Christ when they're around you? Who in your arena of influence does not know Jesus yet? Ask the Lord to give you a heart to lovingly pursue someone with the gospel so they might be caught in the net of God's grace. If you are a follower of Christ, then you were "caught" at some point in your life. If I'm not catching any people with the gospel, then I need to ask Jesus to help me understand why. Maybe my heart needs a change. Maybe I need to apprentice a master fisher of men to see how their lifestyle of evangelism leads them to successful disciple-making. The more introducing people to Jesus becomes a normal part of your life, the more you'll understand the bumper sticker that says, "I'd rather be fishing."

References: *Psalm 89:37; Proverbs 6:19, 12:17, 14:5, 14:25, 19:5, 19:9, 19:28, 21:28; Isaiah 19:20; Mark 1:17; Luke 5:1-11; John 1:7-8, 8:13, 8:18; Acts 1:22, 22:15, 26:16; Romans 1:9, 2:15; 2 Corinthians 1:23; 1 Thessalonians 2:5; 1 Peter 5:1; Revelation 1:5, 2:13, 3:14*

Xerophyte

Desert plants are called *xerophytes.* I have a degree in landscape architecture from the University of Arizona, which is in the middle of the Sonora Desert. Working at the university's desert seed bank was one of the ways I paid for my daily burritos in the dorms. You can learn a lot from plants by collecting their seeds—at least that is what I used to tell myself as I sat categorizing them and wondering what I was doing with my life. Desert plants are absolutely fascinating.

When you are out in 120-degree heat and you see *anything* living on the ground, it is truly amazing. Xerophytes have three basic survival mechanisms to help them survive in hot, dry climates. Each of these tactics profoundly relates to our spiritual journey.

Some plants like cacti and desert pine trees *limit water loss* by their design. Other plants like succulents are designed to *store water*, and a third type has really *deep roots* to tap into water deep within the desert soil. Acacia trees function this way. The Ark of the Covenant, its carrying poles, and the frame of the Tabernacle were all made of acacia wood.

Considering the starkness of the desert and the plants that are somehow able to survive here causes me to pause and ask a similar question of myself: What spiritual strategies do I live by to survive and thrive in the dry spiritual environment of the world? Maybe you grew up in an unbearable family situation. Maybe you work in a depressing or carnal work environment. *All of us in some way have something to learn about how to flourish in the midst of climate conditions we can't control.* How can we adapt spiritually to blossom and influence our environment rather than be dried up like a raisin from the scorching heat of the worldly influences around us? Maybe we can take a page out of the playbook of these really amazing desert plants.

First, are there ways you can "limit your water loss"? Jesus is our Living Water (see John 4:10). What are some routines or patterns you can set up in your life to abide in him so you don't drift or pull away from the Vine that feeds you spiritually (see John 15:1)? Or secondly, maybe we could do a better job of "storing water." Maybe it's time to prioritize memorizing Scripture so that it is written on our hearts and accessible to our minds when we face temptation or trials (see Joshua 1:8). Or third, maybe we need to pray for deeper roots to our spiritual lives. Are you shallow because you rarely spend time in solitude with God? All of the busyness and noise of our culture doesn't help us go deeper; it keeps us shallow. Maybe we need to seek ways to be more like the acacia tree and develop spiritual disciplines that help our roots grow deeper. Shallow roots don't help when droughts come along, that's for sure.

References: Exodus 25; 2 Corinthians 5:17; John 4:10; John 15:1; Joshua 1:8

Yoke

A yoke is a wooden frame that goes across the backs of two animals to attach them together so they can pull a plow in a straight line or pull a cart while sharing the load of the weight. Carrying a backpack in the wilderness or pulling the weight of our gear in a sea kayak can be a burden on our body. Yet God has created us to work. Work is good, not bad. But what is bad is when we work and carry a burden that is too heavy to bear. God is not against effort, but he does not want us to be weighed down unnecessarily. James 1:2-4 asserts: "Consider it all joy, my brethren, when you encounter various trials, knowing that the testing of your faith produces endurance. And let endurance have its perfect result, so that you may be perfect and complete, lacking in nothing." In fact, even Jesus in his fully human frame learned obedience through suffering: "In the days of his flesh, he offered up both prayers and supplications with loud crying and tears to the One able to save him from death, and he was heard because of his piety. Although he was a Son, he learned obedience from the things which he suffered" (Hebrews 5:7-8).

As we experience hard work and struggle this week along the journey, we can be thankful for the opportunity to work hard and trust that the Lord is expanding our faith. This attitude gives us spiritual resilience. We can also remind and encourage each other that, although we may have to strain at the oar or keep putting one foot in front of another as we climb a peak, we can rest assured Jesus offers us help in those moments. "Take my yoke upon you and learn from me, for I am gentle and humble in heart, and YOU WILL FIND REST FOR YOUR SOULS. For my yoke is easy and my burden is light" (Matthew 11:29-30, emphasis mine).

Like oxen in a yoke, if one of the animals tries to walk ahead of the other, it is going to carry the primary burden and get worn out. Jesus calls us to walk shoulder to shoulder with him—in step with his pace. Are you worn out from trying to carry a big burden in your own strength? Ask the Lord to reveal if you have been trying to walk ahead of him in an area of your life. This may be causing you to grow weary. Decide today to cast your burden on him and see how he will bring rest to your soul and new joys to the journey when you humbly submit yourself to his pace.

References: Jeremiah 27:2, 28:2,10,13; Isaiah 9:4, 10:27, 58:6; 1 Kings 12:4,9,10; 2 Chronicles 10:4; 2 Chronicles 10:9,10; Matthew 11:29, Luke 14:19, Lamentations 1:14, 3:27; Numbers 19:2, Acts 15:10, Nahum 1:13, Matthew 11:30; Deuteronomy 21:3, 1 Timothy 6:1

Zeal

Enthusiasm is contagious. The more we aim the frontiers of our life toward glorifying God, the more enthusiastic we become toward his concerns and mission in our world. It is one thing to be enthusiastic, but it is wholly another thing to be enthusiastic about things that matter. A person can be enthusiastic or zealous about all the wrong things and become a menace to society. By recognizing how sinful and prideful we are if left to our own accord, we can avoid this trap. Jesus humbled the disciples through countless out-of-comfort-zone experiences to teach them they must become less and he must become more in their lives. The world needs followers of Christ who are extravagantly zealous for the Great Commission.

Write down a few things you are generally enthusiastic about. What really ignites your passion or makes you talkative when a certain subject comes up? Christ shed his blood for us not so that we would just be zealous, but so we would become enthusiastic about his mission to seek and save the lost. Are we enthusiastic and passionate about the things that ignited Jesus? Often Jesus retreated with his disciples into the wilderness to re-orient their passions toward advancing the Kingdom, rather than advancing themselves. The disciples asked, "Who will be greatest in the Kingdom?" His answer was that he who became least would become the greatest. In the furnace of solitude this week out in the wilderness, ask the Lord to work on your soul like a potter would with a clay pot. Ask him to shape you into a noble vessel with desires, passions, enthusiasm, and zeal for his mission in the world:

> Remember, our message is not about ourselves...All we are is messengers, errand runners from Jesus for you. It started when God said, "Light up the darkness!" and our lives filled up with light as we saw and understood God in the face of Christ, all bright and beautiful. If you only look at us, you might well miss the brightness. We carry this precious message around in the unadorned clay pots of our ordinary lives. That's to prevent anyone from confusing God's incomparable power with us. (2 Corinthians 4:5-7, *The Message*)

References: Numbers 25:11; Deuteronomy 29:20; 2 Samuel 21:2; 2 Kings 10:16, 19:31; Psalm 69:9, 119:139; Proverbs 19:2; Isaiah 9:7, 26:11, 37:32, 42:13, 59:17, 63:15; Ezekiel 5:13, 36:5, 38:19; John 2:17; Romans 10:2, 12:11; Philippians 3:6

CHAPTER 13
IMPLEMENT

Facilitation is a learned art. Implementing your desired outcomes and objectives requires thinking about how you will facilitate the learning process. It's one thing to recognize a teachable moment when it occurs, and it's another thing to make it easy for people to grasp the meaning and pertinence to their own lives. Facilitation is really a big word that simply means to help or assist others in learning.

The opposite of facilitation is to impede learning. Jesus removed impediments to learning. He did this by helping people grasp the meaning through using familiar analogies in nature as a reference point for learning. Jesus also removed obstructions to learning by speaking in the vernacular language of his region. His intolerance to everything that could hinder understanding caused him to creatively draw upon numerous figures of speech to evoke response and action from his followers. A plethora of literature is available regarding Jesus' verbal genius. We will only briefly illustrate some of the main techniques he used. As you think about leading groups on spiritual journeys in the outdoors, consider how you might use these various vocal tools in the way you ask questions, lead discussions, or initiate dialogue. If you have a hard time knowing how to motivate your group to learn, Jesus provides a tool belt that will make the most average of teachers downright effective. Just imitate what he did.

The method of Jesus' teaching in the wilderness took a diversity of forms. For example, there were proverbs, metaphors, riddles, paradoxes, ironies, and questions. There were symbolic analogies, overstatements, puns, and poetry. The variety of his expeditionary and verbal teaching techniques is mind-boggling. This chapter will analyze how he motivated his followers to learn through literary devices and figurative actions.

The Contours of Jesus' Teaching

Forming a mission community was Jesus' strategy to penetrate the world. The essence of his message is in the inaugural messages he preached at the beginning of his ministry. The gospel evangelists agree that Jesus' original message was: "The time has come...The kingdom of God is near. Repent and believe the Good News" (Mark 1:15; parallel passages: Matt. 4:17, Luke 4:16-21, John 1:12-13). How he communicated that simple message is a different story. He is the one who created people with different learning styles, and when we observe Jesus in action we see him brilliantly employing a vast array of strategies to engage every possible type of learning style he created. Yet even with such variety it is not rocket science to learn to teach more like Jesus. His teaching methodology really was quite simple. So far in this book we have put considerably more emphasis on the *setting* in which Jesus taught. Now we will focus on the *style* of how he taught, by identifying some key elements of his pedagogy.

Robert Stein analyzes Jesus' style of teaching in, *The Method and Message of Jesus' Teachings*. Ironically, without the crutch of modern day audiovisual materials Jesus was able to capture the attention his audience better than any contemporary tools we have at our disposal. Rather than taking a broad view of Jesus' impact on people, Stein breaks apart his teaching and analyzes it to show his unmatched creative and verbal genius. In chapter 2, we discussed the parables, which were Jesus' most common form of teaching. But that's just scratching the surface. The rest of this chapter will show a huge variety of other teaching forms. In fact Jesus' teaching style was so intriguing to people that at one point, "The crowds simply forgot about their need for food because of their fascination and interest in [his] teaching."[163]

Overstatements Peel the Onion

Imagine Jesus making this startling statement: "If anyone comes to Me, and does not hate his own father and mother and wife and children and brothers and sisters, yes, and even his own life, he cannot be My disciple" (Luke 14:26). Why such a heart-wrenching statement to force people to evaluate their loyalties? Couldn't he have said it in a more palatable way? Saying it more politically correct could have sounded something like this: "Even natural affection for one's family shouldn't take precedence over loyalty to me." Would his audience have had the same gulp in their throats and grasped the gravity of what Jesus was saying had he chosen a more culturally sensitive way to say this? Apparently Jesus liked to use *overstatements* as a spiritual paring knife to expose the soul's true essence—like peeling off the outer shell of an onion to get to its pungent core.

In a culture where family is just about everything, where community and collectivism is on the top shelf, could Jesus really be saying that I have to be willing to turn away from my family—my safety net? That seems too vulnerable; do I really want to be that exposed? "Can't I just embrace your teaching, Jesus, and not rock the boat in my family by proclaiming you are the Messiah when they don't believe you are?" In Mark 9:43-47, Jesus issues another startling overstatement:

> If your hand causes you to stumble, cut it off; it is better for you to enter life crippled, than, having your two hands, to go into hell, into the unquenchable fire...If your foot causes you to stumble, cut it off; it is better for you to enter life lame, than, having your two feet, to be cast into hell...If your eye causes you to stumble, throw it out; it is better for you to enter the kingdom of God with one eye, than, having two eyes, to be cast into hell.

Couldn't he have just said, "There is no enjoyment of sin in this life that is worth perishing for eternity," and left out the gory details? Instead, he jolts the audience with pictures of cut-off feet and hands and eyeballs being torn out. This was not some sort of Halloween commercial. This was life or death and Jesus wasn't messing around with people's souls. What was the point? Tear out anything in your life that causes you to sin and keeps you from glorifying God. When it comes to spiritual reality, even Jesus' overstatements are *under-statements*. We couldn't handle seeing what he saw regarding the full effects of our sin and the eternal consequences of mankind's disbelief. That's probably one of the reasons why he used overstatements—to crack that window open for a little shock and awe effect.

Exaggeration Confronts Hollow Hypocrisy

In hyperbole, the illustration is so grossly exaggerated that the audience knows it is impossible to fulfill. For example, to "swallow a camel" (Matthew 23:23-24; also note: Matthew 5:29-30 and 5:38-42), or to "first take the log out of your own eye" (Matthew 7:3-5) would be impossible. Often at the end of a hard day of hiking, I've heard kids say, "I'm so hungry I could eat a horse." That's a hyperbole and a great opportunity for a timely trail talk. Just take the opportunity to respond: "Jesus also had strong feelings. Sometimes he exaggerated just like us to make a point when he observed hypocrisy and hardness of heart in people." And then share a few examples and ask them what point he might have been trying to make when he was exaggerating. Young people can relate well with hyperbole because exaggeration is a normal aspect of adolescent development. It's actually quite fun and has its place. Adolescents are especially skilled at hailing hollow hypocrisy, so let's give them a redemptive way to practice it through constructive criticism.

Metaphors Pierce the Heart

Jesus used metaphors all the time. He used analogies to provide vivid illustrations *familiar* to people. He used common household terms like: yeast (see Mark 8:15), salt (see Matthew 5:13; Mark 9:49), light (see Matthew 5:14-16), harvest (see Matthew 9:37-38), snakes (see Matthew 23:33; Matthew 12:34), and foxes (see Luke 13:31-32). One of the most vivid ways I've used metaphors in the wilderness is during an ascent to a summit at night. One moonlit evening in June, my wife, Becky, and I awoke our group of eager high school students to ascend Pyramid Peak in the Weminuche Valley of Colorado. If we started right away, we could reach the peak by sunrise (which is an unparalleled experience in the backcountry). As we hiked, each person had to use their headlamp to cast light on the path to avoid tripping over the rocks. Halfway into the ascent, we stopped and shared Psalm 119:105: "Your word is a lamp to my feet and a light for my path." Several folks were able to draw metaphors from the psalm relating to the experience of walking in the dark. One of them had a serendipitous realization that God desired him to trust and follow him as his Guide—the One who can offer light to his path every day. He remarked that it seems God gives us just enough light to keep us from stumbling, but rarely enough light to see too far ahead. He articulated in his own words the exact picture David paints in this psalm. The "lamp" David would have been referring to was a small oil lamp that could only cast a small ray of light—just enough to keep from stumbling. I love it when people discover truth for themselves like this.

We continued climbing four hours toward the peak. Hiking more efficiently than expected, we reached just below the summit too early: it was still pitch black! The stars were bright and beautiful, but the wind was so cold that we could not stop for long before the sweat on our bodies would chill us—causing hypothermia. The group wanted to wait to see the sunrise, so we clamored down some rocks and tucked ourselves under the cleft of a boulder. We pulled out the emergency sleeping bag and boiled a pot of hot chocolate. Pressing together tightly kept us sheltered from the wind. Hot chocolate was passed around in a water bottle for each to hold for a few seconds, enjoy a sip, and then share with the next person. We managed to stay warm enough; singing, praying, and telling stories, until the sun finally came up. And oh, was it worth it!

This experience of waiting for the sun to rise in the midst of the cold reminded us of the conversation Jesus had with Peter and the disciples as he comforted them before departing to be with the Father. Jesus said:

> Do not let your hearts be troubled. Trust in God, trust also in me. In my Father's house are many rooms; if it were not so, I would have told you. I am going there to prepare a place for you. And if I go and prepare a place for you, I will come back and take you to be with me that you also may be where I am. You know the way to the place where I am going. (John 14:1-4)

In a metaphorical way, our peak experience was worth every bit of the endurance required to experience the stunning sunrise atop the peak. We too will experience trials of many kinds in life, but we need not be troubled. Whatever trials or suffering we endure is worth it because one day we will meet Jesus (the Bright Morning Star) face to face:

> Behold, I am coming soon! My reward is with me, and I will give to everyone according to what he has done. I am the Alpha and the Omega, the First and the Last, the Beginning and the End...I, Jesus, have sent my angel to give you this testimony for the churches. I am the Root and the Offspring of David, and the bright Morning Star. (Revelation 22:12-14,16)

Watching that bright morning star (the sun of our solar system) rise atop Pyramid Peak that morning, as stunning as it was, pales in comparison to seeing Jesus, the *Bright Morning Star,* who will appear at the end of the age. What a sight that will be!

Similes' "Aha!" Power

Simile is one of the simplest forms of teaching Jesus used. A simile compares two things that are unlike each other, but are connected by the word "like," "as," or "than," or by a verb such as "seems." Stein cites several examples:

> Believers are likened to sheep and told to be like serpents in wisdom and like doves in their blamelessness whereas unbelievers are likened to wolves (Matthew 12:40); Jesus' resurrection is likened to Jonah's stay in the belly of a sea monster (Luke 17:6); the believer's faith is likened to a seed (Luke 13:34); Jesus' desire to gather the people of Jerusalem to himself is likened to a mother hen gathering her chicks to herself (Matthew 23:27); and the stately appearance of the Pharisees with their inner spiritual corruption is likened to tombs that outwardly are impressive but inwardly contain corruption (Matthew 23:27-28)![164]

Here is an example of how I have used similes in the wilderness. Often on the last day of the trip before we re-enter civilization, we stop at a stream and make a "mountain sauna" to clean up before we return. It is amazing how dirty a group of people can get in just a few days. And the odors are unforgettable. A sauna consists of a rain fly with rocks around the edges to create a seal. Then you dig a hole in the ground in the middle where we put hot rocks from a fire burning several yards away.

Once everyone is seated under the rain fly, someone whacks the hot rocks from the fire with wet pine branches dipped in water to create a steamy, pine-smelling sauna. There is nothing quite like this experience. The hot steam opens the pores of the skin, and the sweat removes the dirt exquisitely. One can top off the experience by running out of the sauna and lunging into a cold stream to wash off the dirt. After slipping on fresh clothes, one truly feels cleansed. This is another teachable moment to illustrate how good it is to be washed of our sins. John writes, "If we confess our sins, he is faithful and just to forgive us our sins, and cleanse us from all unrighteousness" (1 John 1:9). After sharing this verse with the group, we might ask the question, "If we are honest, do we believe we all get this dirty back at home—carrying a similar odor of sin that carries such a nasty stench at times?" Confession is the route to cleansing.

The leader might reflect further and give the group an opportunity to think about whether they believe this is an appropriate analogy of sin, and whether they think their sin is a daily offense that needs to be washed away. This could lead into a solo hike where everyone is spaced apart to provide time to confess their sins to Christ. This learning event could end with a time of corporate confession or thanking God for the gift of forgiveness we have in Christ. Body odor, a sauna, and the refreshing feeling of being cleansed in a mountain stream are wonderful similes to describe the reality of un-confessed sin, and the joy of forgiveness.

Pithy Proverbs Leave a Permanent Mark

Proverbs are best understood as pithy sayings that contain a memorable statement giving moral or ethical advice (cf. Matthew 6:22, 24; 7:12; Luke 16:10). They are the good kind of graffiti that leaves a permanent mark on our brain. According to Charles Carlston and his commentary on Blaise Pascal's understanding of the use of proverbs:

> The whole point of proverbial wisdom is the communication of the generally accepted, the universal, the tried and true, not the striking or innovative...The challenge of a proverb (if any) thus lies in the realm of action, not thought..."All the good maxims are already current; what we need is to apply them."[165]

At times proverbs are paradoxical (cf. Mark 4:25, 10:43; Luke 14:11), but in general they are short and to the point. Some of Jesus' proverbs relate to the following topics: 1) A person's heart is where their treasure is (see Matthew 6:21); 2) Don't worry about tomorrow (see Matthew 6:34); 3) If you pick up the sword, you will perish by it, i.e., the spiritual battle is not one of flesh and blood (see Matthew 26:52); 4) A kingdom divided against itself cannot stand (see Mark 3:24); 5) Prophets are given little credibility among their closest friends or family (see Mark 6:4); and 6) The mark of the disciple is not in how one starts the journey, but by how he continues and finishes the journey, i.e., if you put your hand to the plow, don't turn back (see Luke 9:62).

Traveling along the trail in the wilderness affords many opportunities to share relevant proverbial sayings. There are proverbs that come from Scripture, as well as proverbs in the form of quotes or sayings that represent reality. Contemporary proverbs can come from songs a person listens to or quotes from famous people they know. Here are a few examples of proverbial sayings relevant to the outdoors:

The mountain is not meant to teach us anything, it is meant to make us something.[166]

While God's glory is written all over his work, in the wilderness the letters are capitalized.[167]

Any error about creation also leads to an error about God.[168]

Secular proverbs are also good door openers for conversation, especially with searching young people):

> There are five basic human needs present in survival. They are water, food, heat, shelter, and spiritual needs. Subtract any two of these and the result is likely to be fatal.[169]

> The roots of education are bitter, but the fruits are sweet.[170]

> Make wisdom your provision for the journey from youth to old age; for it is a more certain support than all other possessions.[171]

> Practice makes perfect.[172]

> One doesn't become [a champion] without sweat.[173]

> To conquer anger is to triumph over one's worst enemy.[174]

> The consequences of anger and vexation are often more grievous than their causes.[175]

> In a stormy night it is good to let out two anchors from a speedy ship.[176]

> Debt reduces the free man to bitter slavery.[177]

> A good reputation is safer than money.[178]

> You can buy no better thing than a staunch friend. (This proverb is a good question for young people in terms of considering what makes a good friend.)[179]

> It is better to grant favors to another than to enjoy the favors of others. (This is a good proverb to spark discussion about the nature of service and generosity.)[180]

Paradox Reconciles Seeming Opposites

In paradox, we observe Jesus saying things that appear contradictory but really aren't. Often Jesus' paradoxical statements were perceived as contradictions because the audience had a false understanding of the principles of the Kingdom of God. For example, Mark 9:35 reads as a paradox: "Whoever wants to be first shall be last." Today we are challenged to consider a similarly remarkable paradox: How are we justified in holding back service from some people (i.e., our lack of mission-commitment to unreached people)—who are the very people whom Jesus served through his death on the cross? This is precisely the reason why we assert the need for thoughtful dialogue regarding how to raise up more cross-cultural missionaries. By ignoring this need we are sitting in the middle of a paradox.

Other selected examples of paradoxes include: The greatest versus the least in the Kingdom of God (see Mark 10:43), the Pharisees who looked good on the outside but were like tombs on the inside (see Matthew 23:27-28), and the widow's mite (see Mark 12:41-44). Pertaining to the widow, Stein remarks:

> Despite the apparent contradiction, the gift of a penny was greater in God's sight than the much larger sums contributed by the rich, and the beautiful veneer of dress and outward piety of the Pharisees and scribes, who were the religious leaders of Israel, was at variance with the inner corruption and spiritual poverty.[181]

Jesus' life itself was a paradox: The King of Israel lived the life of a servant (see Mark 10:14,31,45).

Rock climbing has been a powerful tool to help people learn about God, themselves, and the spiritual life. It effectively illustrates the use of metaphor and paradox. Climbing the rock is like the journey of life. From the base of a rock face, looking up it appears impossible to climb. But with the appropriate equipment and a competent belayer, the climber is assured she can make it. The analogy is simple: The belayer is like God, the rope is like Jesus Christ, and our decision to hook into the rope with a carabiner is analogous to our decision to surrender our lives to Christ, trusting him completely. If a person were to try to climb a difficult pitch without a rope (like journeying through life without a relation-ship with Jesus), then he would most assuredly fall to his death. But if he clips into the rope (makes a decision to trust and believe in Jesus Christ) he is safe to climb—the belayer (God) promises to hold him and get him to the top of the rock (i.e., eternal security).

Yet reaching the top of a rock does not happen without one's own effort. The Heavenly Father enables us, anchors us, and encourages us, but he also desires our best effort: There is an inseparable relationship between work and trust for the climber. In a paradoxical way, we are *safe to risk* with God. Rock climbing models the tension of man's responsibility and God's sovereignty in an experiential and memorable way. Robert Coleman agrees: "In the spiritual dimension of reality, we must believe in order to see. Those who do not trust Christ cannot possibly understand his claims; they are blind. This is the great tragedy of sin."[182]

A Fortiori Appeals to Common Sense

A fortiori is a statement intended to elicit natural agreement among the audience. Essentially, it is an argument from common sense. For example, in the midst of the Sermon on the Mount, Jesus uses this line of reasoning: "Which of you, if his son asks for bread, will give him a stone? Or if he asks for a fish, will give him a snake? If you, then, though you are evil, know how to give good gifts to your children, how much more will your Father in heaven give good gifts to those who ask him!" (Matthew 7:9).

In the Sermon on the Mount, Jesus undoubtedly drew many illustrations from the surrounding hills and meadows. Matthew records Jesus arguing *a fortiori* against the backdrop of the wilderness: "And why do you worry about clothes? See how the lilies of the field grow. They do not labor or spin. Yet I tell you not even Solomon in all his splendor was dressed like one of these. If that is how God clothes the grass of the field, which is here today and tomorrow is thrown into the fire, will he not much more clothe you, O you of little faith?" (Matthew 6:28-30).

Sending out the twelve apostles, Jesus used a similar line of reasoning to prepare them for the sting of rejection and persecution that they would inevitably face. Referring to the religious leaders who would surely try to hand these young men over to the local councils (see Matthew 10:17), Jesus reminded them of how he had already been treated by these same men: "A student is not above his teacher, nor a servant above his master. It is enough for the student to be like his teacher, and the servant like his master. If the head of the house has been called Beelzebub, how much more the members of his household!" (Matthew 6:28-30). Stein sheds further light on this leadership principle *a fortiori*: "If Jesus' authority and influence were not enough to protect him from persecution, how much more will his followers who have less authority and influence be persecuted?"[183]

In the paired parables of the Tower Builder and the Warring King (see Luke 14:28-33) we see an *a fortiori* statement intended to elicit natural agreement among the audience to make a piercing rebuke more palatable. Michael Knowles comments: "The question 'Who among you?' is intended to elicit agreement from the hearer *a fortiori*—that is, given the logical necessity of the anticipated response, how much more, by implication, must the legal or spiritual corollary apply."[184] Regarding the first parable of the Tower Builder, the audience agrees: "Don't advance unless there are sufficient resources." The audience also agrees *a fortiori* with a second statement in the Parable of the Warring King: "Don't go to war unless you know you can win." Again, we would all agree to this wisdom. Yet, following this line of agreement, *Jesus has set us up for a potent rebuke, all the while nodding our heads in agreement.* Consider his two penetrating follow-up questions: 1) Can you afford to follow me?; and 2) Can you afford *not* to follow me? Thus, the surprise of Jesus' statement is this: *Either following him, or refusing to follow him, costs one's whole life!* Brilliant!

Jesus expects his disciples to renounce all and follow him. The issue facing his hearers (and Luke's readers) is not one of risk management. Rather, losing all appears to be *unavoidable* in any case: "The only question is whether one will lose all as a follower of Jesus and for the sake of God's reign, or as one who refuses to follow and obey."[185] There is no risk management plan that limits a person's exposure for exercising faith in Christ. Following him or not following him costs us our lives.

Irony Exposes Motives

Irony is another powerful figure of speech Jesus employed. According to Stein, "irony is the subtle use of contrast between what is actually stated and what is more or less wryly suggested...In this narrow sense, a statement or expression is ironic when its intended meaning is the opposite of the literal meaning of the statement."[186] For example, "The Pharisees and the Sadducees, although religious, are able to interpret the physical signs and predict their implications but are unable to see God's signs in the ministry of Jesus and interpret their significance (Matthew 16:2-3; Luke 12:16-20)."[187] Crafting an ironic statement relevant to young people requires *observing what they value*. For example, let's look at the amount of energy they are willing to expend on the things they love. This shows the irony of what they value in the world compared to an investment of the same passion, time, and energy into efforts of eternal significance.

For example, we might spark a dialogue with young people to help them consider how much time they spend playing Xbox, PlayStation, or Nintendo. Ever since Atari's game "Pong" came out, video games have been increasingly captivating to young people. They are enticed by the adventure and the chance to win against a formidable enemy who is seeking to defeat them. It is ironic that people will spend hours learning how to play a video game in order to conquer an imaginary enemy, yet they lack the desire or discipline to spend even five minutes a day in focused prayer, which is the doorway into the realm of the spirit where the *real battle* rages on. That is very ironic.

I think J.R.R. Tolkien wrote a book series about this irony. It's a story that involves hobbits, elves, orcs, and wizards, but the message is the same. The result was that *some* of the hobbits stopped playing "games" in the shire and got involved in the real battle that threatened all of middle earth. In that fight, the stakes are not imaginary but real—so it is in the spiritual realm.

Does this frivolity relate across cultures or is this just a developed world phenomena? In my view, although young people in the developing world may not struggle as much with video games or other technological distractions, there are still preoccupations with jacks, board games, marbles, soccer, and addictive fascinations with gangs and youth militias. Because we are all cut out of the same sinful seed of Adam, we will all find ourselves in the middle of this irony at times. Amusement is not bad, but if we make all of life out to be entertainment with none of our own skin in the real contest for people's souls, then we are missing out on what it means to carry our cross.

The battle in the spiritual realm is real, the stakes are high—it is not a frivolous game. The powers of darkness seek to defeat and distract us from experiencing abundant life in Christ. If this irony was presented to a group in a compelling non-judgmental way, they might catch on to the real and exciting adventure that awaits them in following Jesus Christ. Jesus invites us to an exciting and courageous journey—much more compelling than the computer-generated adventures available through an Xbox, or the disparaging identity gained from giving one's strength and creativity to a violent gang.

I've observed that when young people retreat for several days in the wilderness, they enjoy a taste of real life, and the distractions of the world lose their grip. They often discover irony in their lives, i.e., what they actually value compared to that which has eternal significance. It is important to follow up with them after a wilderness experience, so they continue to see the futility of the games the world has to offer, compared to the riches we have in Christ: "Praise be to the God and Father of our Lord Jesus Christ, who has blessed us in the heavenly realms with every spiritual blessing in Christ" (Eph. 1:3).

Jesus' Parable of the Persistent Neighbor (see Luke 11:33) provides a cogent example of how he used irony to uncover an accurate understanding of God's character. Kenneth Bailey comments:

> When you go to this kind of neighbor, everything is against you. It is night. He is asleep in bed. The door is locked. His children are asleep. He does not like you and yet you will receive even more than you ask. This is because your neighbor is a man of integrity and he will not violate that quality. The God to who you pray also has an integrity that he will not violate; and beyond this, he loves you.[188]

Herman Waetjen adds:

> Since the sleeper is not motivated on the basis of friendship, the petitioner is confronted with the dishonor of being unable to offer hospitality to his midnight guest. In fact, his dishonor may be compounded in the eyes of his visitor by his neighbor's refusal to observe the reciprocity of village friendship. His only recourse is to resort to conduct that will succeed in acquiring the bread he needs to offer hospitality to his unexpected visitor. The irony is that he must become shameless in order to save his honor.[189]

The irony is that, although shamelessness is regarded as dishonorable, one must become shameless in order to save his honor! This begs the question, "In what ways do we shamelessly petition in prayer or practical service toward others in order to save our honor in Christ?" Do we have integrity to shamelessly seek the Lord on behalf of others?

As we consider the implications of this ironic parable, we quickly discern its mission-application in terms of our responsibility as ambassadors of Jesus. First, we are called to prayerfully and boldly urge others to join us in missions to serve those in need. Secondly, if we are in the position of the "neighbor," we must not ignore the petitioner; otherwise we become dishonorable in the ways of the Kingdom. *If we avoid becoming shameless for the sake of the lost, then we become shameful in the ways of the Kingdom.* According to this parable, becoming shameless in prayer and service will help restore integrity in regard to our responsibility in the Great Commission.

Humor Causes Interpersonal Breakthroughs

Jesus also used humor to motivate his disciples. He joked about the logic of putting a lamp under a bowl (see Mark 4:21) and throwing pearls to swine (see Matthew 7:6). He told a tale regarding the foolishness of putting a new patch of cloth on an old garment (see Matthew 9:15-17). He often said tongue-in-cheek, "He who has ears let him hear" (see Matthew 11:15). If Jesus spoke this same message to young people today, we might hear him say: "Would it so dull your life, if for a minute you turned off your iPod or Wii and listened to your Maker whisper into your ear?"

Jesus' use of humor highlights how much we need clowns in the Body of Christ. Those gifted in humor have a unique role in ministry to help us remember that if we take ourselves too seriously we will likely experience personal turmoil and miss opportunities for spiritual breakthroughs. For example, Jesus used humor with precise timing when the disciples were at critical breakthrough moments. On the heels of the earth-shattering Mount of Transfiguration experience, an argument arose among the disciples about which one of them would be the greatest. Luke's account conveys how Jesus recognized this as a breakthrough moment and used humor to achieve his goal: "Jesus, knowing their thoughts, took a little child and had him stand beside him. Then he said to them, 'Whoever welcomes this little child in my name welcomes me; and whoever welcomes me welcomes the one who sent me. For he who is least among you all—he is the greatest'" (Luke 9:47-48).

Johan Hovelynck and Luk Peeters have seen this humor-principle at work regarding the role of humor in outdoor experiences with young people: "As far as timing is concerned, humor seems most beneficial when participants are close to a breakthrough."[190] Humor can bring a new perspective to tense situations like the disciples' embarrassing, "Who shall be the greatest," antic. Describing the phenomenon of uttering a joke into a petulant situation, they write: "In this respect, the irritated [person] and the joking [person] have similar concerns. Both are probing how safe it is to address more personal matters in the group."[191] They continue:

> Our exploration reveals some beneficial as well as unwanted aspects of humor in adventure education. First, we argued that humor may play a positive role in developing relationships that are conducive to learning about self and one's identity in relation to others. It tends to support the initial contact in the earlier stages of group development, in later stages provides a means to test the grounds for further disclosure and carefully explore more personal communication without becoming overly vulnerable, and represents a rather innocent form of coping with counter-dependency. Second, humor can contribute to the learning process itself as it may, one, facilitate a workable distance to more sensitive learning issues and, two, present new and unexpected perspectives that dislodge old, restrictive frames.[192]

Jesus presented new perspectives and dislodged restrictive frames particularly during the Sermon on the Mount. Here is one of Jesus' sayings, easily applied on a wilderness journey: "You are the light of the world. A city on a hill cannot be hidden. Neither do people light a lamp and put it under a bowl. Instead they put it on its stand, and it gives light to everyone in the house. In the same way, let your light shine before men, that they may see your good deeds and praise your Father in heaven" (Matthew 5:14-16).

One can imagine how humorous and unintelligent it would be to keep one's flashlight shining in a pocket while walking in the darkness down a rocky path. In the wilderness, the necessity of light is pronounced: Putting your flashlight in a pocket while stumbling down a dark path lacks common sense. An application of this humorous interlude might be: If we rarely shine and share Jesus in our arena of influence at home in our community or city, isn't this also as senseless as putting a flashlight in our pocket while trying to walk a narrow path in complete darkness? Have we been deceived to believe this is an acceptable pattern in our lives at home in the city? Jesus uses humor to reveal that this lacks basic common sense.

Confronting these types of well-worn paths of disobedience and deceit can be challenging for a leader because we struggle with them as well. For this reason, though, humor has at times a paramount role in speaking the obvious while keeping the audience's heart open through laughter. In my experience, if someone can laugh at something, they are more likely to accept it. In other words, "Humor provides a testing ground for more direct communication about emotionally laden issues."[193]

CHAPTER 14
INVOLVE

Variation and Participation

Another recognizable feature of Jesus' teaching style was the effort he took to *vary* teaching and motivate his listeners to *participate*. Jesus varied his teaching through presentations, discussions, lecture-style, and questioning sessions. He offered answers to questions from his audience and even submitted answers to questions that he knew were on people's hearts but *remained unspoken*. He used the element of surprise, told countless stories, demonstrated truth through object lessons, and quoted ancient and contemporary sources. He asserted maxims, offered challenges, rebuked, offered commentary on Scripture, told riddles, argued, and at times remained silent. The lesson we learn from all of this variety and effort Jesus expended to involve people in the learning process is that *people tend to learn better when they apply and do something with what they learn*. Robert Zuck provides a list of some of the ways Jesus initiated *participation* in order to promote learning. I've italicized the action verbs to highlight the *elements of participation and involvement* in Jesus' teaching approach:[194]

1. The disciples *climbed* in a boat while he taught (see Mark 3:9).

2. The disciples *baptized* converts (see John 4:2).

3. He *sent* the disciples to a nearby Samaritan village (not a town they were familiar with) to *buy* food (see John 4:8).

4. He told a demon-possessed man to *go tell* his family of his healing (see Mark 5:19).

5. He sent twelve groups in pairs to *exorcise* demons, *heal* the sick, *preach*, and *teach* (see Matthew 10:1-4; Mark 6:7-13; Luke 9:1-6) with detailed instructions (see Matthew 10:5-40).

6. He had the disciples *report* their ministry (see Mark 6:30; Luke 9:10) and then took them away for a *retreat* (see Mark 6:31-32; Luke 9:10).

7. He directed the disciples to *seat* five thousand people down in groups (Matthew 14:19-20).

8. He took Peter, James, and John with him to *climb* the Mount of Transfiguration (see Matthew 17:1).

9. He told Peter to catch a fish and *take a coin* out of its mouth (see Matthew 17:27).

10. He sent messengers into a Samaritan village to *prepare* accommodations (see Luke 9:52).

11. He *commissioned* seventy-two in groups of twos to go *heal* sick and *preach* (see Luke 10:1-17).

12. He sent two disciples to Bethpage to *get a colt* for him to ride (see Matthew 21:1-3).

13. He sent his disciples to *prepare* a Passover meal (see Matthew 26:17-19).

14. He commanded his disciples to *make disciples* of all nations (see Matthew 28:18-20).

15. He commanded Peter to *feed* his sheep (see John 21:15-17).

This is just a small sampling of the ways Jesus quickly moved people from listening to doing. Even the best of teachers know it's when you teach others something that you really begin to understand its inner workings intimately. *Jesus is the creator, founder, initiator, and originator of experiential learning.* And he wanted his disciples to go do the same. After washing their feet to teach them the paramount importance of getting their hands dirty as servants of the Kingdom, he said with timeless lucidity: "I have set you an example that you should do as I have done for you" (see John 13:15). The apostle John wrote down many examples of Jesus teaching this way, but even what he wrote down was just the tip of the iceberg. Hear the apostle John's enthusiastic exclamation point at the end of his account, which highlights that Jesus was constantly a *doer* of the Word: "Jesus did many other things as well. If every one of them were written down, I suppose that even the whole world would not have room for the books that would be written" (John 21:25).

The Art of Asking Questions

Evangelism and discipleship is simply *doing* the text of the Bible—putting into life and action the living words of God. Let's look at a few specific ways Jesus brought the text to life for people. Jesus bear-hugged people with his words. He warmly softened and moved them toward humility so they could experience the blessing of a relationship with God in their daily lives. Jesus was also the master of constructing well-crafted questions that caused people to squirm like an uncomfortably long but loving hug from your Aunt Sue.

During the Sermon on the Mount, he asked the crowd, "If the salt loses its saltiness, how can it be made salty again?" (Matthew 5:13). Another time on the outskirts of Caesarea Philippi (a city named after Caesar, who claimed the status of a god), Jesus asked his disciples a poignant question regarding their loyalty. First, he asked them *who do the people say that I am?* It is easier to discuss first what *others* think of Jesus—this provides a non-threatening starting point. But then Jesus probed deeper and asked the disciples to pony up and answer, "Who do *you* say that I am?" (Mark 8:27-32, emphasis added). Pressed to the precipice of commitment, Peter jumped out of his foxhole and brought everything out into the open saying, "You are the Christ." The trajectory of this young man's whole life changed in response to this simple but eternally profound question.

As a leader, are you bold enough to ask people these kinds of questions? Say "yes" and life becomes really adventurous.

This simple yet crafted line of questioning created space for Peter to jump off the cornice of belief to start carving turns in his trust that Jesus was the Son of God. Because of his courage, he became an example and leader to the rest of the disciples. Don't miss that you as an outdoor leader have similarly ordained opportunities. By asking tough questions, you are creating a wide-open space for courageous leaders in your group to step out on a limb and express their loyalty to Jesus. *In doing so, you may have just seeded the raising up of a leader who will change the world like Peter did!*

Jesus also used questions to prod people to honestly express their opinions and desires. For example, "Who of you by worrying can add a single hour to his life?" (Matthew 6:27). By starting the question with, "Who of you?" people have to look around and decide if they want to take a risk and come out of their shell. Like a seed that sprouts a green shoot of life when its outer shell tears open, spiritually motivated questions crack the shell of people's hearts and give them an opportunity to believe. Jesus-type questions erode the outer shell and open a window of opportunity for people to step out in faith and confess with their mouths that Jesus is Lord. When Jesus asked the blind man, "Do you believe that I am able to do this?" (Matthew 9:28), he was pushing for an expression of faith. Again, he pressed for a faith response from his disciples by asking, "Where shall we buy bread for these people to eat?" (John 6:5). These types of questions scrape off the outer shell of the soul so life can burst forth.

Jesus often used *rhetorical questions* to motivate thinking without putting the hearer on the spot to provide an answer. One isn't necessarily expected to answer a rhetorical question. For example, at a wedding you might hear someone say, "'I am' is the shortest sentence in the English language. Could it be that 'I do' is the longest one?" If you were just about to get married, how would you answer that question? You wouldn't. These questions are often so large there aren't any clichés available to ward off their effect. This non-threatening technique allows people to see their error or immaturity without unnecessary embarrassment. Jesus' rhetorical questions typically evoked the audience to compare the Kingdom of God to the world. For example, consider this string of rhetorical questions that gives the religious elite no room for a chestnut response:

> When he said this, all his opponents were humiliated, but the people were delighted with all the wonderful things he was doing. Then Jesus asked, "What is the kingdom of God like? What shall I compare it to? It is like a mustard seed, which a man took and planted in his garden. It grew and became a tree, and the birds of the air perched in its branches." Again he asked, "What shall I compare the kingdom of God to? It is like yeast that a woman took and mixed into a large amount of flour until it worked all through the dough." (Luke 13:17-21)

Good rhetorical questions leave people quiet or dumbfounded, anxious for the asker to release the pressure valve and answer his or her own question. We see Jesus doing this here brilliantly. First, he asked the questions, "What is the Kingdom of God like? What shall I compare it to?" The people were humbled and had no response at all—they were aching for Jesus to answer his own question. This heightens learning because it creates a "need to know." If you don't know the answer to a question, curiosity kicks in and you suddenly have "ears to hear."

To practice using rhetorical questions on the trail, just make a list of things you see people enamored with in your neighborhood, workplace, or school campus. Then write a few rhetorical questions from your list and throw them out in the open when a timely opportunity arises. When a person is complaining about how hard their life is or how much God has apparently let them down, you might ask them gently, "So, has God ever done anything for you?" This is not a question easily answered but directly confronts their dangerous pride. Don't be surprised if silence follows such a large question like that. Also, don't be afraid to ask others if they've ever said to themselves, "Why me God?" This is a favorite, enslaving rhetorical question that we mumble to ourselves sometimes. Jesus asked rhetorical questions to free people from bondage with the light of truth. So can we.

Inductive Approach to Asking

Asking relevant questions is truly a provocative art. We can easily miss an opportunity to engage and draw out true seekers by asking thoughtless questions, possibly causing defensiveness rather than openness. For instance, it is common in leading Bible studies to start off asking questions that are subtly looking for a specific/right answer. This shuts down the discovery process. If people don't have confidence that what they have to share is "right," they are likely to avoid participating in the discussion.

An inductive approach to dialogue is more beneficial in helping people find out for themselves the truth of a passage. This approach requires you as the discussion leader to craft questions that are open-ended (i.e., not yes/no). The following section provides examples of well-crafted non-threatening questions. Learning to write questions like this will help you create an atmosphere of learning in your group. In the following examples, I will note in *italics*, the key words that *promote* dialogue.

Observation

Observation questions are a starting point in the inductive study process. We might begin with questions that ask for a *list*, or to identify facts in the passage. One subtle way to draw participants into the discussion is to use open-ended words like "*some*." For example, a good observation question for a study of Mark 2:1-12 might be: "According to the passage, list *some* of the people who are in this story. What are *some* of the things we learn about each of them?" These are non-threatening questions even for the most biblically illiterate person because they are open-ended, and anyone may answer the questions with a degree of confidence.

Negatively, if I had asked, "From the passage, who are the people in the story? What do we learn about each of them?" there would have been considerably more silence in the group because few people want to be wrong in front of their peers by answering questions that are fishing for one "right" answer. The difference in the good questions is very subtle. Using the word "*some*" instead of the word "are" in those questions encourages participation and enables personal discovery.

Interpretation

Leading the study further, we need to consider the interpretation of the text and we'll follow the same pattern. Interpretive questions explore the "why" behind the passage. Yet the word "why" is a very threatening word because it implies there is only one right answer, and it may push for personal commitment too early in the discussion. So we must be extra careful in using questions containing the word "why." Interpretation questions progress the group from observations to meaning. We are hoping to help our group discover the significance of the *observations* to understand the gist of the biblical author's original intended meaning. Words like "*might*," "*what*," and "*some*" are helpful in making these questions more open-ended.

For example, using the same passage above, we might ask: "From the passage, what are *some* reasons why Jesus *might* have spoken to the paralyzed man about sin before dealing with his physical need? What reasons do we think Jesus *might* have had for going ahead and healing the man?" These questions allow people to explore some of the reasons he might have done this even if they have little conception as to what his reasons really were. This highlights the art of questioning. As you guide the discussion, you must have confidence that it's okay for others to explore *probable* meanings in the process of discovering the *actual* meaning.

A closed-ended example of these questions that would likely inhibit folks from entering into the dialogue would have been: "From the passage, why does Jesus speak to the paralyzed man about sin before dealing with his physical need? Why does he heal the paralyzed man?" See if you can discover the subtle difference in the bad wording of these questions. Say out loud to yourself both the good and bad questions above and then circle the questions you think would more likely keep discussion going. Which ones might send an unfortunate hush over the crowd? If a person is afraid his answer might be wrong, he will usually keep silent, which truncates the searching process. At the end of the day you have to make sure your group interprets the passage correctly. If the discovery process is moving slowly, I encourage leaders to keep asking clarifying questions until the group figures out the true meaning. Unless you absolutely must, don't give in to their frustration (or yours) and make a definitive statement to interpret it for them. As much as possible, help the group discover the interpretation themselves. Let them wrestle with it.

Application

Finally, if we wanted to lead a group into a practical application of the text, we would follow the same principles. In application questions, the leader is working to help the group identify *how to build the truths of the text into their lives.* These questions probe what the passage says about God, about people, about sin, etc. A good application question pushes for ways individuals and the group can put the text into action. It will help group members *integrate* the relevance of the text to their *personal lives* and to the *group* as a whole. For example, using the same passage of Scripture, we might ask the following questions to promote a relevant application (key words that fuel open discussion are italicized): "In this account, Jesus talks about his ability to forgive sins. Do we think that forgiveness of sins is a need that people *might* have today? Are there any *ways* you have experienced this need in your life? What are *some ways* that forgiveness *has been* important to you?"

You would probably experience an entirely different response if the questions were asked in this manner: "From the passage, Jesus talks about his ability to forgive sins. Is forgiveness of sins a need people have today? Why or why not? Is this a need you experience in your life? How is forgiveness important to you?" Again, the differences are almost unnoticeable at first glance in all of these examples, but the responses will likely be vastly different. What makes these questions so bad? See if you can identify the words that will shut people down from sharing. I have experimented with both forms of questions and observed the contrast between productive discovery-oriented Bible studies (which employ well-crafted, open-ended questions) versus observing complete paralysis in a group discussion due to thoughtless closed-ended questions. This is one of the most important skills you need to master if you are going to involve people in the learning process.

Responding to Questions

Jesus not only asked questions, but he also answered inquirers. He often answered questions with another question. This was not because he wanted to sound like some Confucian *guru*. He knew the *motivation* behind the person's question was the key to their heart. There is a theological rationale for how to respond to questions. *One of my goals in responding to questions is to find out why a person is asking the question.* For instance, if a person asks you, "How can we really know the Bible is true?" you might respond, "Before we talk about that, can I ask you another question? What are some reasons why you want to know if the Bible is true?" This exposes the motive of the questioner. Often people ask questions to avoid commitment—they ask to keep a distance. So Jesus returned questions with a question to lovingly reveal their true motive. In doing so, he winsomely drew people to himself. Obviously, we don't want to answer every question with another question, but if you sense a person's question has an edge of resistance or pride to it, then don't miss the chance to address the motive of their heart by asking them to give you some reasons *why* they want to know the answer to their question first.

Puns

Robert Stein helps us see several other ways that Jesus used variation and creativity to encourage participation of his audience in the learning process. One of my personal favorites is how Jesus used puns to scrape the plaque off of people's intellectual teeth. A pun is simply a "play on words" that toys with two like-sounding words or one word that has two different meanings.[195] We'll look at some ways you can use puns in the context of outdoor adventure. But, before this, let's look at several examples of how Jesus used puns. In Matthew 23:23-24, Jesus says to a group of Pharisees:

> Woe to you, teachers of the law and Pharisees, you hypocrites! You give a tenth of your spices—mint, dill and cummin. But you have neglected the more important matters of the law—justice, mercy and faithfulness. You should have practiced the latter, without neglecting the former. You blind guides! You strain out a gnat but swallow a camel.

In the Aramaic language, "camel" and "gnat" look and sound alike. The word for gnat is *galma* and the word for camel is *gamla*. So in the original language he said, "You blind guides, you strain out a *galma* but turn around and swallow a *gamla!*"[196]

Another time, presumably at the base of rock-strewn Mount Hermon, Jesus said, "And I say, you are Peter and on this rock I will build my church" (Matthew 16:18). In the Greek language, *Petros* and *petra* are used for "Peter" and "rock." Stein comments: "In Aramaic, however, the play on words is even more pronounced, since the same term *kepha* served as both the proper name and the word for rock."[197] We even see this today with names like "Stone" which is both a proper name and an alternative term for "rock." Here are a few more examples of how Jesus busted out a pun to make something more memorable:

1. John 3:8: "In Aramaic the word for 'wind' and the word for 'Spirit' are the same—ruha."[198]

2. Luke 9:59-60: In essence Jesus says, "Let the spiritually dead bury their own physically dead."[199]

3. Mark 1:17: Jesus makes a connection between "Fishing for fish" and "fishing for people."[200]

4. Mark 8:35: The way Jesus uses the words "save" and "lose" highlights both a physical and spiritual meaning of those words.[201]

Puns are a powerful tool to cause people to think. Setting aside time to think and make sense of their lives is one of the most glaring needs for people today. I learned of the power of puns from a good friend, Dave, who is a pun master. Whenever we are together, he causes me to think more about the everyday matters of life because he speaks puns so readily. He keeps me on my toes. Since I know he uses puns, my interest is piqued so I don't miss them when they sneak out. Just as explaining a joke takes away most of its bang, puns also have a greater effect when you don't have to draw attention to them. Puns make people think; and they can even help set a tone of learning among a group once you've established a reputation for dropping puns like Jesus did.

During a week on the trail, there are numerous opportunities for arousing interest through a well-timed pun. At times, I've shared one along the trail and then suggested the group try to come up with some puns along the way. It's a great distraction when hiking is tough, and it helps them be more aware of the journey by trying to find words to express the realities they experience. It's an acquired taste because puns don't come easily at first. You have to think.

For example, one evening after setting up camp above tree line, I began to cook a pot of noodles for dinner. Our base camp was set at the base of Pyramid Peak in the Weminuche Wilderness area of Colorado, and we were preparing to make an ascent to the peak the next morning. In a matter of minutes, dark clouds flooded over the ridge bringing rain, sleet, lightning, and very high winds of nearly one hundred miles per hour. We immediately moved the group into two rain flies and instructed them to hold on to the sides of the fly so that it would not blow away. My guide partner and I donned our headlamps and placed large rocks around each fly to hold them down. The storm raged for hours; lightning flashed, hail pelted the flies, and it was so windy that the stoves could not create enough heat to boil water to cook the pasta. So all we had to eat was the dessert. At about 3:00 a.m. we heard a "rip" followed by shrill screams in the rain fly next to us. I rushed out to look, and saw that the wind had torn the fly in half and part of it had blown off the mountain. Exposed to the raging elements of the storm, we quickly helped the kids from that rain fly (soggy sleeping bags and all) pile into the other one; stuffing them in like sardines. Some of the kids (several of whom were very unsure about their belief in Jesus before this point) began to pray and ask God to "save us from the storm!" We made it through the night—each camper with a handful of fabric in his or her fist to make sure the fly did not blow away.

The next morning was a prime opportunity to lighten the mood with a pun. While we were sitting in a circle eating our breakfast, I said, "Well, guys, there is just one word to describe what we went through last night: *In Tents!*" Only some of the kids got my play on the word "intense" and its connection to the fact that we had been squeezed like sardines in our "tents" all night, but this was a light-hearted way to transition into a quiet time to contemplate a relevant storm-passage in Scripture. We drew their attention to how they could identify with the disciples who were caught in a furious squall on the Lake of Galilee.

Very early one morning in the San Juan Mountains, I was leading a group to a crossing at Ute Creek. The stream spilled out of snowfields high above the valley and came up to our knees. After teaching the group how to walk across the stream safely, I clamored to the middle of the creek in case anyone might fall. The group was afraid of the freezing water and the strength of the current. With much coaxing, we finally got everyone across. Cold and wet, we sat down to warm up our feet (my legs were as pink as watermelons from the icy stream). This was a prime opportunity for a pun:

Well, folks, how was that experience for you? Did anyone get "cold feet"? Ha, Ha...No, I mean did any of you get "cold feet"? Were you scared to cross the stream? You know, often in my life, when I face something that is new and risky, I am tempted to get "cold feet," and avoid going through with it. All of us back at home will face icy "rivers" (decisions or opportunities) in our lives that seem scary. We might get "cold feet" and want to give up or go the other way.

There once was a time when God asked his people to "cross over" into the beautiful Promised Land he had prepared for them. They decided to send out twelve spies to see if there were any obstacles. When the spies returned, they painted a frightening picture of what lay ahead. They described a land filled with giants who could crush them "like grasshoppers." Ten of the spies got "cold feet," and said they weren't going to follow through with the plan God had given them. Only Caleb and Joshua stood up without fear and committed to crossing the river. Well, the people ended up listening to the cowardly ten spies, and because of that decision, none of the people who grumbled against God were allowed to enter in to the Promised Land. Instead, they had to wander around for forty years in a desert. So what do we learn from this? God honors courage when we step out in faith and are willing to take risks to follow him, like you did in crossing the freezing stream. When we obey him, we are blessed beyond measure. If we are willing to cross through "rivers" and challenges the Lord leads us to, we can be assured that he is with us!

[Then a few days later, after we had traveled over peaks—seeing the beautiful scenery, one could come back to this topic again]:

Remember a few days ago when we crossed that raging river? Just think; if we had gotten "cold feet" and not crossed over, think of all the beauty and adventure we would have missed. The past couple days have been amazing...we've ascended peaks, gone swimming in mountain lakes, enjoyed the warm sun in alpine meadows...If we had given in to our "cold feet" and decided not to cross the stream, we would have really missed out. I bet once the Israelites eventually obeyed God and went into the Promised Land, they must have regretted all that they had missed because of their disobedience and lack of courage. Is there any decision you are facing where you are fearful to commit? If God is asking you to follow him in some area of your life right now, you will be blessed when you obey him.

Riddles Reveal Reality

From a cold prison cell, John the Baptist realized his life was coming to an end. When facing one's death it is common to ask weighty questions about the meaning and purpose of life. In this state of mind, John the Baptist sought a friend's solace. With sincere concern, he sent his disciples to ask Jesus, "Are you the one who was to come, or should we expect someone else?" (Matthew 11:3). Although one might hope for a display of more faith from Jesus' cousin, John the Baptist, we observe from this passage that he was sincerely wondering if he had lived his life in vain. Jesus knew his heart, but he also knew the people (and John the Baptist) were confused about why he was not initiating the Kingdom of God like the people expected, i.e., in a *forceful* way. With love and respect Jesus sent his cousin a message sandwiched with a riddle. First, he gave John's friends a reassuring message to take back to him in prison: "The blind receive sight, the lame walk, those who have leprosy are cured, the deaf hear, the dead are raised, and the good news is preached to the poor. Blessed is the man who does not fall away on account of me" (Matthew 11:5-6). Then while John's friends were still within earshot, Jesus turns to the crowd and tells them a riddle about *John* and the *nature of the Kingdom of God*:

> From the days of John the Baptist until now, the kingdom of heaven has been forcefully advancing, and forceful men lay hold of it. For all the Prophets and the Law prophesied until John. And if you are willing to accept it, he is the Elijah who was to come. He who has ears to hear, let him hear. (Matt. 11:12-15)

Jesus' riddle defined reality for John the Baptist in terms of what he *couldn't* see. Many envisioned a forceful inauguration of the Kingdom. Yet Jesus' way of war was one of humility, and self-sacrifice. And lest we be shocked or critical of his blindness, we should also recognize that you can't find anything that resembles Jesus' battle strategy anywhere in Sun Tzu's widely read *Art of War* either. This was a radically different approach. In perfect riddle-form, Jesus' response to John's question was a resounding, "Yes" (the battle is being won forcefully), but the conflict was on *his* terms and was going to look quite different than expected. The apostle Paul later commented as well on the nature of this cosmic quarrel, in a letter to the church at Philippi:

> Who, being in very nature God, did not consider equality with God something to be grasped, but made himself nothing, taking the very nature of a servant, being made in human likeness. And being found in appearance as a man, he humbled himself and became obedient to death—even death on a cross! Therefore God exalted him to the highest place and gave him the name that is above every name, that at the name of Jesus every knee should bow, in heaven and on earth and under the earth, and every tongue confess that Jesus Christ is Lord, to the glory of God the Father. (Philippians 2:5-11)

Jesus' riddles had a ringing rhythm of a pattern called *reveal and conceal*. A.B. Caneday has reflected on this apparent pattern in the riddles of Jesus. The Parable of the Soils provides a poignant example:

> Because Jesus' sayings and deeds both reveal and conceal simultaneously, eyes and ears must be vigilantly alert. For Jesus provokes hostility or submissive belief. One will be hardened like the religious officials, or one will become enamored with Jesus as the crowds [were and then] fall away quickly under troubles brought on by the gospel, or one will be choked to unfruitfulness by entanglement in the concerns of the "things of men." Or one will grasp the "things of God" and be variously fruitful in the gospel.[202]

The way Jesus used puns and riddles, shows his awareness and attentiveness to the surroundings and state of being of others. This is the art of outdoor leadership. This is the essence of shepherd leadership. Learning how to help people become aware of God's activity and his voice in the world is our aim. And one way Jesus did this was through riddles. His rhythm of reveal and conceal caused people to question their true beliefs—which is like taking a seed of the gospel and planting it in the good soil of a humble heart. Those who have ears to hear, hear.

Props Stir Us Like a Good Drama

You can't put on a play or roll out a blockbuster movie without actors and actresses to carry the plot. Yet what often distinguishes between a good and great theatrical performance is the design of the set, the costumes, and the props that bring the story to life. Similar to the role of the performers in a play or movie, a teacher is of paramount importance for delivering a message, but often what distinguishes between an average and excellent teacher is how they use props to stir people's emotional response. Corrie ten Boom was famous for saying a teacher should always have a prop to coincide with her message in order to increase involvement in the learning process. Tangible visual aids greatly enhance learning because they provide a paradigm or schema on which to hang what we are learning.

In the outdoors, we have more props than we could ever use in a thousand lifetimes! At our fingertips we have gear, branches, stones, rivers—you name it. Finding a prop is not difficult in the natural setting. The problem is that we often miss the opportunity because we simply don't look around for an object to connect with what we are teaching. Many of the prophets like Hosea, Isaiah, Jeremiah, and Ezekiel used figurative actions, symbolism, and object lessons to dramatically communicate truth. For example, Jeremiah, in chapters 27 and 28, walked around with a wooden yoke to dissuade the Judeans from joining in an alliance with Egypt.

It's up to you to find a prop to enhance your message. Chapters 11-12 offer some examples of creation analogies and object lessons. Now, it's your turn. I believe the best teaching in the outdoors is still to come...maybe you'll be the one who picks up where I've humbly left off and offer new ideas for advocates of experiential learning in the future. Where do you start? All you need to do is pause and look around; props illustrating Kingdom certainties are literally everywhere.

CHAPTER 15
INTEGRATE

J.E.R.E.M.I.A.H. Guide Preparation Plan

In the world's eyes, Jeremiah was not a success. But from God's perspective, he was the epitome of it. Jeremiah was faithful to God and completely obedient. He had integrity and carried out his calling regardless of the personal cost. The core value God wanted Jeremiah to uphold through his whole life was to tell people to repent and turn back to God. Being a shepherd leader of people requires us to have a proper view of success. Christian outdoor leaders are shepherds at the core. Like Jeremiah, we aren't aiming to please men. Paul eloquently asserts this leadership maxim as well: "Am I now trying to win the approval of men, or of God? Or am I trying to please men? If I were still trying to please men, I would not be a servant of Christ" (Galatians 1:10).

Sometimes in order to help someone who is spiritually unhealthy we have to poke or prod or say hard things. The New Testament is chocked full of Jesus' hard sayings, and the Old Testament is teeming with prophets who spoke the hard things in order to help people restore their relationship with God. Jeremiah stands out as one of those prophets. I also like Jeremiah as a model for guiding because he was young and fairly inexperienced when God called him. Our competence comes from God. God graciously spoke these words to Jeremiah when he called him out to lead: "Before I formed you in the womb I knew you, before you were born I set you apart; I appointed you as a prophet to the nations" (Jeremiah 1:5). In all humility and honesty, Jeremiah replies, "Ah, Sovereign LORD...', 'I am only a child" (Jeremiah 1:6). Then God tells him to take courage and lead because he will be with him every step of the way. His age and experience were apparently irrelevant.

Discipling others is not easy. In the context of outdoor ministry it is a challenge to say the least. To be responsible not only for the spiritual journey, but the physical safety of others is a large task. But take heart, God is with you. All we need to do is focus on having integrity in our relationship with God and lean on him every step of the way. He will give you what you need. But recognize that as you take on the responsibility of leading others in the wilderness, you are called to *shepherd* them. And that may require you to speak into others' lives and say some hard things. We respect and admire Jeremiah not because he was successful in the ways of the world. Rather, we admire him because of his tough love. He obeyed God and called people to fear God, repent, and turn back to him. Our core goal is to help people become whole through humbly submitting to the authority of their Maker. As a Christian outdoor leader, I want to be more like Jeremiah, even if that comes with considerable personal cost. It is worth it.

So how do we become a guide with the tenacious resilience and focus of Jeremiah? From my own experience I have distilled a few suggestions that help me prepare to lead others as well as to stay focused on soul care in the midst of the adventure. Jeremiah was a hardened follower of God in all the right ways. He was faithful, feared God and not man, and seemed to be able to overcome even the most ridiculous of challenges. Jeremiah is a prototype for outdoor leaders to emulate. The following acronym "JEREMIAH" helps me remember some of what it takes to be an adequately prepared guide, responsible for others. Hopefully this tool will help you become the leader you desire to be as well.

J – Journal

Some people naturally love to journal and others don't do it at all. I've been all over the map in my walk with Christ, but generally I think journaling is more helpful than not. It's not that I necessarily look back over my journals very often, but the act of writing things down somehow helps me think and listen to God more intentionally.

Every so often when I read something that really resonates, I jot it down so I can come back to it for further thought. For Christian outdoor leaders there are a few other reasons why journaling is crucial. There are at least **four main reasons I have for keeping a journal. First, it enhances my own devotional life with Jesus**. I can keep track of conversations we have together. I note the Scripture he speaks to me, and the prayers I pray while I wait for him to answer. A journal can be a collection of letters you write to God, expressing your heart, asking real-life questions, and being honest about your sin through confession. Consistent honest communication is the mark of true friendship, and a journal can be a helpful way to enjoy and remember your friendship with God over the years.

To get started you might journal your prayers as a four-layer conversation: Usually we begin by *talking to God*, then *God listens to us!* Imagine that Christ is listening to you intently as you pray to him because he is! Next, in real conversations the other person *speaks back to you*. This is also true with prayer. After we speak to God and he listens to us, then *he speaks back to us*. He is conversational—he has personal words for us. And the last stage of a conversation is to listen to God. He speaks to us, but *do we listen to him*? What Scripture does he bring to mind? What questions might he be asking you? What do you sense the Holy Spirit saying to you as you pray? Journaling your conversations like this can be a helpful tool in learning how to pray more intimately. Jesus said to his disciples: "I have much more to say to you, more than you can now bear" (John 16:12). We have God's Word available to us in the Bible and the Holy Spirit has much to say to us as we personally commune with him. I recommend Walter Wangerin Jr.'s book *Whole Prayer* if you would like to grow more in your conversational relationship with God through prayer like this.

A second reason for journaling is that it helps you become a better learner. By keeping a learning log of my experiences leading small groups, I can become a better leader in the future. All of our effort can't be spent on helping others learn. We, too, need to recognize the primary reason the Lord has given us the opportunity to lead others is for him to get at our heart. He doesn't really need us to lead others; he could choose anyone to do that. But he has chosen us by his grace to have opportunities to lead. The person he is aiming to reach through our leadership is us! He calls us to lead others mainly to draw us close to him. By journaling, I protect myself from arrogance or pride that comes from an overemphasis on helping *others* learn. I need to first place myself at the feet of Jesus as a *learner*. That's what the word "disciple" means.

Thirdly, I like to keep a catalogue of Bible studies and trail talks or teachable moments I commonly use on the trail. The more you can organize this into a useful system, the more benefit it will be to you in the context of the ever-changing climate of outdoor adventures. In the middle of a pressure-cooker moment, you don't want to be digging around for a piece of paper at the bottom of your bag in the watertight compartment of your sea kayak. It's better to have a small journal to which you can easily refer. Journaling is also a good way to evaluate and assess your Bible studies and activities to improve them for the future. There is so much that happens throughout a week in the wilderness it would be hard to remember everything without writing some of it down. What were the good questions I used to set up quiet times? Which ones flopped? Which topics sparked memorable discussions? Referring back to my journal after returning home from an outdoor adventure, I can work to improve how I teach the Bible with more clarity and winsomeness. Improvement is a never-ending journey. There is always something new to master in our pursuit to glorify God through excellence.

A fourth reason I like to journal is to keep a logbook for each trip I lead. This includes the type of landscape in which it occurred, the skills I used heavily, whether I was training others or being trained on this experience. I jot down a brief description of the route, the distance covered, the weather, dates, and the year. Then I take time to write down a brief description of each person on the trip and highlights of what I saw him or her learn and take away from the trip. I include quotes they said, transformation I witnessed, and follow-up I anticipate being helpful for them as they return to their daily lives in the city. At the end of each trip before we leave the wilderness, I have each participant fill out a one-page storyboard to debrief what happened to them. The stuff people write will both crack you up and make you cry. If you want more help in these areas, refer to the resources page at www.outdoorleaders.com/resources.

E - Eat

One of the first things you do while evaluating an injured patient in the wilderness is to ask them what their most recent food "input" was? When did they last have a meal and what did it consist of? Do they have low blood sugar from lack of food intake? Could they be having an allergic reaction to something they've eaten? Since our body is a temple of the Holy Spirit (see 1 Corinthians 6:9), God wants us to be careful with what we put into it. Eating well can refer to our diet, but it can also be a good analogy for spiritual health as well. Both apply to outdoor leadership. If you are going to be leading people in adventurous settings with potential dangers, then you need to be as healthy as possible so you will be able to facilitate a safe environment. We need to pay attention to good nutrition so our bodies are functioning at their optimal capacity so we can be a blessing to others. Similarly, we need to eat spiritual food that will give us strength and wisdom to provide a spiritual covering for others.

Another question we ask patients in the wilderness is what their last "output" was. This can be a little embarrassing for folks because we want to know the last time they went to the bathroom and if there was anything odd about it. As uncomfortable as that is, it is essential to determine what is wrong with them. Are they dehydrated or constipated? Could they have a parasite or bacterial infection? Similar to diagnosing a potential gastrointestinal problem, there is a spiritual analogy connected to our "outputs" as well. The Bible talks about the fruit of the Spirit as well as the fruit of sin and disobedience. If we are putting rubbish into our minds by what we watch, do, or listen to, then it should be no surprise rubbish will come out in our behavior or personality as well.

Yet if we eat well by putting in our soul those words that bring freedom, then we will see the evidence of this in the spiritual fruit that bursts out of us. If your outputs are displaying fruit of the Spirit, then by the grace of God this is probably because you are putting healthy spiritual food into your heart, mind, and soul. Jesus offers us spiritual food through abiding in his Word. To be a healthy, resilient leader who can offer life and peace to others, we must first ensure our last input of food (both diet and spiritual sustenance) was good and reflects God's love for us, since we are a temple of his Spirit. And correspondingly, if our last "output" reveals the fruit of walking in the flesh rather than the Spirit, then we need to stop ourselves from conforming to the world, repent, and go back to the Vine of Jesus Christ. He renews us by the nectar of his Word as it flushes through our mind (see Romans 12:1-2). Then the output of our life will change to fruit of the Spirit: love, joy, peace, patience, kindness, goodness, faithfulness, gentleness, and self-control (see Galatians 5:22). Eugene Peterson's *Eat This Book* is a helpful resource in developing a deeper understanding of Spiritual Theology, which is a biblical framework to help us focus on what we "take in" to our souls. For further study, you might also refer to the following passages related to what we "eat":

Here is some helpful Scripture on this topic:

Ezekiel 4:10, Numbers 11:18, Exodus 12:20, Deuteronomy 12:22, Genesis 2:17, Deuteronomy 15:22, Ezekiel 3:1, Leviticus 6:16, Exodus 29:33, 2 Kings 4:43, Numbers 18:10, Leviticus 22:10, 2 Kings 4:40, Luke 17:8, 2 Kings 6:28, 1 Corinthians 8:13, Isaiah 7:22, Mark 6:37, Leviticus 17:12, 10:14, 25:22, Deuteronomy 12:15, Genesis 3:17, Leviticus 8:31

R - Run

"I believe God made me for a purpose, but he also made me fast. And when I run I feel his pleasure."[203] —Eric Liddell

I find that when I am exercising regularly and caring for the body God gave me, I tend to be more disciplined in just about every other area of my life. It's a funny thing about restraint...when we commit to being disciplined in one area of life, this often leads more easily to discipline in other areas as well. The opposite of fitness is misuse. God has given us our bodies and he desires for us to be good stewards of them. As an active outdoor leader, when we do this we are able to enjoy the benefits of fitness and we gain the ability to bless others in their time of need, because we've stayed in decent shape. If I'm not in shape then I may become a liability rather than a blessing to the group. A lack of attention to this area of life can lead to insecurity, which distracts me from leading others.

As an outdoor leader we don't have an Hippocratic oath like doctors do, but if I could make one up it would include a pledge to do all I can to safely and effectively introduce people to Jesus Christ and help them grow in their faith through guided outdoor adventures. Although risk management is a topic beyond the scope of this book, being in shape physically is one the best things you can do to mitigate risks and be prepared to handle emergencies. It is essential if you are going to be leading people in the outdoors to give adequate attention to your physical health, especially in the areas of building up strength and endurance.

Being physically fit enables you to be at ease with the possibility of having to run or paddle out of the backcountry for an emergency. And I find that the more competent an outdoor leader is in general, the more confident and relaxed they are in their leadership position. Physical fitness is not the goal, but a means to our goal to provide safe and effective outdoor adventures for those who've put their trust in us. To be the leader you aspire to be, you'll need to get in shape and remain disciplined to the degree that matches the intensity of the kind of wilderness trips you intend to lead. That's just common sense, and it feels really good too. For further study, I recommend reading, *The Image of God in the Human Body: Essays on Christianity and Sports* by Donald Deardorff III and John White.

E – Explain

(A Twelve-Step Technique)

Great teachers often measure their effectiveness by the learning that results in their audience. This is not the only way to evaluate great teaching, because sometimes people just don't want to learn and you can't fault the teacher for that. Outdoor leadership offers many opportunities for teaching, so in my opinion it is important to strive for excellence in our ability to explain things well. Eloquent teaching requires identifying goals or dreams for our interaction with the group. Explaining biblical truth to a group should not be taken lightly. The apostle Peter sets a very high standard for us as Christian outdoor leaders: "Each one should use whatever gift he has received to serve others, faithfully administering God's grace in its various forms. If anyone speaks, he should do it as one speaking the very words of God" (1 Peter 4:10-11). Since we are accountable to God for what we teach, let's make sure we are careful to keep the Bible as our curriculum, and trust the Holy Spirit to be the one who illumines and opens the eyes of people's hearts. We don't have to be super-teachers, we are simply asked to allow the Bible to speak for itself and do our best to present the message of Scripture with winsomeness and accuracy like Jesus did.

The outcomes listed in Chapter 6 could be a beginning point for you to formulate a personal goal or dream for your curriculum with a group. After identifying the goals, you need to make sure you have a good grasp on your audience. Where are they coming from? How are issues of timing, setting, and current events relevant to understanding the state of your audience? After choosing your outcome and determining your starting point to engage the audience, you need to think through how you are going to present your message so it holds a tension between training (or *criticism* of a widely held belief that is wrong), and the *action* you want them to take in response to what you are teaching them.

There is no single way to teach for transformation. In my opinion, most teaching is more about who you are than the style in which you teach. However, I will offer a suggested *twelve-step technique* to help you become a more eloquent teacher in the context of outdoor ministry (a one-page synopsis of this model is available at www.outdoorleaders.com/resources).

1) Whenever you introduce a topic or open up a dialogue around a teachable moment, start with an *opening hook* sentence. This phrase needs to start with where your audience is in order to get their attention.

2) The next trick of the trade is to state creatively in a short phrase *why they need to know* what we are about to share with them. This appeals especially to imaginative learners.

3) The next thing you want to do is *initiate a slight disequilibrium* in the group. This is often best achieved by sharing some novel illustration (object lesson) or information that casts a new perspective on something familiar to them. It is key to attach some tangible benefit they will experience from embracing what is being learned. One of the ways this is achieved through experiential learning is to create a learning environment where people have to cooperate with one another to interact with what you are teaching them. This way even though they may be slightly out of their comfort zone, they feel like everyone else is learning this together. This greatly enhances learning for most people.

4) Next, after you've established the benefits for learning what you are about to teach, provide an *Anticipatory Set* (discussed in Chapter 7) to set the stage for the work required to learn something new. Here you are simply telling them what they are about to learn.

5) At this stage, provide a *simple and unique problem to solve* that is relevant to your topic. This primes the pump for considerable creative thinking you want to see flow through the group as you teach this new concept. When you get to this point,

you're ready to present a few principles to the group (this is the main body of your teaching). The rest of your teaching process might look like this:

6) *Coach:* Choose up to three main points to keep it focused.

7) *Illustrate:* Offer an illustration or story to demonstrate an example of each main point.

8) *Do Drills*: Involve everyone in an activity that is hands on. Encourage relational learners who ascertain by participating to make observations of what they are learning from the hands-on exercise.

9) *Debrief:* Encourage analytical learners to break apart the principle, story, or argument into its various parts for understanding. Use exploratory questions to help analytical learners verbalize what they've learned and what they would like to do with their knowledge.

10) *Apply:* (Conclusion to tie your theme together) Facilitate personal reflection on the relevance of what we have learned today (sensing learners) for an everyday situation. How am I helping participants experience a feeling of accomplishment today through processing the experience?

11) *Generalize and transfer to future endeavors*: How am I motivating my apprentices and what response do I expect of them from today's topic? What are the potential spin-offs or benefits of learning this skill or knowledge? This appeals especially to dynamic learners. If you've asked questions to help them express what they've learned and they are able to articulate an application, they have learned what you set out to teach them— you have succeeded. Celebrate!

12) *Evaluate:* Spend some time evaluating your a) strengths, b) growth areas, c) questions that arose that would require you to do some further study for next time you teach this topic.

M – Memorize

The Psalmist writes: "I have hidden your word in my heart that I might not sin against you" (Psalm 119:11), and "The commands of the LORD are radiant, giving light to the eyes" (Psalm 19:8). Peter exhorts believers to be prepared in and out of season to give a reason to others for the hope and joy we experience (see 1 Peter 3:15). If you think about most professions, there is usually a baseline expectation of knowledge in order to be able to practice that profession. Doctors, lawyers, engineers, and architects even have a board exam where they have to display proficiency in a large body of knowledge related to their field. Without memorization it would not be possible to function in any of those professions adequately, because while practicing in those fields there is not always enough time to refer to a book of professional standards to solve problems, make decisions, or give guidance.

Although in my opinion, outdoor leadership is an *art* not a *profession* in the classic sense of the word (because there could never be a standardized exam required as a prerequisite to practice outdoor leadership), this is still a good analogy for understanding the benefits of memorizing God's Word. Just as in any field, the vocation of ministry or soul care cannot be practiced very well if you always have to rely on a manual. There is a certain amount of effort that needs to be invested to develop the confidence to practice this art of ministry. Memorizing Scripture is an important discipline for anyone who is a follower of Christ. Its benefits are astounding both as a defense against the lies and deceit of the world and as an offensive tool to intercede for others with the power of the gospel. To shepherd others well, we need to develop a habit of committing Scripture to memory.

Memorizing the Bible makes God's Word accessible in our minds and readily available to teach, correct, rebuke, and train others (see 2 Timothy 3:16). Just like the vocations listed above, we still might have to refer to our "trade manual" (the Bible) to brush up on the specifics. But the great thing about memorization is, even if you can't recall the specific wording of a passage, you will probably be able to find the chapter or verse. I don't mind if a lawyer or engineer needs to look something up to double check his knowledge, that's just being human. But I wouldn't be very comfortable entrusting the safety of my family to a doctor who never passed a board exam.

Because we live under grace, no one is forcing us to memorize Scripture or study it for that matter. But James did say that not many of us should presume to be teachers of the Word, because we are held to a higher standard (see James 3:1). If you want to take on the responsibility of leading others, I highly encourage you to take this mantle of responsibility seriously. The spiritual disciplines of study and memorization are not meant to be a burden but a joy. Be in awe of the privilege it is to lead others spiritually. This leads us to a grateful attitude, which fans into flame the freedom to excel still more (see 1 Thessalonians 4:10, 1 Corinthians 14:12)!

Scripture for further study: Joshua 1:8, Psalm 19:7-11; 119:9-16

I - Inquire

God is inviting each of us to daily *cultivate the soil of our hearts through a passionate relationship with Jesus Christ.* In the same way we are *not* fashioned to become weary of pursuing the relationship we have with our spouse if we're married, we are also not designed to tire of inquiring of God. Paying attention to Christ through companionship is an unparalleled privilege and honor. I don't believe it is a coincident that in Mark 3:13, the first mark of discipleship Jesus highlighted was that they were simply called to "be with him." Our starting point as a Christian is to be seated with Christ: "And God raised us up with Christ and seated us with him in the heavenly realms in Christ Jesus, in order that in the coming ages he might show the incomparable riches of his grace, expressed in his kindness to us in Christ Jesus" (Ephesians 2:6-7).

We see Jesus commending Mary on her choice to sit at his feet, whereas he rebuked Martha for choosing to stay busy while he was in her presence. Spiritual formation is incredibly needed in the Body of

Christ today to ensure we are forming our identity based upon *who* we are in Christ, rather than on what we can *do* for him. The former leads to sustainability and effectiveness whereas the latter leads to burn out. Leading others through outdoor adventures will surely tax your mind, body, and soul. So the way we stay healthy and joyful regardless of whether things are going well or not is to always choose what Mary did: "Mary has chosen what is better, and it will not be taken away from her" (Luke 10:42).

A – Artistry

"I knew at that moment that life was not a work of art.
And that this moment could not last."
— Norman Maclean, *A River Runs Through It*

An intriguing work of art hangs on the wall. Staring reflectively into it, one is elevated out of the narrow perspective of her circumstance. She considers the more lofty ideals that busyness has crowded out of her soul. This is the affect a masterful oil painting can have on us. But relationships are not works of art in the same way. Moments pass by, people move on. You can't capture life and hang it on a wall; it is more organic than that. Yet, ironically, it is precisely because of this reality that we ought to approach life more like an artist approaches her canvas. Color and texture only derive meaning when the artist's hand moves it across the page into something recognizable. There is a method to the mess.

There is thought and heart that goes into the creation of something. I approach guiding others in the wilderness like an artist by first painting a picture in my mind of what the week could possibly look like in terms of building relationships with God and others on the trip. Like a canvas, the landscape is waiting for us to walk through it. Similar to painting a picture, outdoor leaders get to map out a route their group will probably remember for the rest of their lives. That's much more valuable than a Rembrandt on the wall. I hear many people say after their week in the wilderness that this was the "best week" of their lives. That is how an artist feels when she

301

puts down her brush and stands back with pleasure to see the story she's spread out on the canvas. *That is also how a guide feels when she has approached her trip with a prayerful and theological rationale for how she led the experience.*

If we don't have a *theological palette* from which to dip our brush or to put color into our adventure, we run the risk of limiting the memories of our trip to sentimentality. If you think back over the most vivid memories of your life, one can become either sentimental or deeply transformed. Norman Maclean, in *A River Runs Through It*, recognizes this as he and his brother and father sit reveling in an unforgettable day of fishing together in the Montana wilderness. Rather than trying to hold onto the moment like a work of art that could be placed on a wall, Norman recognizes that "this moment could not last." Rather than holding onto that memory as mere sentiment, he allows it to become something much bigger to his soul. This moment led him later to write down the story of his life in a way that could impact generations. The apostle Paul viewed the canvas of his ministry similarly: "Brothers, I do not consider myself yet to have taken hold of it. But one thing I do: Forgetting what is behind and straining toward what is ahead" (Philippians 3:13).

The potential impact you have as a spiritual guide to others depends on the picture you are trying to paint and the decisions you make to strain toward what is ahead. By having a vision for those you're shepherding and by carefully crafting those experiences you will share together, you are leaving behind something much greater than a canvas on the wall or a picture in an album. You are leaving a legacy that can affect generations after you are gone.

H – History Telling

Most people I know don't have an insatiable desire to read an historical non-fiction book. Historical fiction maybe, but most people are bored by history. This is both sad and concerning as we think about how much history has shaped our societies. One of my passions is trying to figure out how to teach history in a compelling way. The most influential leaders throughout history had a strong foundation in understanding the facts of history and the consequences (both good and bad) of repeating it.

I believe postmodern people are more apt to be drawn into history backwards. Simply put, if we can find ways to connect events and experiences of today with corresponding historical lessons from the *recent* past they will be more apt to follow how yesterday's lessons have impacted our situation today. Teaching history starting with a "way back then" approach (starting in the ancient past and then working up to today) loses postmodern people somewhere around the time of Pharaoh. They are mentally out to lunch before you can say "King Tut" (unless you teach about him by singing the 1979 *Saturday Night Live* version of "King Tut" sung by Steve Martin and the *Toot Uncommons* who were actually members of the *Nitty Gritty Dirt Band*). That might keep folks with you to the middle of the Late Bronze Age.

Jeremiah the prophet was a great student of history, as were most of his contemporaries. The prophets had a firm grasp on what the people of God had done in the past and the consequences that had followed the actions of their ancestors. So much of these prophets' lives was about proclaiming what was going to happen to people if they didn't learn the lessons from their history and repent. And Jeremiah used a myriad of object lessons from creation to teach his contemporaries the importance of learning from history.

It is scary how much history repeats itself. We need more Christian leaders raised up among our younger generation who understand history enough to prevent some parts of both secular and church history from repeating itself. I know some people may think it's an off-the-wall goal to make history-learning a desired outcome for a *wilderness camp*. But consider: Where else do people have enough quiet and headspace to consider the valuable lessons of history? To demonstrate the value of highlighting lessons from history as a potential goal for your outdoor adventure, let me give you an example of how one might help people learn lessons from history *backwards*. This is probably more suited for an advanced group of participants but if one of your goals is leadership development, then this could be a poignant topic to discuss with people who have been deeply impacted by post-modern thinking:

1) Begin with the real/relevant questions of today; bands or musicians that write thoughtful lyrics are a good starting point. Think of a band you like and start with them. What are these lyrics saying? What questions do they ask? What do they protest? The lyrics of songs that young people listen to will give you a clue to their nagging questions or concerns.

2) Take those contemporary questions or problems and explore history backwards to show the reality of sin/depravity in current and *recent* history. Show how depravity and brokenness today is linked to recent historical sin and then keep working backward showing how the problems that impassion us today are nothing new...they are similar to a month ago, a year ago, a decade ago, a century ago, a millennia ago, and from the very genesis of human history.

3) Illustrate: Demonstrate how an honest appraisal of general history over the past few hundred years and beyond uncovers every person's "need" for repentance and why the blood of Jesus Christ was necessary. The world is messed up and we need a Savior.

4) Show how our deepest "desires" today are only found in Christ (the King), and in the context of biblical community (his Kingdom).

5) Present the idea that Jesus has extended us grace, and we must extend that same grace to others. All people are in process; history teaches us that sin and depravity are always a part of humanity because of the fall of man. Don't let that sucker-punch you with despair, just expect it and be a part of the solution today, not the problem. It's not going away until Jesus returns.

6) Apply ways we can abide in Christ so we don't repeat the negative stories of history. Give a grand and positive vision of how, through faith, spiritual disciplines, worshipping regularly in community, and submitting ourselves to Scripture and those in authority, the church can truly serve as salt and light to the world. This is where the rubber meets the road.

This is a way to help postmodern minds see how history has shaped today. You can also talk about Scripture in this way by telling God's story backwards (from today to Genesis). A way I try to accomplish this on wilderness camps is by setting up "life stories" to give everyone a chance during the trip to share what has shaped them and made them who they are today. We usually give each person twenty to thirty minutes to share their story and then another twenty to thirty minutes for follow-up questions from the group to get to know them even better. This helps us see the story of people's lives—both past and present. If you have Christians on your trip, they will likely talk about their need for a Savior and how Jesus has been the answer to their longings. For people who have not committed their lives to Jesus, sharing life stories is a great way for them to feel valued and loved for who they are. It also may help them see more clearly what has shaped their life, and it gives them space to honestly consider whether they are truly content without Christ.

Adventure is truly God's invention. The Bible clearly claims that the concepts of outdoor ministry and outdoor leadership originated with God himself. Not everyone will embrace my declaration that Jesus Christ is the founder of outdoor leadership, but regardless of one's convictions about the origins of this dearly loved field, I hope that anyone who has read these pages will be able to humbly stand in awe of the One who lovingly wrote the Book on outdoor leadership— the One who loves us so much that he made the earth for us to enjoy and explore—Jesus Christ: "For in him all things were created: things in heaven and on earth, visible and invisible, whether thrones or powers or rulers or authorities; all things have been created through him and for him" (Colossians 1:16).

With humble gratitude I offer these final words from C.S. Lewis, one of this centuries largest and bravest thinkers: "Aim at heaven and you will get earth thrown in. Aim at earth and you get neither." My hope and prayer is that all who tread the paths of pristine wilderness be moved to worship the Creator of these magnificently beautiful places. After all, *he deserves* our humble reverence:

"I know that everything God does will endure forever; nothing can be added to it and nothing taken from it. God does it so that men will revere him." –Solomon (Ecclesiastes 3:14)

Epilogue

We live in an increasingly urbanized world. Three-fifths of the world's population will likely live in sprawling urban landscapes by the year 2030. Demographically, many people's daily experiences do not include time alone or adequate space to enjoy the music of their Creator.

The Bible demonstrates that the physical setting of creation, which Jesus supremely designed from eternity past, was his most extensively used classroom for illustrating Kingdom truth to his friends as well as the masses. It is no wonder he was the Master of illustrations from creation because he is the Author of creation! From the moment God created the seas and earth, seed-bearing plants, animals, and humans, he began crafting *the theater* in which the life-changing wilderness experiences of the Bible would someday take place. He has always planned to use these spaces and landscapes to teach us something. And that did not end with the ascension of Christ. The wilderness still calls out to us today.

It is hard for us westerners to understand how much "the land" shaped the identity of the ancient Hebrews. Even today, eastern people ardently identify themselves with their land. Westerners have been shaped by a different story, so we have a tendency to focus more on the wilderness as a *metaphor* than taking the biblical accounts literally and grappling with the reality that a bulk of these life-changing events in the Bible happened *in* the wilderness—not in a metaphorical sense, but in the literal outdoor setting of the wilderness.

Wilderness is more than a metaphor, isn't it? It is a place to go—to experience fresh air, the sounds of gurgling streams and breaking waves, the singing of birds, claps of thunder, flashes of lighting, physical challenges, sleeping under the stars, living in community, packing light, climbing peaks, paddling through storms, and journeying through desert canyons. The Bible is like an IMAX theater for watching how many of the world's most memorable leaders were transformed through wilderness adventures.

We often find comfort in metaphors and discomfort in *reality*. It's easy to share with a friend about a personal "wilderness experience" (referring to an emotional or spiritual thing we've been feeling), but how often do we actually *go away to experience* a true wilderness experience *in* the wilderness terrain? The wilderness is a *place* for transformation, not just a metaphor to describe one's personal struggles in life. The wilderness can be used as a metaphor for our spiritual trials, but I would assert that the desert metaphor will gain all the more meaning in your spiritual life if you actually spend time *out in* the wilderness every once in a while. There is something special about sojourning *in* the outdoors for the purpose of conversing with the Almighty.

This book is just the beginning of a much bigger conversation needed today. As with any theological endeavor we are diving into a deep sea of possibilities, so I think I've probably raised as many questions as provided answers. C.S. Lewis once said, "[You will not] get anywhere by looking at maps without going to sea. Nor will you be very safe if you go to sea without a map."[204] I hope that this book will inspire you and many others to courageously set sail toward a sea of possibilities in your arena of influence whether it is in the marketplace, in the church, in youth ministry, in missions, with your peers, or with your own kids. And as C.S. Lewis wisely exhorts—while setting sail into fresh ways of making disciples, make sure that you tenaciously cling to the map of God's Word to keep you on course.

I sincerely hope that some who read this book will see other ways to enhance this young, but growing, field of Christian outdoor leadership. We need more books, articles, idea sharing, networking, and vision casting for why this field of ministry is needed in both the Christian and secular marketplace. Having solid theological grounds for why outdoor ministry works will help you cast this vision to others. Being able to articulate a 30 second elevator speech for the rationale undergirding Christian outdoor leadership will be helpful to others who don't understand its value. We must be able to answer people's questions well. We need to excel in what we do so that there is no difference between the standard of excellence we strive for as compared to our secular friends who practice outdoor leadership. Anything less than excellence is a poor witness, and the world will be quick to point that out.

I encourage leaders who resonate with this style of ministry and its relevance to youth ministry and other kinds of ministries to view your self as a *stepping-stone*, like the early pilgrims who discovered America viewed themselves. They believed their role was to serve future generations by laying a foundation for them to walk on. As we pioneer the field of Christian outdoor leadership, we too are merely stepping-stones. I believe those who embrace this attitude will influence many. The limits to what you can accomplish for God's glory are far less if you don't care who gets the credit for advances and successes in the field. We need team players that are aiming at getting glory for God, plain and simple.

In the imagery of Tolkien's *Lord of the Rings: The Return of the King*, the signal fire above Minas Tirith has been lit to call for support from the warriors of Rohan at a crucial time. If you feel called to Christian outdoor leadership in a small or large way, I invite you to light a signal fire in your church, organization, or university to cast a vision for more experiential approaches to ministry. May you be part of a string of signal fires stretching across both hemispheres to put in motion a massive return to Jesus' shoulder-to-shoulder style of adventurous, experiential, and relational evangelism.

ONLINE RESOURCES

One of my favorite aspects of outdoor leadership is that no day is the same when you are on a journey. Variables are always changing and there is no cookie-cutter approach to the art of outdoor leadership. For that reason, I invite your participation! Please feel free to take a regular peek at our free online resources. The website is designed to be like a Swiss Army knife for Christian leaders who want to learn more about apprenticing others the way Jesus did in the outdoors. My hope and dream is that thousands more Christian leaders will begin to see the value of sharing a purposeful adventure with others. Our website is continually adding new resources for you to download and share for building up the Kingdom. If you ever have any feedback or questions please feel free to contact our team or e-mail me through our website. If you'd like to open up our Swiss Army knife of resources just visit www.outdoorleaders.com/resources.

Visit www.outdoorleaders.com/resources to download these FREE visual resources to hang on your wall or stuff in your notebook for easy reference:

CHRISTIAN OUTDOOR LEADERSHIP OUTCOMES ABCDE MODEL:

As an outdoor leader, you will be more effective if you know what you are hoping to see happen in your group. *ABDCE* is an acronym for five of the most common spiritual outcomes that result from outdoor adventures. If you choose one or two of the *ABCDE* outcomes as an umbrella theme for your trip, you'll notice more intentionality in everything you do. Then, if you choose one of the ten W.I.L.D.E.R.N.E.S.S. learning objectives suggested in *Christian Outdoor Leadership: Theology, Theory, & Practice*, your teaching content will have a sharper aim at your audience and result in a lasting effect. "Aim small, miss small!"

S+T+IC=K MODEL:

How did Jesus make his teaching STICK? The content of his teaching usually catches our attention, but what about the context? If you want to emulate the teaching techniques of Jesus you have to pay attention to your surroundings. He didn't teach in a vacuum. The one-two punch of his teaching style was the way he combined **S**etting and **T**iming with **I**ntentional **C**ontent to tie the **K**not of learning. He evoked a response. He closed the deal. So before you teach toward a desired outcome, consider how you'll tie the elements of **S**etting and **T**iming together with **I**ntentional **C**ontent into a nice **K**not to evoke a response.

W.I.L.D.E.R.N.E.S.S. LEARNING OBJECTIVES:

These objectives are steps toward achieving your *ABCDE* outcomes. For example, in a soccer game the outcome or "end" you hope for is to *win* the game. Each goal you score is an *objective* toward that end. If you don't score any goals then you won't achieve your desired outcome either. Reaching the desired outcome is somehow intimately and mysteriously linked to our effort. Our 10 W.I.L.D.E.R.N.E.S.S. objectives are more focused steps to help us move toward the *ABCDE* desired outcomes for our trip. For a more expanded explanation, refer to chapter 6 in *Christian Outdoor Leadership: Theology, Theory, and Practice.*

12 STEPS TO EXPLAINING WITH ELOQUENCE:

Eloquent teaching requires identifying a goal or dream for your interaction with the group. The apostle Peter sets a very high standard for us as Christian outdoor leaders: "Each one should use whatever gift he has received to serve others, faithfully administering God's grace in its various forms. If anyone speaks, he should do it as one speaking the very words of God (1 Peter 4:10-11)." Since we are accountable to God for what we teach, lets make sure that we are careful to keep the Bible as our curriculum, and trust the Holy Spirit to be the one who illumines and opens the eyes of people's hearts. We don't have to be super-teachers, we are simply asked to allow the Bible to speak for itself and do our best to present the message of Scripture with winsomeness and accuracy.

A RATIONALE FOR OUTDOOR ADVENTURE MINISTRIES BASED ON A THEOLOGY OF JOURNEY IN THE BIBLICAL TEXT:

A catalogue of wilderness journeys throughout the Bible, where the text explicitly identifies transformation occurring as a result of the journey.

SYNOPSIS OF JESUS CHRIST'S TEACHING PASSAGES THAT OCCURRED IN THE OUTDOORS

A synopsis of Jesus' teaching that occurred in the outdoors.

WILDERNESS MINISTRY STARTUP KIT FOR CHURCHES AND MISSION ORGANIZATIONS:

A how-to guide for starting a wilderness ministry program in your church or mission organization.

ROP LIST (A DIRECTORY OF RECOMMENDED OUTDOOR PROGRAMS):

A growing and dynamic list of recommended camps, organizations, universities, seminaries, and churches that provide quality outdoor ministry, adventure camping, and Christian outdoor leadership training.

STORY BOARD QUESTIONNAIRE FOR POST-ADVENTURE FOLLOW UP:

After your outdoor adventure is completed, it is a good idea to help people write down memories and transformational insight that they learned while out in the wilderness. This one-page form is a helpful tool for both closure of the experience and follow-up afterward.

INDEX

END NOTES

[1] Aland Kurt, ed., *Synopsis of the Four Gospels*, United Bible Societies, 1982

[2] Of the 366 pericopes in the Gospels, 276 involve some aspect of Jesus' teaching. Of those 276, the breakdown is as follows: Indoor (43 pericopes), Outdoor (142 pericopes), Uncertain location (91 pericopes). More than half of Jesus' recorded teachings occurred in the outdoors. Of the teaching that took place in the outdoors, 89 percent occurred outside of the city and 11 percent was outdoors but in a city. Only 16 percent of his recorded teachings designate an indoor setting in the text. Of his indoor teaching, 69 percent occurred in some sort of home or residential dwelling, 25 percent in synagogues, and less than 5 percent was in other buildings or Herod's palace. We are uncertain of the location of 33 percent of Jesus' blocks of teaching. A synopsis of these passages is available at:
www.outdoorleaders.com/resources

[3]Starbuck, Edwin D., *The Psychology of Religion: An Empirical Study of the Growth of Religious Consciousness*, quoted in Joseph Kett, *Rites of Passage: Adolescence in America 1790 to the Present* (New York: Harper & Row, 1977, p. 62)

[4] Benson, Warren, and Senter, Mark, editors, *The Complete Book of Youth Ministry*, Chicago: Moody Press 1987, 62.

[5] Ibid., 64.

[6] Mathews, Basil, and Mott, John R., *World Citizen*. New York: Harper & Brothers, 1934: 96

[7] Benson and Senter, *The Complete Book of Youth Ministry*, 64.

[8] Clark, Francis E., *Christ and the Young People*, New York: Revel, 1916, 14.

[9] Ibid., 11.

[10] Ibid., 12.

[11] Benson and Senter, *The Complete Book of Youth Ministry*, 67.

[12] Ibid., 67.

[13] Ibid., 69.

[14] Ibid., 69.

[15] Clark, Chap, *Hurt: Inside the World of Today's Teenagers*. Grand Rapids: Baker Academic, 2004, 171.

[16] Yung, Hwa, Some *Challenges for Leadership Development for Mission in East Asia*, Transformation, 21/4 Oct.
2004, 234-237.

[17] Global Training Network:
http://www.globaltrainingnetwork.org/resources/gtn-brochure/, accessed November 5, 2010.

[18]Johnson, Todd "World Christian Trends 2005," IFMA/EFMA, St. Louis, September 2004, p. 5.

[19] Neill, James, and Dias, Katica, "Adventure Education and Resilience." *Journal of Adventure Education and Outdoor Learning* 2, no. 1 (2001): 41.

[20] Klatzky, R.L., (1975). *Human Memory: Structures and Processes*. San Francisco: W.H. Freeman & Co.

[21] Lewis, C.S., *Surprised by Joy: The Shape of my Early Life*. London: Harcourt Brace & Company, 1955, 16.

22 Philips, J.B., *Ring of Truth: A Translator's Testimony*. London: Hodder and Stoughton, 1967, 54.

23 Swift, Fletcher Harper, *Education in Ancient Israel: From Earliest Times to A.D. 70*. Chicago: The Open Court Publishing Company, 1919, 60.

24 Ibid., 60.

25 Ibid., 85.

26 Ibid., 85.

27 Hinsdale, B.A., *Jesus as a Teacher and the Making of the New Testament*. St. Louis: 1895, 16.

28 Clark, Chap. *Hurt: Inside the World of Today's Teenagers*, 171.

29 Visit www.outdoorleaders.com/resources for the catalogue of passages.

30 Funk, Robert W., "The Wilderness." *Journal of Biblical Literature* 78, no. 3 (September 1959): 209.

31 The Wilderness Act was passed by the U.S. Congress in 1964 and continues to be the guiding piece of legislation in the United States for all wilderness areas. It is also referred to by many other developed countries as a helpful guide. The Act defines Wilderness as follows:
1) lands designated for preservation and protection in their natural condition...Section 2(a)
2) an area where the earth and its community of life are untrammeled by man...Section 2(c)
3) an area of undeveloped Federal land retaining its primeval character and influence, without permanent improvement or human habitation...Section 2(c)
4) generally appears to have been affected primarily by the forces of nature, with the imprint of man's work substantially unnoticeable...Section 2(c)
5) has outstanding opportunities for solitude or a primitive and unconfined type of recreation...Section 2(c)
6) shall be devoted to the public purposes of recreation, scenic, scientific, educational, conservation, and historic use...Section 4(b)
In other words, the wilderness is a place where one's senses indicate he is surrounded by the pristine natural world, i.e., the sounds, smells, and view tell him he is *surrounded by the God-made rather than the manmade*.

32 Funk, Robert W., Full quote: "It should be stressed at the outset that 'the wilderness' often bears a non-local, mythical sense in primitive Near Eastern mythologies and that this meaning is carried over in part into Biblical thought. In the latter it is also developed as a theological phrase with reference to Israel's original encounter with a rebellion against Yahweh. It is not, however, a question of either/or...the question...therefore, is whether this topographical-mythical-theological phrase was localized in proximity to the holy land and the holy mountain, Zion."

33 McCloskey, Michael J., and Spalding, Heather, "A Reconnaissance-Level Inventory of the Amount of Wilderness Remaining in the World." *AMBIO* 18, no. 4 (1989): 222.

34 Orr, James, M.A., D.D. General Editor, "Entry for 'DESERT.'" "International Standard Bible Encyclopedia." <http://www.searchgodsword.org/enc/isb/view.cgi?number=T2652>. 1915. Many of the Hebrew language concepts discussed in this section are guided by Orr's exegetical expertise on these Hebrew terms for "wilderness".

[35] Orr, "Entry for DESERT'". 1915. Note these other verses where *jeshimon* occurs in biblical poetry: (Psalms 78:40; 106:14; Isaiah 43:19,20).

[36] Thayer and Smith. "Greek Lexicon entry for Eremos." "The New Testament Greek Lexicon."
<http://www.searchgodsword.org/lex/grk/view.cgi?number=2048>

[37]Ibid.

[38] Louw, Johannes P., and Nida, Eugene A., editors, *Greek-English Lexicon of the New Testament Based on Semantic Domans, Second Edition.* New York: United Bible Societies, 17.

[39] Sarna, Nahum, *The JPS Torah Commentary,* ed. Sarna, Nahum (Philadelphia: The Jewish Publication Society, 1989), 290-91.

[40] Ibid., 84.

[41] Coleman, Robert, *The Master's Way of Personal Evangelism,* p. 79-80. See also Mark 2:1-12, Matthew 9:1-8 and Luke 5:17-26.

[42] Cowan, Rebecca, "Stress Camping Experience." *YouthWorker Journal,* no. 2 (Summer 1985): 45.

[43] Bruce, F.F., *The New International Commentary on the New Testament,* edited by Gordon D. Fee, *The Epistle to the Hebrews; Revised.* Grand Rapids: Wm. B. Eerdmans Publishing Company, 1990, p. 108-109.

[44] Derby, Josiah, "The Wilderness Experience." *Jewish Bible Quarterly* 26, no. 3 (1998): 194.

[45] Ibid., Deuteronomy 8:3-4 recounts the miracle that the Israelite's clothing did not rot and their feet did not blister.

[46] Bruce, F.F., *The Hard Sayings of Jesus.* Downers Grove: Intervarsity Press, 1983: 26.

[47] Jordan, Clarence and Doulos, and Lane, Bill, *Cotton Patch Parables of Liberation* (Scottsdale: Herald Press, 1976), 20.

[48] Stein, Robert, *An Introduction to the Parables of Jesus.* Philadelphia: The Westminster Press, 1981: 67.

[49] Dodd, C.H., *The Parables of the Kingdom.* (New York: Charles Scribner's Sons, 1961), 5.

[50] Trench, Richard, *Notes on the Parables.* (Grand Rapids: Zondervan Publishing House, 1948), 15.

[51] Ibid., 5.

[52] Dodd, *The Parables of the Kingdom,* 7.

[53] Trench, *Notes on the Parables,* 11.

[54] Knowles, Michael P., *Challenge of Jesus' Parables.* Grand Rapids: W.B. Eerdmans Publishing Company, 2000: 286.

[55] Lockyer, Herbert, *All the Parables of the Bible.* Grand Rapids: Zondervan Publishing House, 1963: 18.

[56] Ibid., 17.

[57] Editor, "Historical Voices on Learning from Creation," *Green Cross,* April, 1996.

[58] Ibid.

[59] Ibid.

[60] Seitz, Oscar Jacob, "Love Your Enemies, the Historical Setting of Matthew 5:43f, Luke 6:27f." *New Testament Studies* 16 (October 1969): 39.

[61] Dallas Willard, *The Spirit of the Discipline: Understanding How God Changes Lives* (New York: HarperCollins Publishers, 1988), 77.

62 Foster, Richard, *Celebration of Discipline: The Path to Spiritual Growth* (New York: Harper & Row Publishers, 1978), 2.
63 Beames, Simon, "Critical Elements of an Expedition Experience." *Journal of Adventure Education and Outdoor Learning* 4, no. 2 (2004): 153.
64 Bonhoeffer, Dietrich, *The Cost of Discipleship*. New York: Macmillan Publishing Co., Inc, 1963: 241.
65 Ibid.
66 Scaer, Peter J., "Jesus and the Woman at the Well: Where Mission Meets Worship." *Concordia Theological Quarterly* 1, no. 67 (January 2003): 15. John 4:31-34 says, "The disciples urged him, 'Rabbi, eat.' But he said to them, 'I have food to eat which you do not know.' So the disciples said to one another, 'Could someone have brought him something to eat?' Jesus said, 'My food is to do the will of the one who sent me and to finish his work.'"
67 Tiede, David L., "Luke 6:17-26." *Interpretation* 1, no. 40 (January 1986): 64.
68 Creighton, Lacy. *American Society of Missiology Series*, eds. Gerald H. Anderson, Robert T. Coote, Norman A. Horner, James M. Phillips, *Mission Legacies; Biographical Studies of Leaders of the Modern Missionary Movement* (New York: Orbis Books, 1994), p. 363.
69 Knowles, *Challenge of Jesus' Parables*, 301.
70 Sarna, Nahum, *The JPS Torah Commentary*. Edited by Nahum Sarna. New York: The Jewish Publication Society, 1989: 113.
71 Beames, "Critical Elements of an Expedition Experience," 150.
72 Kellert, Stephen R., Yale University; *A National Study of Outdoor Wilderness Experience*. School of Forestry and Environmental Studies, 1998: 29.
73 Ibid., 30.
74 Bonhoeffer, *The Cost of Discipleship*, 231.
75 Dodd, C.H., *The Parables of the Kingdom*. New York: Charles Scribner's Sons, 1961: 9. This pertains particularly to the employer who pays the same wages for an hour's work.
76 Dodd, *The Parables of the Kingdom*, 10-11.
77 Bruce, F.F., *The Hard Sayings of Jesus*: 211. "We are not afraid when the earth heaves and the mountains are hurled into the sea: so Psalm 46:2, NEB, describes a real or figurative convulsion of nature which leaves men and women of God unshaken because he is their refuge and strength."
78 Jeremias, Joachim, *The Parables of Jesus*. (New York: Charles Scribner's Sons, 1962), 21. Italics added.
79 Hunter, Archibald, *Interpreting the Parables*. Philadelphia: Westminster Press, 1960: 14.
80 Ibid.
81 Cheston, Sharon E., "Spirituality of Encouragement." *Journal of Individual Psychology* 56, no. 3 (Fall 2000): 302.
82 Berleant, Arnold, "The Wilderness City: An Essay on Metaphorical Experience," A. Haapala, ed., *The City as Cultural Metaphor: Studies in Urban Aesthetics* (Lahti, Finland: International Institute for Applied Aesthetics, 1998): 31.
83 Coleman, *The Master's Way of Personal Evangelism*: 139-140. See also Acts 9:1-31; 22:1-21; 26:1-18.

[84] Coleman, *The Master's Way of Personal Evangeli*sm: 99. See also Matthew 8:5-13 and Luke 7:1-10

[85] Noebel, David, *Understanding the Times: Collision of Today's Competing Worldviews.* Manitou Springs: Summit Press, 2006: 16.

[86] Doucette, Patricia, "Walk and Talk: An Intervention for Behaviorally Challenged Youths." *Adolescence* 39, no. 154 (Summer 2004): HTML, http://web24.epnet.com/citation.asp?tb=1&_ug=fim+0+cp+1+dbs+reh%2C rfh%2Crlh/ (accessed 11/14/2005).

[87] Cowan, Rebecca, "Stress Camping Experience." *YouthWorker Journal*, no. 2 (Summer 1985): 42.

[88] Ibid., 43

[89] Wangerin, Walter Jr., *Whole Prayer: Speaking and Listening to God* (Grand Rapids: Zondervan Publishing House, 1998.

[90] Bruce, F.F. ,*The New International Commentary on the New Testament, The Epistle to the Hebrews; Revised*, 136.

[91] Bounds, E.M., et al., *E.M. Bounds on Prayer* (New Kinsington: Whitaker House, 1997), 76. Bounds indicates he is drawing his theological view from James 4:2-3.

[92] Knowles, *Challenge of Jesus' Parables,* 297.

[93] Ibid., 298.

[94] Beames, "Critical Elements of an Expedition Experience," 150-151.

[95] Scaer, Peter J., "Jesus and the Woman at the Well: Where Mission Meets Worship," *Concordia Theological Quarterly* 1, no. 67 (January 2003): 18.

[96] Murray, Andrew, *With Christ in the School of Prayer; George Muller, and the Secret of His Power in Prayer.* http://www.ccel.org/ccel/murray/prayer.html, accessed 5 Nov. 2010: 99.

[97] Bruce, A.B., *The Training of the Twelve* (New York: Hodder and Stoughton, 1871), 100.

[98] Coleman, Robert, *The Master Plan of Evangelism* (Grand Rapids: Fleming H. Revell, 1963), 27.

[99] Barclay, William, *The Master's Men.* (Nashville: Parthenon Press, 1959), 18. "The Galileans have never been destitute of courage" (Josephus, Life, 17; Wars of the Jews 3, 32).

[100] Coleman, *The Master Plan of Evangelism,* 53.

[101] Barclay, *The Master's Men*, 19. See also Luke 22:8.

[102] Ibid., 19. See also John 6:66-69.

[103] Ibid., 21. The Great Promise: "Thou art Peter, and upon this rock I will build my church" (Matthew 16:18), The Great Rebuke: "Get thee behind me, Satan" (Matthew 16:22-23; Mark 8:32-33).

[104] Ibid., 23-24. Regarding the Great Commission: "It was Peter who was the first to enter the tomb and find it empty" (John 20:6), regarding the Great Realization: (Acts 10).

[105] Ibid., 31.

[106] Ibid., 31, 39.

[107] Ibid., 41-44.

[108] Ibid., 42. See also John 1:40-42.

[109] Ibid.

[110] Ibid.

[111] Ibid., 49.

112 Another example of this principle is found in Jesus' response to John the Baptist when from prison he sent his disciples to ask Jesus, "Are you the one who was to come, or should we expect someone else?" (Matthew 11:3).

113 Ibid., 50.

114 Ibid., 48.

115 Bruce, A.B., *The Training of the Twelve* (New York: Hodder and Stoughton, 1871), 19-20.

116 Ibid., 100.

117 Betz, Otto, *What We Know about Jesus* (Philadelphia: Westminster Press, 1968), 75-76.

118 Ibid.

119 Coleman, Robert, *The Great Commission Lifestyle: Conforming Your Life to Kingdom Priorities* (Grand Rapids: Fleming H. Revell, 1992), 59.

120 Bruce, A.B., *The Training of the Twelve*, 29.

121 Coleman, *The Great Commission Lifestyle: Conforming Your Life to Kingdom Priorities*, 58. See also Matthew 9:37,38.

122 Bruce, *The Training of the Twelve*, 180.

123 Ibid., 112-113.

124 Ibid., 35-36.

125 Coleman, *The Master Plan of Discipleship*, 31.

126 Coleman, *The Master Plan of Discipleship*, 56-57.

127 http://en.wikipedia.org/wiki/Anchorite

128 Merton, Thomas, *The Wisdom of the Desert: Sayings from the Desert Fathers of the Fourth Century*. New Directions, 1960. Print: 3.

129 O'Hannay, James, *Wisdom of the Desert* (Las Vegas: IAP, 2009). O'Hannay (All four points are ideas drawn from excerpts from pages 10-14).

130 Bratton, Susan, *Christianity, Wilderness, and Wildlife: The Original Desert Solitaire* (Scranton, Pa: University of Scranton Press, 1993), 244.

131 O'Hannay, *Wisdom of the Desert*, 11.

132 Ibid., 18

133 Nomura, Yushi, and Nouwen, Henri J. M., *Desert Wisdom: Sayings from the Desert Fathers* (Maryknoll, N.Y: Orbis Books, 2001), 68.

134 Regnault, Lucien, *The Day-to-Day Life of the Desert Fathers in Fourth-Century Egypt* (Petersham, Mass: St. Bede's Publications, 1999), 240.

135 This information can be found in *Paradise of the Holy Fathers*. (This is a reprint of a translation of an ancient syriac manuscript made by E. A. Wallis Budge, curator of Egyptian and Assyrian Antiquities in the British Museum, and first published in 1904): http://evlogeite.com/?p=224.

136 Ibid. (This list is a direct quote from this resource originally published in 1904.)

137 Mott, 96.

138 Hendricks, Howard, *Teaching to Change Lives* (Portland: Multnomah Press, 1987), 13.

139 Morosco, Robert E., "Matthew's formation of a Commissioning Type-Scene Out of the Story of Jesus' Commissioning of the Twelve." *Journal of Biblical Literature* 103, no. 4 (December 1984): 542.

140 Keijo Eriksson, "In Search of the Meaning of Life: A study of the Ideas of Senior Compulsory School Pupils on Life and its Meaning in an Experiential Learning Context." *British Journal of Religious Education* 22, no. 2 (Spring 2000): 120.

END NOTES

[141] Ibid.

[142] Ibid., 122-123

[143] Borrie, William, and Roggenbuck, Joseph, "Providing an Authentic Wilderness Experience? Thinking beyond the Wilderness Act of 1964." In *Coalition for Education in the Outdoors Third Research Symposium Proceedings held in Bradford Woods, IN, January 12-14, 1996*, edited by Aldo Leopold Wilderness Research Institute, 34-44 : U.S. Department of Education Educational Resources Information Center (1996): 35.

[144] Ibid., 36. Quoting Henry David Thoreau, 1854.

[145] Rickelle Smyth, interview by Ashley Denton, April, 2004, email.

[146] Borrie, William T., and Roggenbuck, Joseph W., "Providing an Authentic Wilderness Experience? Thinking beyond the Wilderness Act of 1964." In *Coalition for Education in the Outdoors Third Research Symposium Proceedings held in Bradford Woods, IN, January 12-14, 1996*, edited by Aldo Leopold Wilderness Research Institute, p. 34-44: U.S. Department of Education Educational Resources Information Center (1996): 37.

[147] Cara Alexander, interview by Ashley Denton, April, 2004, email.

[148] Holly. Mountain View Backcountry, Fort Collins, CO: June 2010.

[149] Riley. Mountain View Backcountry, Fort Collins, CO: June 2010.

[150] Borrie and Roggenbuck, "Providing an Authentic Wilderness Experience? Thinking beyond the Wilderness Act of 1964," 37

[151] Andy. Mountain View Backcountry, Fort Collins, CO: June 2010.

[152] Luckner, John L.; Nadler, Reldan S. *Processing the Experience; Strategies to Enhance and Generalize Learning*. Dubuque: Kendall/Hunt Publishing Company, 1997. Quoted in *Outdoor Leadership: Theory and Practice*: Bruce Martin, Christine Cashel, Mark Wagstaff, Mary Breunig: Books. 258.

[153] Farrell, Greg et. al., *Roots: From Outward Bound to Expeditionary Learning*, ed. Emily Cousins (Dubuque: Kendall/Hunt Publishing Company, 2000), 79-81.

[154] Petzoldt, Paul, et. al., *The New Wilderness Handbook* (New York: W.W. Norton Company, 1984), 56.

[155] Ibid., 57.

[156] Martin, Bruce et. al., *Outdoor Leadership Theory and Practice* (Champaign: Human Kinetics, 2006), 182.

[157] Petzoldt, *The New Wilderness Handbook*, 57.

[158] Brett DeYoung, "Wilderness Camping and Leadership Development" (Master's thesis, Cincinnati Bible Seminary, Cincinnati, Ohio), 1987: 4.

[159] Norman Rose, "Moral Development: The Experiential Perspective," *Journal of Moral Education* 21, no. 1 (1992): 33.

[160] Bratton, Susan, *Christianity, Wilderness, and Wildlife: The Original Desert Solitaire*. (Scranton, Pa: University of Scranton Press, 1993), 244

[161] Cashel, Christine et. al., "Personality Preferences of Outdoor Participants," *Educational Resources Information Center*, 1996. http://www.eric.ed.gov/ERICDocs/data/ericdocs2/content_storage_01/00 00000b/80/22/f4/ee.pdf. (Accessed January 25, 2006): 138.

[162] Swift, *Education in Ancient Israel: From Earliest Times to A.D. 70*, 26.

[163] Stein, Robert, *The Method and Message of Jesus' Teachings* (Louisville: Westminster John Knox Press, 1994), 7. The biblical reference is Mark 6:35-36.

164 Ibid., 15.
165 Carlston, Charles E., "Proverbs, Maxims, and the Historical Jesus." *Journal of Biblical Literature* 99 (1980): 88-89, Quotation from Pascal, *Pensees* VI: 380.
166 Chambers, Oswald, *My Utmost for His Highest* (Grand Rapids: Discovery House Publishers, 1935), October 1.
167 Nash, Roderick Frazier, *Wilderness in the American Mind* (New Haven: Yale University Press, 2001), 125.
168 Editor, "Historical Voices on Learning from Creation." *Green Cross*, April, 1996, Creation Care Publication: 1, quoting Thomas Aquinas.
169 Brahler, Gwen, and Denton, Ashley, and Fuchs, Greg, *Rocky Mountain Region Backcountry Trail/River Reference Manual*, 2001: 15, quoting *Survival in the Wilderness*.
170 Aristotle; cited Diogenes Laertius, *Lives*, V. 18.
171 Bias, cited in Diogenes Laertius, *Lives*, I.88.
172 *Discourses*, I.xxiv.2.
173 *Discourses*, I.xxiv.2.
174 Publilius Syrus, *Sentences*, [B] 87.
175 Marcus Aurelius, *Meditations*, XI.18.8.
176 Pindar, Olympian *Odes*, VI.101.
177 Publilus Syrus, *Sentences*, [A] 11). Cf. Also Eccl 5:9; 7:12; 10:19.
178 Publilius Syrus, *Sentences*, [B] 75.
179 Publilius Syrus, *Sentences*, [A].
180 Bion, cited in Diogenes Laertius, *Lives*, IV.49.
181 Stein, *The Method and Message of Jesus' Teachings,* 20.
182 Coleman, *The Master's Way of Personal Evangelism*, 89-90. See also John 9:1-38.
183 Stein, *The Method and Message of Jesus' Teachings*, 21.
184 Knowles, 291.
185 Ibid., 294.
186 Stein, *The Method and Message of Jesus' Teachings*, 21.
187 Ibid., 22.
188 Bailey, Kenneth E., *Poet & Peasant and Through Peasant Eyes*. 2 vols. (Grand Rapids: William B. Eerdmans Publishing Company, 1999), 133.
189 Waetjen, Herman C., "The Subversion of 'World' by the Parable of the Friend at Midnight." *Journal of Biblical Literature* 4, no. 120 (2001): 713.
190 Hovelynch, et. al., "Laughter, Smiles and Grins: The Role of Humor in Learning and Facilitating." *Journal of Adventure Education and Outdoor Learning* 3, no. 2 (2003): 181.
191 Ibid., 178.
192 Ibid., 181.
193 Ibid., 178.
194 Zuck, Roy, *Teaching as Jesus Taught* (Grand Rapids: Baker Books, 1995), 174-175. All fifteen of these examples are referenced by Zuck.
195 Stein, *The Method and Message of Jesus' Teachings*, 12-13.
196 Ibid., 13-14.
197 Ibid.
198 Ibid.
199 Ibid.
200 Ibid.

END NOTES

[201] Ibid.

[202] Caneday, A.B., *He Wrote in Parables and Riddles: Mark's Gospel as a Literary Reproduction of Jesus' Teaching Method* (Orlando: Evangelical Theological Society Papers. Theological Research Exchange Network, 50th National Conference), p. 37. Italics added.

[203] http://www.imdb.com/title/tt0082158/quotes?qt0456355, accessed 11/4/2010. Chariots of Fire quote (1981).

[204] Lewis, C.S. *Mere Christianity* (New York: HarperSanFrancisco, 1996), 154-155.

Made in the USA
Lexington, KY
29 November 2011